KU-627-315

50 Self-Help Classics

C334198056

This new and updated edition first published in 2017 by Nicholas Brealey Publishing
An imprint of John Murray Press
First edition published in 2003

An Hachette UK company

1

Copyright © Tom Butler-Bowdon 2003, 2017

The right of Tom Butler-Bowdon to be identified as
the Author of the Work has been asserted by him in accordance
with the Copyright, Designs and Patents Act 1988.

All rights reserved.
No part of this publication may be reproduced, stored in a
retrieval system, or transmitted, in any form or by any means without
the prior written permission of the publisher, nor be otherwise circulated in
any form of binding or cover other than that in which it is published and
without a similar condition being imposed on the subsequent purchaser.

British Library Cataloguing-in-Publication Data
A catalogue record for this book is available from the British Library.

ISBN 978-1-47365-828-8
eBook (UK) ISBN 978-1-85788-474-6
eBook (US) ISBN 978-1-47364-448-9

Printed and bound by Clays Ltd, St Ives plc

John Murray Press policy is to use papers that are natural, renewable
and recyclable products and made from wood grown in sustainable forests.
The logging and manufacturing processes are expected to conform
to the environmental regulations of the country of origin.

Nicholas Brealey Publishing
John Murray Press
Carmelite House
50 Victoria Embankment
London EC4Y 0DZ
Tel: 020 3122 6000

Nicholas Brealey Publishing
Hachette Book Group
Market Place Center, 53 State Street
Boston, MA 02109, USA
Tel: (617) 263 1834

www.nicholasbrealey.com
www.butler-bowdon.com

50 Self-Help Classics

Second Edition

Your shortcut to the most important ideas on happiness and fulfilment

Tom Butler-Bowdon

NICHOLAS BREALEY
PUBLISHING
London • Boston

Richard Koch

Ellen J. Langer

Alain de Botton

William Bridges

Pierre Teilhard de Chardin

Henry David Thoreau

Clayton Christensen

Wayne Dyer

Marcus Aurelius

The Dalai Lama & Howard C. Cutler

Lao Tzu

Mihaly Csikszentmihalyi

Maxwell Maltz

Anthony Robbins

Thomas Moore

Paulo Coelho

Marie Kondo

norman vincent peale

DAVID BROOKS

The Dhammapada

Stephen Covey

The Bhagavad-Gita

Shakti Gawain

Ralph Waldo Emerson

Florence Scovell Shinn

Daniel Goleman

James Allen

BOETHIUS

The Bible

Abraham Maslow

David D. Burns

Robert Bly

Viktor Frankl

Deepak Chopr

Charles Duhigg

Joseph Murphy

M. Scott Peck

Clarissa Pinkola Est“es

Louise Hay

Martin Seligman

James Hillman

Joseph Campbell with Bill Moyers

Samuel Smile

Richard Carlson

Marianne Williamson

Brené Brown

Dale Carnegie

John Gray

Susan Jeffers

Benjamin Franklin

Contents

Preface
Second Edition

On many levels, *50 Self-Help Classics* is a special book for me. The self-help literature that I discovered in my twenties turned my life around and changed my thinking. I fell in love with it, reading every title I could get my hands on to boost my career and improve my relationships. But as I got deeper into the genre, and saw how amazing it is, I wondered: why there was no guide to it? Perhaps it was because self-help had a slightly low-brow reputation, but this seemed totally unjustified.

Despite a heritage going back to Samuel Smiles and Orison Swett Marden in the nineteenth century, in the late 1990s self-help books seemed like a new thing. A string of mega-selling titles, from *The 7 Habits of Highly Effective People* to *Don't Sweat the Small Stuff* to *Awaken The Giant Within*, had made self-help a "hot" publishing genre, yet it still lacked critical appreciation. *50 Self-Help Classics* was my attempt to fill this gap. The book sold extremely well, and ended up being translated into 20 languages. Though the majority of self-help authors were American, it was clearly a global phenomenon.

Though I had never planned to become a writer, self-help pulled me into its orbit, virtually demanding that I leave a successful career and devote myself to it full-time. True to the self-help mantra, so beautifully expressed in Paulo Coelho's *The Alchemist*, that one must "follow your dream," I was very happy to do so. It felt like a vocation.

As it happened, *50 Self-Help Classics* proved to be just the entry point to a larger exploration of personal development, and the foundation of a bestselling series. The book was followed by *50 Success Classics*, a survey of the success and motivational literature, and then *50 Spiritual Classics*. Later books in the series, such as *50 Psychology Classics*, *50 Philosophy Classics*, and *50 Economics Classics* may seem to be about drier topics, but this isn't so; what drives every title is the *potential of the individual*. Success is always about expanding the mind and seeing new possibilities, and the *50 Classics* series is my contribution to that end.

Almost 15 years have passed since *50 Self-Help Classics* was published. What, if anything, has changed in the self-help field? Many would argue that the genre has been superseded by psychology and its more scientific approach to understanding why we think and act as we do. Indeed, when I wrote about Daniel Goleman's *Emotional Intelligence* and Martin Seligman's *Learned Optimism*, such titles were a sign of things to come in terms of personal development becoming more grounded and scientific. A person who 20 years ago might have been happy to get a lift or a set of life pointers from a classic work such as *How to Win Friends and Influence People*, today might be drawn to a book by a distinguished psychologist instead. It should be no surprise that serious titles such as Daniel Kahneman's *Thinking, Fast and Slow*, which reveal how our brains work and which therefore help us change our behaviors, are now found at the top of bestseller lists.

Yet to say that self-help has been overtaken by psychology would be wrong. There is still a place for great self-help writing, although it is more likely to support its claims by reference to research. Charles Duhigg's *The Power of Habit* and Brené Brown's *Daring Greatly*, which I look at in the new edition, are good examples. Yet self-help books can offer something that goes beyond psychology. David Brooks' *The Road to Character* is really a work of ethical philosophy with a powerful message about personal change across a lifetime. Marie Kondo's deceptively simple *The Life-Changing Magic of Tidying Up* aims to transform the reader's life through changing our attitude to things and spaces; if our homes have the air of a Shinto shrine, peace, order, and happiness reign. What self-help books do really well is combine aspects of different areas, including psychology, philosophy, spirituality, motivation, and even business (see, for example, Clayton Christensen's *How Will You Measure Your Life?*), and the best ones create an intimate connection with the reader. You really *can* change your life, the author tells us, and I will show you how.

This combination of education and inspiration is what originally drew me to the self-help genre, and as I put together this new edition of *50 Self-Help Classics*, with its new chapters on the books mentioned above, it is still what holds me in its thrall.

Tom Butler-Bowdon

Acknowledgments

50 Self-Help Classics was originally published by Simon & Schuster in Australia. Nicholas Brealey acquired rights to the book in 2003, which was then revised for UK and US publication.

This new, updated edition took shape at Nicholas Brealey Publishing, now part of Hachette UK. At Hachette I thank editorial director Holly Bennion, sales manager Ben Slight and editorial assistant Louise Richardson, the rights team headed by Joanna Kaliszewska, and designer Joanne Myler who came up with the great new cover. Thanks for your work championing the *50 Classics* series, along with Hachette offices in the United States, Australia, the Far East, and India.

I am grateful to the many people who have touched by the book and wrote to tell me so. Writing it was a personal, deeply inspiring experience. I'm grateful to the people who supported my efforts to be a writer at that time, including my parents Marion and Anthony, the Lucas family, and many friends and colleagues.

I salute all the writers and figures who created the self-help genre, and am grateful for the ideas of the living authors included in the book.

Introduction

"The greatest discovery of my generation is that a human being can alter his life by altering his attitudes."
William James (1842–1910)

"Habits of thinking need not be forever. One of the most significant findings in psychology in the last twenty years is that individuals can choose the way they think."
Martin Seligman, Learned Optimism

You will have heard many times that "you can change your life by changing your thoughts and your mental habits," but have you ever stopped to consider what that means? This book identifies some of the most useful ideas from writings specifically devoted to personal transformation—from the inside out.

I have called these books "self-help classics." You may already have an idea of what self-help is, but that understanding should be deepened by the range of authors and titles covered in these pages. If there is a thread running through the works, it is their refusal to accept "common unhappiness" or "quiet desperation" as the lot of humankind. They acknowledge life's difficulties and setbacks as real, but say that we cannot be defined by these. No matter how adverse the situation, we always have room to determine what it will mean to us, a lesson given us in two books covered here, Viktor Frankl's *Man's Search for Meaning* and Boethius' *The Consolation of Philosophy*. To consciously decide what we will think, not allowing genes or environment or fate to determine our path—this is the essence of self-help.

A conventional view of self-help is that it deals with problems, but most of the self-help classics are about *possibilities*. They can help reveal your unique course in life, form a bridge between fear and happiness, or simply inspire you to be a better person. Samuel Smiles wrote the original *Self-Help* in 1859. He feared that people would think his book a tribute to selfishness. In fact it preached reliance on one's own efforts, the never-say-die pursuit of a goal that did not wait on government help or any other kind of patronage. Smiles was originally a

1

political reformer, but came to the conclusion that the real revolutions happened inside people's heads; he took the greatest idea of his century, "progress," and applied it to personal life. Through telling the life stories of some of the remarkable people of his era, he tried to show that anything was possible if you had the gall to try.

Abraham Lincoln is sometimes mentioned in self-help writing because he embodies the idea of "limitless" thinking. Yet his thoughts were not applied to himself—he considered himself an ungainly depressive—but to the potential he saw in a situation (saving the Union and freeing America of slavery). Lincoln's vision was not vainglorious; he lived for something larger.

At its best, self-help is not about the fantasies of the ego, but involves the identification of a project, goal, ideal, or way of being where you can make a big difference. In so doing, you can transform a piece of the world—and yourself along with it.

The self-help phenomenon

> "... the symbols of the divine show up in our world initially at the trash stratum."
> *Philip K. Dick,* Valis

The self-help book was one of the great success stories of the twentieth century. The exact number purchased is impossible to calculate, but this selection of 50 classics alone has sold over 150 million copies between them, and if we consider the thousands of other titles the final number would run to more than half a billion.

The idea of self-help is nothing new, but only in the twentieth century did it become a mass phenomenon. Books like *How to Win Friends and Influence People* (1936) and *The Power of Positive Thinking* (1952) were bought by ordinary people desperate to make something of their lives and willing to believe that the secrets of success could be found in a paperback. Maybe the genre took on its lowbrow image because the books were so readily available, promised so much, and contained ideas that you were unlikely to hear from a professor or a minister. Whatever the image, people obviously had a new source of life guidance and they loved it. For once, we were not being told what we couldn't do but only that we should shoot for the stars.

A self-help book can be your best friend and champion, expressing a faith in your essential greatness and beauty that is sometimes hard to get from another person. Because of its emphasis on following your star and believing that your thoughts can remake your world, a better name for self-help writing might be the "literature of possibility."

Many people are amazed that the self-help sections in bookstores are so huge. For the rest of us there is no mystery: Whatever recognizes our right to dream, then shows us how to make the dream a reality, is powerful and valuable.

The books
This list of classics is the result of my own reading and research, and might be quite different if another person were to undertake the same project. The focus is on twentieth-century self-help books, but much older works are also included because the self-help ethic has been with us through the ages. The Bible, The Bhagavad-Gita, and Marcus Aurelius' *Meditations* are examples of works that may not have been thought of as self-help before, but I hope I can argue the case for their inclusion.

Most of the contemporary writers are American, and while this may seem like cultural imperialism, in reality self-help values are universal. There are a number of strands to self-help that offer specific guidance, for example on relationships, diet, selling, or self-esteem, but the books covered here relate to the broader personal development aims of self-knowledge and increasing happiness. Through the selections I try to give a sense of the huge diversity of the genre. Many of the titles were easily selected because they are both famous and influential. Others are included because they fill a niche through their ideas. Every book had to have a level of readability and "spark" that defies the time and place that it was written.

At the end of *Women Who Run with the Wolves*, Clarissa Pinkola Estés lists a great array of books that might be of interest to readers. She asks, "How do they go together? What can one lend the other? Compare, see what happens. Some combinations are bomb materials. Some create seed stock."

The same could be said of the self-help classics. However, to help draw out some themes, below I have grouped the works into areas that may help you find what you are after. There is an additional list, "50 More Classics," at the end of the book.

The Power of Thought
Change your thoughts, change your life

James Allen, *As a Man Thinketh*
David Brooks, *The Road to Character*
David D. Burns, *Feeling Good: The New Mood Therapy*
Daniel Goleman, *Emotional Intelligence: Why It Can Matter More than IQ*
Louise Hay, *You Can Heal Your Life*
Ellen J. Langer, *Mindfulness: Choice and Control in Everyday Life*
Joseph Murphy, *The Power of Your Subconscious Mind*
Norman Vincent Peale, *The Power of Positive Thinking*
Florence Scovell Shinn, *The Game of Life and How to Play It*
Martin Seligman, *Learned Optimism*

Following Your Dream
Achievement and goal setting

Dale Carnegie, *How to Win Friends and Influence People*
Deepak Chopra, *The Seven Spiritual Laws of Success*
Paulo Coelho, *The Alchemist*
Stephen Covey, *The 7 Habits of Highly Effective People*
Charles Duhigg, *The Power of Habit*
Benjamin Franklin, *Autobiography*
Shakti Gawain, *Creative Visualization*
Susan Jeffers, *Feel the Fear and Do It Anyway*
Maxwell Maltz, *Psycho-Cybernetics*
Anthony Robbins, *Awaken the Giant Within*

Secrets of Happiness
Doing what you love, doing what works

Mihaly Csikszentmihalyi, *Flow: The Psychology of Optimal Experience*
The Dalai Lama and Howard C. Cutler, *The Art of Happiness: A Handbook for Living*

The Dhammapada (Buddha's teachings)
Wayne Dyer, *Real Magic: Creating Miracles in Everyday Life*
John Gray, *Men Are from Mars, Women Are from Venus*
Richard Koch, *The 80/20 Principle: The Secret of Achieving More with Less*
Marie Kondo, *The Life-Changing Magic of Tidying Up*
Marianne Williamson, *A Return to Love*

The Bigger Picture
Keeping it in perspective

Marcus Aurelius, *Meditations*
Boethius, *The Consolation of Philosophy*
Alain de Botton, *How Proust Can Change Your Life*
William Bridges, *Transitions: Making Sense of Life's Changes*
Richard Carlson, *Don't Sweat the Small Stuff . . . And It's All Small Stuff*
Viktor Frankl, *Man's Search for Meaning*
Lao Tzu, *Tao Te Ching*

Soul and mystery
Appreciating your depth

Robert Bly, *Iron John*
Joseph Campbell with Bill Moyers, *The Power of Myth*
Clarissa Pinkola Estés, *Women Who Run with the Wolves*
James Hillman, *The Soul's Code: In Search of Character and Calling*
Thomas Moore, *Care of the Soul: A Guide for Cultivating Depth and Sacredness in Everyday Life*
M. Scott Peck, *The Road Less Traveled*
Henry David Thoreau, *Walden*

Making a Difference
Transforming yourself, transforming the world

The Bhagavad-Gita
The Bible
Brené Brown, *Daring Greatly*
Clayton Christensen, *How Will You Measure Your Life?*

Ralph Waldo Emerson, *Self-Reliance*
Abraham Maslow, *Motivation and Personality*
Samuel Smiles, *Self-Help*
Pierre Teilhard de Chardin, *The Phenomenon of Man*

Over to you

"In the last analysis, the essential thing is the life of the individual. This alone makes history, here alone do the great transformations take place, and the whole future, the whole history of the world, ultimately springs as a gigantic summation from these hidden sources in individuals."
Carl Gustav Jung

Once upon a time we lived in tribal groups that guided our lives and supplied us with our physical, social, and spiritual needs. As "civilization" emerged it may have been the Church or the State that assumed these roles; today, you may depend on the company for which you work for material security and a sense of belonging.

Yet history shows that every kind of institution and community eventually crumbles, and when it does the individual is exposed. This is forced change, and as the world speeds up the likelihood of its happening to you increases. Therefore you need to know more about yourself, be aware of how to manage change better, and have a plan for your life that does not depend on an institution. Whether you want to change the world or just change yourself, you are right in suspecting that no one is going to do it for you. In the end, it is all up to you.

The other key pressure on us, strange as it may seem, is the expansion of choice. Most of us cherish freedom, but when we actually get the opportunity to make our own way it can be terrifying. Many of the works covered in this book deal with the paradox that the more choices we have, the greater our need for focus. Anyone can get a job, but do you have a purpose?

The twentieth century was about fitting in to large organizational structures—by conforming well you became successful. Yet Richard Koch shows us in *The 80/20 Principle* that success now and in the future comes from being more yourself; if you are willing to express your uniqueness, you will inevitably contribute something of real value to the world. This has a moral dimension to it (Teilhard de Chardin referred to "the

6

incommunicable singularity that each of us possess"), but also makes economic and scientific sense: Evolution happens by differentiation, not by matching up to some general standard, and therefore the rewards of life will always go to those who are not simply excellent but outstanding.

The future of self-help

"I contradict myself. I am large. I contain multitudes."
Walt Whitman

At the heart of the self-help literature are two basic conceptions of how we should see ourselves. Titles like Wayne Dyer's *Real Magic*, Thomas Moore's *Care of the Soul*, and Deepak Chopra's *The Seven Spiritual Laws of Success* assume the existence of a changeless core inside us (called variously the soul or the higher self) that guides us and helps us to fulfill a purpose unique to us. In this conception, self-knowledge is the path to maturity.

Then there are titles such as Anthony Robbins' *Awaken the Giant Within* and Benjamin Franklin's *Autobiography*, which assume that the self is a blank slate on which you can write the story of your life. There is no one better than Friedrich Nietzsche to sum up this attitude:

"Active, successful natures act, not according to the dictum 'know thyself', but as if there hovered before them the commandment: will a self and thou shalt become a self."

The self-knowing and the self-creating person are, of course, only abstractions; a person will always be an interesting combination of the two. Both viewpoints, nevertheless, contain the assumption that the self is independent and unitary ("one"). Yet in the twenty-first century we have multiple roles, are members of many communities, and express a variety of personas, so our experience is of complexity. Where does self-help fit into such a context?

In his book *The Saturated Self*, Kenneth Gergen suggested that the old idea of the unitary self has had to evolve to take account of our many-mindedness, or what he called the "multiphrenic personality." Another writer, Robert Jay Lifton in *The Protean Self: Human Resilience in an Age of Fragmentation*, says that to prevent the feeling of being pulled in all directions we have to develop a tougher and more sophisticated self, aware of all its many dimensions; only this "protean self" will cope with a vastly complicated world. For Lifton, the unitary self is not dead but in a time of challenge.

However, will even this more evolved understanding of the self be able to cope with technological advance? What sort of people will emerge from a twenty-first century that can use genetic and other technologies to alter the personality and increase intelligence? If we will have the ability to change the self to such an extent, what is "self-knowledge" as Plato imagined it?

Scientists are confident that many children born now will have a life expectancy of well over 100 years, even 140 or 150. Will living that long make your sense of identity more coherent, or will 15 decades of change—relationships, families, careers, world events—shatter any feelings of continuity and security? Scarier still is the possibility that we may be able to keep alive the "software" of our brain long after our body has given up, then perhaps have it transplanted into a new corpus.

The ever more sophisticated application of technology to the human body and brain is clearly going to make the question "What is the self?" even more significant. In this *Blade Runner* future, the idea of self-knowledge will get ever more interesting.

Self-help books emerged from the evaporation of certainty and the collapse of tradition. But the literature always assumed that we knew what the self was. As this assumption is questioned, future self-help books will have to be guides to the self itself.

Reader bonus

Readers are invited to receive a bonus commentary on Srikumar Rao's excellent *Happiness at Work*. Just send an email to tombutlerbowdon@gmail.com with "Self-Help Bonus" as the subject.

50 Self-Help
Classics

As a Man Thinketh

1902

"*Of all the beautiful truths pertaining to the soul that have been restored and brought to light in this age, none is more gladdening or fruitful of divine promise and confidence than this—that you are the master of your thought, the molder of your character, and the maker and shaper of your condition, environment and destiny.*"

"*Good thoughts and actions can never produce bad results; bad thoughts and actions can never produce good results . . . We understand this law in the natural world, and work with it; but few understand it in the mental and moral world—although its operation there is just as simple and undeviating—and they, therefore, do not cooperate with it.*"

"*Law, not confusion, is the dominating principle in the universe; justice, not injustice, is the soul and substance of life; and righteousness, not corruption, is the molding and moving force in the spiritual government of the world. This being so, we have to but right ourselves to find that the universe is right.*"

In a nutshell

We don't attract what we want, but what we are. Only by changing your thoughts will you change your life.

In a similar vein
Joseph Murphy, *The Power of Your Subconscious Mind* (p248)
Florence Scovell Shinn, *The Game of Life and How to Play It* (p272)

CHAPTER 1

James Allen

With its theme that "mind is the master weaver," creating our inner character and outer circumstances, *As a Man Thinketh* is an in-depth exploration of the central idea of self-help writing. James Allen's contribution was to take an assumption we all share—that because we are not robots we therefore control our thoughts—and reveal its fallacy. Because most of us believe that mind is separate from matter, we think that thoughts can be hidden and made powerless; this allows us to think one way and act another. However, Allen believed that the unconscious mind generates as much action as the conscious mind, and while we may be able to sustain the illusion of control through the conscious mind alone, in reality we are continually faced with a question: "Why cannot I make myself do this or achieve that?"

In noting that desire and will are sabotaged by the presence of thoughts that do not accord with desire, Allen was led to the startling conclusion: "We do not attract what we want, but what we are." Achievement happens because you as a person embody the external achievement; you don't "get" success but become it. There is no gap between mind and matter.

We are the sum of our thoughts

The logic of the book is unassailable: Noble thoughts make a noble person, negative thoughts hammer out a miserable one. To a person mired in negativity, the world looks as if it is made of confusion and fear. On the other hand, Allen noted, when we curtail our negative and destructive thoughts, "All the world softens towards us, and is ready to help us."

We attract not only what we love, but also what we fear. His explanation for why this happens is simple: Those thoughts that receive our attention, good or bad, go into the unconscious to become the fuel for later events in the real world. As Emerson commented, "A person is what he thinks about all day long."

Our circumstances are us

Part of the fame of Allen's book is its contention that "Circumstances do not make a person, they reveal him." This seems an exceedingly heartless comment, a justification for neglect of those in need, and a rationalization of exploitation and abuse, of the superiority of those at the top of the pile and the inferiority of those at the bottom.

This, however, would be a knee-jerk reaction to a subtle argument. Each set of circumstances, however bad, offers a unique opportunity for growth. If circumstances always determined the life and prospects of people, then humanity would never have progressed. In fact, circumstances seem to be designed to bring out the best in us, and if we make the decision that we have been "wronged" then we are unlikely to begin a conscious effort to escape from our situation. Nevertheless, as any biographer knows, a person's early life and its conditions are often the greatest gift to an individual.

The sobering aspect of Allen's book is that we have no one else to blame for our present condition except ourselves. The upside is the possibilities contained in knowing that everything is up to us; where before we were experts in the array and fearsomeness of limitations, now we become connoisseurs of what is possible.

Change your world by changing your mind

While Allen did not deny that poverty can happen to a person or a people, what he tried to make clear is that defensive actions such as blaming the perpetrator will only run the wheels further into the rut. What measures us, what reveals us, is how we use those circumstances as an aid or spur to progress. A successful person or community, in short, is one who is most efficient at processing failure.

Allen observed, "Most of us are anxious to improve our circumstances, but are unwilling to improve ourselves—and we therefore remain bound." Prosperity and happiness cannot happen when the old self is still stuck in its old ways. People are nearly always the unconscious cause of their own lack of prosperity.

Tranquillity = success

The influence of Buddhism on Allen's thought is obvious in his emphasis on "right thinking," but it is also apparent in his suggestion that the best path to success is calmness of mind. People who are calm, relaxed, and purposeful appear as if that is their natural state, but nearly always it is the fruit of self-control.

These people have advanced knowledge of how thought works, coming from years of literally "thinking about thought." According to Allen, they have a magnet-like attraction because they are not swept up by every little wind of happenstance. We turn to them because they are masters of themselves. "Tempest-tossed" souls battle to gain success, but success avoids the unstable.

Final comments

Some 100 years after its first publication, *As a Man Thinketh* continues to get rave reviews from readers. The plain prose and absence of hype are appealing within a genre that contains sensational claims and personalities, and the fact that we know so little about the author makes the work somehow more intriguing.

To bring its message to a wider audience, two updated versions of the work that correct the gender specificity of the original have been published: *As You Think*, edited by Marc Allen (no relation), and *As a Woman Thinketh*, edited by Dorothy Hulst.

James Allen

Allen was born in Leicester, England, in 1864. At 15 he was forced to leave school and go out to work; his father, who had left for the United States following the failure of the family business, had been robbed and murdered. Allen was employed with several British manufacturing firms until 1902, when he began to write full time. Moving to Ilfracombe on the south-west coast of England, he settled down to a quiet life of reading, writing, gardening, and meditation.

As a Man Thinketh was the second of 19 books that Allen wrote in a decade. Although considered his best work, it was only published at his wife's urging. Other books include From Poverty to Power, Byways of Blessedness, The Life Triumphant *and* Eight Pillars of Prosperity. *Allen died in 1912.*

Meditations

2nd century

"*Begin each day by telling yourself: Today I shall be meeting with inter-ference, ingratitude, insolence, disloyalty, ill-will and selfishness—all of them due to the offenders' ignorance of what is good or evil. But for my part I have long perceived the nature of good and its nobility, the nature of evil and its meanness, and also the nature of the culprit himself, who is my brother (not in the physical sense, but as a fellow-creature similarly endowed with reason and a share of the divine); therefore none of those things can injure me, for nobody can implicate me in what is degrading.*"

"*Love nothing but that which comes to you woven in the pattern of your destiny. For what could more aptly fit your needs?*"

"*Everything—a horse, a vine—is created for some duty. This is nothing to wonder at: even the sun-god himself will tell you, 'This is a work I am here to do,' and so will all the other sky-dwellers. For what task, then, were you yourself created? For pleasure? Can such a thought be tolerated?*"

In a nutshell

Don't get caught up in trivia or pettiness; appreciate your life within a larger context.

In a similar vein

Boethius, *The Consolation of Philosophy* (p34)
Richard Carlson, *Don't Sweat the Small Stuff* (p78)

CHAPTER 2

Marcus Aurelius

Marcus Aurelius Antoninus was emperor of Rome from 161AD until his death 19 years later. By the time he came to power, Rome was under threat: constant warring with "barbarians" on the frontier, disease brought back by soldiers, pestilence, and even earthquakes. Try to imagine the President of the United States being so philosophical in the midst of such crises. Yet despite the circumstances, after his death Marcus Aurelius would come to be idealized by the Romans as the perfect emperor, a genuine philosopher-king who provided the last real nobility of rule before the savagery of his son Commodus' reign and the anarchy of the third century.

A student of Stoic philosophy, Marcus Aurelius refused to be made miserable by the difficulties of life. Stoicism was a Greek school of thought originating around 300BC. In simple terms, it taught that submission to the law of the universe was how human beings should live, and emphasized duty, avoidance of pleasure, reason, and fearlessness of death. Stoics would also have full responsibility for their actions, independence of mind, and pursue the greater good over their own. The emperor would have been comfortable with today's United Nations and other world bodies that stand for cooperative effort: Stoics had an international outlook and believed in universal brotherhood.

As well as the world, the thoughts of the Stoics spanned time, as this excerpt from the *Meditations* demonstrates:

"All things fade into the storied past, and in a little while are shrouded in oblivion. Even to men whose lives were a blaze of glory this comes to pass; as to the rest, the breath is hardly out of them before, in Homer's words, they are 'lost to sight alike and hearsay'. What, after all, is immortal fame? An empty, hollow thing. To what, then, must we aspire? This, and this alone: the just thought, the unselfish act, the tongue that utters no falsehood, the temper that greets each passing event as something predestined, expected, and emanating from the One source and origin."

This was written over 19 centuries ago, yet it is somehow even more relevant when we know how ancient it is. Marcus Aurelius' life itself bears the statement out; not many now will have cause to remember his skill or otherwise as a leader, but his *Meditations*, quiet thoughts written by firelight in the midst of campaigns, live on in hearts and minds.

The *Meditations* are alive with perceptiveness about the basic unity of all things in the universe, including its people. They tell us that the effort to see through another's eyes is nothing less than an expansion of one's world—and a unifying of it. To despise, avoid, or judge a person is simply an obstruction of Nature's law. The realization that to move human relations to a higher level we must do the opposite of these things formed the basis of the emperor's thought.

On every page of the *Meditations* is this theme of accepting things and people how they are, not how we would like them to be. There is sadness in this view, as the following brief comment suggests: "You may break your heart, but men still go on as before." One does get the impression of reading the thoughts of a lonely man, but then Marcus Aurelius' ability to see life objectively saved him from any real disillusionment:

"Be like the headland against which the waves break and break: it stands firm, until presently the watery tumult around it subsides once more to rest. 'How unlucky I am, that this should have happened to me!' By no means; say, rather, 'How lucky I am that this has left me with no bitterness; unshaken by the present, and undismayed by the future.'"

The great worth of Stoic philosophy is its ability to help put things into perspective so you can remember the things that matter; the *Meditations* is, if you like, an ancient and noble *Don't Sweat the Small Stuff*. The person who can see the world as it really is also carries the ability to see beyond that world. We are here and we have a job to do, but there is a feeling that we came from another place, and will eventually go back to it. Life can be sad and lonely, seemingly one thing after another, but this should never dull our basic wonder at our existence in the universe:

"Survey the circling stars, as though you yourself were mid-course with them. Often picture the changing and rechanging dance of the elements. Visions of this kind purge away the dross of our earth-bound life."

16

Final comments

What can we make of the fact that Marcus Aurelius was the father of Commodus, whose accession and brutal reign broke the tradition of non-hereditary kingship? If the philosopher was such a great man, how could he have fathered such a brute?

The *Meditations* is not just another self-help book with easy answers—its very theme is imperfection. We can never know exactly why things happen, why people act the way they do, but it is not up to us to judge anyway; there is a larger meaning to events and lives that escapes us. This knowledge itself is a comfort.

This is a short book that is a source of sanity in a mad world, and today's reader will also love the beautiful prose that makes it stand out against modern philosophical and self-help writings (Maxwell Staniforth's translation is particularly good). Buy a copy and you will make use of it for life.

Marcus Aurelius

When Hadrian, one of Rome's most successful emperors, died in 138AD, he appointed as his successor Antoninus Pius, who in turn, on Hadrian's instructions, adopted the 17-year-old Marcus Aurelius as his successor. The young man's future was confirmed when he was married to Faustina, a daughter of Antoninus Pius. As well as carrying out courtly duties, he devoted himself to the study of law and philosophy. Taking power at age 40, Aurelius voluntarily divided rule with his brother Lucius Verus, who was to die eight years later.

Though peaceful by nature, Aurelius was forced continually to defend the Empire's territories against the Germanic tribes, including the Marcomanni and the Quadi. A single manuscript, now lost, is the source of the Meditations. *Marcus Aurelius had never intended that it be published. The year 1559 saw its first printing, almost 14 centuries after the emperor's death in 180. While Ridley Scott's film* Gladiator *portrays the emperor being murdered by Commodus, there is no historical evidence for this.*

The Bhagavad-Gita

*"We are born into the world of nature; our
second birth is into the world of spirit."*

*"But he who, with strong body serving mind,
Gives up his power to worthy work,
Not seeking gain, Arjuna! Such an one
Is honourable. Do thine alloted task!"*

*"He whose peace is not shaken by others, and before
whom other people find peace, beyond excitement and
anger and fear—he is dear to me."*

*"If thou wilt not fight thy battle of life because in
selfishness thou art afraid of the battle, thy resolution
is in vain: nature will compel thee."*

*"I have given thee words of vision and wisdom more secret
than hidden mysteries. Ponder them in the silence of thy
soul, and then in freedom do thy will."*

In a nutshell

Seek peace inside yourself, do the work that is yours, and wonder at
the mysteries of the universe.

In a similar vein
Deepak Chopra, *The Seven Spiritual Laws of Success* (p90)
The Dhammapada (p128)

CHAPTER 3

The Bhagavad-Gita is the record of a conversation between a young man and God (in the form of Krishna). The young warrior Arjuna, from the royal Pandava family, is in a state of panic on the morning of a battle. The "enemies" he is expected to fight are cousins whom he knows well.

In this desperate predicament, Arjuna turns to his charioteer Krishna for help. The answers he gets are not exactly what he wants to hear, but it is Krishna's opportunity to tell a mortal about how the universe operates and the best approach to life.

The Gita is a small but much-loved part of the vast Hindu epic the Mahabarata, a poetic chronicle about two warring groups of cousins, the Kauravas and the Pandavas. The title means Celestial Song or Song of the Lord, and Juan Mascaró (whose translation is used here) has described it as a "symphony" that represents a peak of Indian spirituality.

The beauty of this work is that it operates on various levels—poetry, scripture, philosophy, self-help guide—and here we will focus on the last of these.

The meaning of Arjuna's predicament

Arjuna does not want to get involved in this battle, and why would he? The reader cannot but agree that it is madness to wage war against one's own relatives. The story is allegorical, however; it is about action and non-action, and introduces us to the concepts of *karma* and *dharma*.

Arjuna wonders, quite reasonably, why he should bother to do any-thing good, or to do anything at all, in a world that is so bad. Joseph Campbell says in *The Power of Myth* that part of maturity is saying "yes" to the abominable or the evil, to recognize its existence in your world. What he calls "the affirmation of all things" does not mean that you can't fight a situation, only that you can't say that something does not have the right to exist. What exists does so for some reason, even if

19

that reason is for you to fight it. It would be nice to withdraw from life, to be above it all, but you can't. Because we are alive, we can't avoid action or its effects—this is *karma*.

If we must throw ourselves into life, what should be our guide? There is action motivated by desire, and action undertaken out of a sense of purpose.

The first type seems easier, because it allows you to live without questioning and requires little self-knowledge. In fact it goes against the grain of universal law, usually leading to the departure of spirit from our lives. Purposeful action seems more complicated and obscure, but is in fact the most natural way; it is the salvation of our existence and even the source of joy. The word for this is *dharma*.

Reason

The Bhagavad-Gita is a great book because it embodies the reasoning mind, capable of choosing the way of purpose over the automaticity of a life led by desire. If Arjuna simply follows his desire not to fight, he learns nothing. Instead, Krishna tells him to "fight the good fight"— this is his duty, his purpose, his *dharma*.

Freed from indecision, Arjuna is subsequently told that his opponents "have it coming to them" anyway; Arjuna is merely the instrument of divine *karma*.

The reader should not dwell too long on why God is recommending war. The point of the story is that the young warrior, in questioning his own action and existence, displays reason. Nowadays we tend to equate reason with intelligence. This is lazy thinking, because it means that a mouse or a computer, displaying the ability to "work something out," is at our level.

Reason is actually the process by which we discover our place in the larger scheme of things, specifically the work or actions by which our existence is justified and fulfilled. It is what makes us human beings.

The Gita is no flight into the mystical; in showing the path to reason, it reveals our highest faculty and greatest asset.

Work

The Bhagavad-Gita draws attention to the three "constituents of nature," Tamas (darkness), Rajas (fire), and Sattva (light). A Rajas style of life is full of action and endless business, with fingers in too many pies, hunger for more, lack of rest, and lust for things and people. It is about gaining and attaining, a life focused on "what is mine and what is not yet mine."

Sound familiar? This is living according to "outcome," and while it may be of a higher order than Tamas (inertia, dullness, lack of care, ignorance), it is still one of mediocrity. And the life of light, Sattva? You will know you are living it when your intentions are noble and you feel peace in your actions. Your work is your sanctuary and you would do it even for no reward at all.

This holy book's key point about work is that unless you are doing the work you love, you are darkening your soul. If this seems impossible, love what you are doing. Freedom—from fear and anxious worry over "results"—will follow. The wise always have an outcome or result in mind, yet their detachment from it makes them all the more effective.

The Gita says that higher even than the peace of meditation is the peace that comes from surrender of the fruit of one's actions; in this state we are free from the rigidity of set expectations, allowing the unexpected and remarkable to emerge.

The steady self

You may be relaxing in front of the television when a report comes on about the year's Academy Awards, telling of the glitter and glory of the Oscars and exclusive post-ceremony parties. Someone remarks, "This is where the rest of the world would like to be." Beneath the superficial enjoyment of the report, suddenly you get a sense of inferiority. "Who cares if people say it's shallow, I want to be there! What have I done with my life that I am not on the list for that party? Am I really going back to my job on Monday morning?"

There is a phrase in psychology for this thinking: "object referral." This means having a focus on others and seeking their approval. Hollywood is famously a shrine to external valuations of worth, where you are always wondering what people will think of your next audition, performance, or deal. This is basically a life of fear and, when things don't turn out as you had hoped, of desperation. The Gita teaches that you can achieve a state where you don't need any external commendation to make you feel right; you know you are of real worth.

One of the main routes to this level of being is meditation, which brings detachment from emotions like fear and greed. Through it we discover a self that is not subject to change, that is, in Deepak Chopra's words, "immune to criticism . . . unfearful of any challenge, and feels beneath no-one." This surely is real power, compared to what we can acquire in the world of action.

In your baser conscious desires you are just like everyone else; in the meditative state you grasp your uniqueness. What we do following meditation does not normally generate negative *karma*, because we are emerging from a zone of purity and perfect knowledge. "With perfect meditation comes perfect act," says The Bhagavad-Gita.

The book repeatedly comments that the enlightened person is the same in success or failure, is not swayed by the winds of event or emotion. It is a manual on how to achieve steadiness, which ironically comes from appreciating the ephemeral nature of life and the relentless movement of time. Though the universe may be in a constant state of flux, we can train our mind to be a rare fixed point. The book is a brilliant antidote to the feelings of smallness and insignificance that can swamp even the most confident in modern life.

Final comments
Those prejudiced against religious books as "mystical rubbish" may be shocked to discover that The Bhagavad-Gita is one of the great works on the sovereignty of the mind.

God tells Arjuna:

> *"I have given thee words of vision and wisdom more*
> *secret than hidden mysteries.*
> *Ponder them in the silence of thy soul, and then in*
> *freedom do thy will."*

Even though God is all powerful, man has free will. The Gita has delivered this message with force across the ages because, perhaps ironically, it is done through poetry, the language of the heart.

This is a perfect self-help book because it is not scholarly or compli-cated but remains a source of the most profound wisdom, offering a path to steadiness of mind and joy in one's work that could not be more relevant amid the speed and pressure of life in the twenty-first century.

The Bible

"Thou shalt decree a thing, and it shall be established unto thee: and the light shall shine upon thy ways." (Job 22:28)

"The Lord is my shepherd, I shall not want; he makes me lie down in green pastures.
He leads me beside still waters; he restores my soul." (Psalm 23)

"Finally, brethren, whatever things are true, whatever things are honest, whatever things are just, whatever things are pure, whatever things are of good report; if there be any virtue, and if there be any praise, think on these things." (Philippians 4:8)

"I can do all things through Christ who strengtheneth me." (Philippians 4:13)

"He giveth power to the faint; and to them that have no might he increaseth strength." (Isaiah 40:29)

"If God is for us, who can be against us?" (Romans 8:31)

"What things soever ye desire, when ye pray believe that ye receive them, and ye shall have them." (Mark 11.24)

In a nutshell

Love, faith, hope, the glory of God, the perfectibility of man.

In a similar vein
The Bhagavad-Gita (p18)
The Dhammapada (p128)

CHAPTER 4

The way people view the Bible usually falls into one of three categories: a sacred religious text; a vast historical work; or a collection of great stories. However, our attachment to these tired slots can prevent us from seeing it anew as a collection of ideas, ones that helped create our concept of what a human being might be.

Progress

It is easy to forget just how much the Old and New Testaments are responsible for the world we live in today. In his book *The Gifts of the Jews: How a Tribe of Desert Nomads Changed the Way Everyone Thinks and Feels*, Thomas Cahill wrote:

"Without the Bible we would never have known the abolitionist movement, the prison-reform movement, the anti-war movement, the labor movement, the civil rights movement, the movement of indigenous and dispossessed peoples for their human rights, the anti-apartheid movement in South Africa, the Solidarity movement in Poland, the free-speech and pro-democracy movements in such Far Eastern countries as South Korea, the Philippines, and even China. These movements of modern times have all employed the language of the Bible."

Perhaps the crucial change in the way we think was the idea of progress. In the distant past time was invariably seen as cyclical; the great creation stories were so important to these early cultures' understanding of themselves that little attention was paid to the future. The idea that tomorrow could be better than today was alien. There were many gods, but they were impersonal and capricious and none had any particular vision for the human race.

This changed with the direct revelation of the commandments through Moses on Mount Sinai. While this new singular God was to be feared, He was a God who not only always had our best interests at heart, but had a long-term vision for His people. He was the God who led the Jews out of slavery in Egypt to the Promised Land, who would work through history in order to create his own ends—the God of progress.

Though we take it for granted today, this progressive worldview has defined western culture and been adopted by nearly all non-western cultures too. It is, as Cahill says above, the force behind all the great emancipation movements that, often employing the language of the Book of Exodus, grew out of the thought that "it does not have to be this way." This thought is also the light that guides most of the self-help literature.

The power of love

If the Old Testament has been the inspiration for groups through the millennia, the New Testament became a symbol of personal salvation. The Old was revolutionary because it put fresh emphasis on the individual, but the New took this to its logical extreme by saying that individuals could not only change the world, but had a duty to do so. Its challenge to transform the world in God's image, using Jesus as the example, made it a manual for active love. Again, a love that heals and creates—like progress—is something totally taken for granted now. But as Andrew Welburn put it in *The Beginnings of Christianity*: "Love is the revelation of God to the individualised, self-conscious man, just as power and wise order were the revelation of God to ancient, pre-self-conscious humanity."

The Bible's theme of the power of love marked a new era of humankind. On his way to Damascus to help suppress the Christians, Saul of Tarsus (who later became St. Paul) was "blinded by the light." This wonderful story of personal transformation illustrated the strange new idea that love could be stronger than position or power.

Faith

The collections of deities that preceded the Judaic concept of one god were mostly reflections of human desire. If you didn't get what you wanted, it was obvious that the gods were displeased with you. Moses' God was more complicated, requiring the worshipper to have faith in order to fashion His ends and demonstrate omnipotence. The Judaic and Christian God became one not simply of creation and destruction, but of co-creation.

Look at the story of Abraham: Told by God to go to a mountain to make a sacrifice, he does so but realizes that the sacrifice will be his only son. Amazingly, he is willing to go through with it. At the last minute God has him replace the boy with a ram caught in a nearby bush. Abraham's success at this incredible test of faith is rewarded by generations of his descendants living in prosperity.

Yet this was not simply a test of allegiance to God, and not just about Abraham. Humanity itself had passed a test: we could choose no longer to be animals quivering with fear, tied to the physical world, but could reflect God in becoming beings with calm faith.

The Bible and individuality

Other religions and philosophies had seen the world either as an illusion or a drama in which we played a role, but Christianity, by making the individual the unit through which the world would develop and fulfill its potential, made history important—it became the story of humankind's efforts to create heaven on earth.

Above all, Christianity freed believers from having to accept their lot in life. It was profoundly egalitarian: Human beings were no longer captive to other humans, nor to capricious gods, the "fates," or the "stars." This emphasis gave people the groundbreaking idea that they could no longer be defined by factors such as class, ethnicity, or lack of money.

The revolutionary opportunity of the Bible, particularly the New Testament, was to see and understand the "incommunicable singularity of being which all possess" (Teilhard de Chardin). While the broader vision of the Bible is the creation of a community of humankind, it can only be one in which each person has the opportunity to express this singularity to the full. Whatever you think of him, this belief is what fired Pope John Paul II to be so strongly anti-communist—he saw a system that was willing to sacrifice a person's uniqueness to some larger community.

Final comments

The Bible deserves to be seen with new eyes. We no longer have to see it as being about original sin and sacrifice, or as spawning a heavy church hierarchy and holy wars. We should be reminded of its simpler messages of compassion and fulfillment and refinement of ourselves, a morality requiring no imposition on others. Though fascinating as a historical book with great stories, we should do the Bible justice by remembering that it was the original manual for personal transformation.

Iron John

1990

"The male in the past twenty years has become more thoughtful, more gentle. But by this process he has not become more free. He's a nice boy who pleases not only his mother but also the young woman he is living with."

"The word special is important to the naïve man, and he has special relationships with certain people. We all have some special relationships, but he surrounds the special person with a cloying kind of goodwill. The relationship is so special that he never examines the dark side of a person."

"The Iron John story retains memories of initiation ceremonies for men that go back ten or twenty thousand years in northern Europe. The Wild Man's job is to teach the young man how abundant, various, and many-sided his manhood is. The boy's body inherits physical abilities developed by long-dead ancestors, and his mind inherits spiritual and soul powers developed centuries ago."

In a nutshell

Through old stories we can resurrect the ancient and deep power of the masculine.

In a similar vein

Joseph Campbell with Bill Moyers, *The Power of Myth* (p72)
Clarissa Pinkola Estés, *Women Who Run with the Wolves* (p156)
Thomas Moore, *Care of the Soul* (p242)

CHAPTER 5

Robert Bly

Robert Bly is a respected American poet. How did he come to write a self-help bestseller? Bly had been giving talks on mythology to supplement his income, and found that the Brothers Grimm tale "Iron John" hit a nerve with men. His resulting book about this age-old story helped establish the men's movement, and his seminars inspired its drum-beating, tree-hugging stereotype.

The modern man

In early seminars, Bly asked men to re-enact a scene from The Odyssey, in which Odysseus is instructed to lift his sword as he approaches the symbol of matriarchal energy, Circe. Peace-loving men were unable to lift the sword, so fixed were they on the idea of not hurting anyone. These were men who had come of age during the Vietnam war, and they wanted nothing to do with a manhood that, to feel its aliveness, required an enemy. In place of the single-mindedness of the 1950s male, they had receptivity to different viewpoints and agendas.

The world is a much better place for these "soft males" — they are lovely human beings, Bly admits — but such harmony-minded men are also distinguished by their unhappiness, caused by passivity. Bly tried to teach them that flashing a sword didn't necessarily mean that you were a warmonger, but that you could show "a joyful decisiveness."

Iron John is about taking men back, through myth and legend, to the source of their masculinity, and finding a middle path between the greater awareness of the "sensitive new age guy" and the power and vitality of the warrior.

The story

The Iron John story has been around in one form or another for thousands of years. In a nutshell: A hunter answers a challenge from the king to go to a part of the forest from which men don't normally return. The hunter goes into the forest and his dog is taken by a hand that shoots out of a lake. Slowly draining the lake with a bucket, he finds at the bottom a hairy wild man, who is taken back to the town castle and imprisoned.

The king's son is playing with a golden ball when it accidentally rolls into the cage holding the wild man. At length, the prince does a deal in which he gets the ball back, but only after he has released the hairy man in the cage. This deal marks the beginning of the boy's manhood: He is willing to separate himself from his parents and retrieve his "golden ball" (that alive feeling of youth) through discovering his masculine energy.

Who or what is a wild man?

Bly makes an important distinction between the wild man and the savage man. The savage is the type who wrecks the environment, abuses women, and so on, his inner desperation being pushed out on to the world as a disregard or hatred of others. The wild man has been prepared to examine where it is he hurts; because of this he is more like a Zen priest or a shaman than a savage. The wild man is masculinity's highest expression, the savage man its lowest.

A civilized man tries to incorporate his wildness into a larger self. When the prince in the story risks all and goes into the forest with the wild man, the parents simply think that their boy has been taken by the devil; in fact it is a profound initiation, an awakening. Bly's message is that the modern obsession with making childhood a cocoon of light closes children off to sources of power. Addictions and psychological disorders mirror society's inability to accommodate the "dark side."

Bly believes that New Age thinking about harmony and higher consciousness holds a dangerous attraction to naïve men. Mythology beckons us to enter fully into life, with all its blood and tears; the way we achieve full realization of ourselves is to focus on "one precious thing" (an idea, a person, a quest, a question) and the decision to follow it at any cost is the sign of maturity. When we make a clear choice, the king inside us awakens and our powers are finally released.

Re-awakening the warrior

Warrior energy, if not honored or channeled, ends up being expressed as teen gang warfare, wife beating, paedophilia, and feelings of shame.

If used rightly, it can become a source of delight to everyone in its refinement. How else, Bly asks, can we explain the unconscious admiration for a glorious knight or a man in a starched white uniform and medals? This image represents the civilization of warrior energy.

The author also calls for the warrior spirit and occasional "fierceness" to be used in relationships. He quotes psychoanalyst Carl Jung, who said that American marriages were "the saddest around because the man reserved all his fighting for the office." At home he was a pussycat. Fierceness involves protecting what is rightfully yours, and women want to know what a man's boundaries are.

Coming to ground

A man may spend his twenties and thirties as a sort of "flying boy"; in his imagination, nothing can hold him down. But for a man to be made whole, there has to be something that rips him open, a wound that allows his soul to enter. In many myths, a wild animal gets close enough to a young man to gore his leg; in the Iron John story, it is a knight who chases after the prince and stabs him in the leg. As he falls off his horse, the golden hair he has hidden from everyone underneath the helmet is revealed. Until then he has seemed two-dimensional. Appreciation of pain and sorrow, Bly says, is as vital to a man's potentiality as is having the ability to soar through the air.

A hunger for the masculine

The male initiation ceremonies of all cultures form a deepening, a forced discovery of the dark side. Women can't initiate men. In many cultures, a boy is taken from the women who have so far managed his life and made to live among older men for a while. Modern society has few structures for initiation, and boys can spend their teenage years prolonging their freedom, manifested in wild behavior, rudeness to parents (particularly the mother), and clothing and music that attract attention.

Millions of men have grown up with an environment of feminine energy—which isn't a problem in itself, but boys also need the masculine. Men start to think more about their fathers as they get older, and mythology has much to say about the heaviness of "entering the father's house," leaving behind the expectation of lightness and comfort to face grim reality. Bly says that Shakespeare's Hamlet, for instance, is an elaborate metaphor for this process of moving from the mother's side to the father's.

Colors of a life

In Iron John the prince, disguised as a knight, rides a red then a white then a black horse. These colors have a logical symbolic progression in relation to a man's life: The "redness" of his emotions and unbridled sexuality in younger years; the "whiteness" of work and living according to law; and the "blackness" of maturity in which compassion and humanity have the chance to flower.

Bly comments that in the later years of his presidency, Lincoln was a man in black. He had seen it all. No longer ruled by his emotions (red) or some external set of principles or law (white), he had ceased to blame and had developed a brilliant, philosophical sense of humor. You tend to know a man who has begun to move into the black because he is really trusted. There are no hidden corners, because he has fully incorporated his shadow.

Final comments

Why has Bly's retelling of a fairy tale appealed to millions of western men?

The Iron John story has been told around campfires for millennia. Unfortunately, like an inheritance that lies uncollected, many men do not know exactly what they have missed, but this book's impact suggests that many overdue claims for genuine masculinity are now being made—and women and the rest of society will be better off for it too.

Men who may laugh at a book like this are probably those who need it most. The most destructive types tend to be those with the least developed powers of self-examination, and women should welcome any efforts to revive a forceful, but non-destructive, spirit of masculinity. What *Iron John* has done for men, *Women Who Run with the Wolves* (Clarissa Pinkola Estés) has achieved for women, and is highly recommended.

Iron John bears reading twice or more, especially if you are unfamiliar with mythology. This was Bly's first book of prose, but it includes a good selection of his excellent poems.

Robert Bly

Born in 1926 in Madison, Minnesota, to a farming family, Bly went to Harvard for his BA and received an MA from the University of Iowa. He is one of the most renowned living American poets, and has edited a number of collected works, mentored many young poets, and made non-English poetry more widely available through his translations. He was a leader in the anti-Vietnam war movement.

Bly has written other mainstream books, including The Sibling Society, *which argues that we now live in an "adolescent" culture,* The Maiden King: The Reunion of Masculine and Feminine, *with self-help author Marion Woodman, and* A Little Book on the Human Shadow. *He lives in Minnesota.*

The Consolation of Philosophy

6th century

"Contemplate the extent and stability of the heavens, and then at last cease to admire worthless things."

". . . lack of self-knowledge is natural in other living creatures, but in humans is a moral blemish."

"So although the general picture may seem to you mortals one of confusion and turmoil because you are totally unable to visualize this order of things, all of them none the less have their own pattern, which orders and directs them towards the good."

"'This is why,' she went on, 'the wise man ought not to chafe whenever he is locked in conflict with Fortune, just as it is unfitting for the courageous man to be resentful when the din of battle resounds. For each of them the difficulty offers the opportunity; for the courageous man it is the chance of extending his fame, and for the wise man the chance of lending substance to his wisdom.'"

In a nutshell

No matter what happens to you, you always have freedom of mind.

In a similar vein
Marcus Aurelius, *Meditations* (p14)
David Brooks, *The Road to Character* (p50)
Viktor Frankl, *Man's Search for Meaning* (p162)

CHAPTER 6

Boethius

I t is difficult to overestimate the place of *The Consolation of Philosophy* in the self-help canon. Though Boethius is not a household name today, for over a millennium in the Christian West his work was second only to the Bible in popularity.

Boethius' life was one of incredible privilege. Born Anicius Manlius Severinus Boethius into an aristocratic family in the late Roman Empire, he was adopted by the statesman Symmachus, whose daughter he married. Groomed for power, he received the best education and was made Consul while still in his late twenties. As well as being a pillar of the Roman Senate and society, he was esteemed as a scholar, making translations and commentaries of Aristotle that would keep alive the classical tradition through the Middle Ages. But his aim to translate all the works of Plato and Aristotle and to harmonize their ideas into one work would never be fulfilled. For Boethius lived in interesting times.

The Roman Empire had metamorphosed into "Christendom," split between East (Constantinople) and West (Ravenna). While he maintained most of the old Roman institutions, the ruler of Italy was now not a Roman, but a "barbarian," the Ostrogoth Theodoric. Boethius was appointed Master of Offices in Theodoric's court, a sort of chief-of-staff who could smooth relations between the Senate and the new regime. However, a court intrigue saw Theodoric accuse Boethius of treason and, despite assertions of innocence, he was sentenced to death by torture.

The life that had previously had everything now lay in ruins. How could his beloved philosophy help him now? This awful predicament made him uniquely suited to answer the question, and it was on death row that *The Consolation* was written.

The wheel of Fortune
The book begins when a despondent prisoner in his cell (whom we take to be Boethius himself) is visited by an apparition, Lady Philosophy.

Having heard the prisoner rail against the injustice of his situation, Philosophy begins reasoned arguments on why he should not blame Fortune.

Fortune comes and goes as she chooses, and therefore should never be depended on. The prisoner has associated "happiness" with his high position, public esteem, and wealth, but Philosophy argues that these things cannot be the real source of happiness if they have led him to where he sits now. If one is to depend on Fortune, one should expect her departure as much as her arrival, just as seasons come and go. In his rage, Boethius has forgotten how the world is ordered.

And how is it ordered? Philosophy gets the prisoner to agree that the highest good we can seek is God, and that our pursuit of external things including fame, wealth, or power are *de facto* graspings for this source of true happiness. Unlike Fortune, God is unchanging and is accessed through looking inward. Paradoxically, the person who seeks to know God attains self-knowledge.

Still somewhat despondent, the prisoner complains that the wicked often win out over the good. However, Philosophy questions this, noting that if the wicked achieve their ends they become as animals, whereas if the good succeed they rise above being human to the level of gods. So evil can never really win, since "success" in evil does not lead anywhere, whereas all attempts at good take us higher.

Fate and Providence

The book builds up to even bigger questions concerning Providence and free will. Told that there is no chance in the universe, that Providence orders everything perfectly, the prisoner rightly demands: "How then do humans have free will?" Philosophy explains that "God sees in the present the future events which proceed from free choice." God knows what will happen if you make a particular choice, but does not interfere in the choice made, unless asked for guidance.

The prisoner learns that whereas Providence effortlessly organizes the universe as a whole, Fate concerns the movement of individual beings within time. Those who are closer to God live in greater accord with Providence and can therefore depend on it for help; those who believe they are on their own are wholly tied to their fate and are— again paradoxically—in lesser control of their destiny. Those who appreciate stillness know the mind of Providence; those who apprehend nothing but turmoil and chaos can only see the harshness of Fate.

Meaning from misery

Philosophy tries to show Boethius that there is no better person than he, who had enjoyed wealth, power, fame, and all the advantages of high birth, to be forced to consider the ultimate worth of material things. These are no protection against what has befallen him, and in fact set him up for his fate. In his last days, writing as "the prisoner," he sees his life in perspective. His achievements, he realizes, are not as important as the self-knowledge he is now gaining.

It dawns on Boethius that his life thus far has been about the power of mastery, or willful self-creation. In the course of the year in prison he replaces the mastery fixation of the adolescent/adult with an appreciation of the universe's unity and oneness; he transforms himself from grasping politician to wise elder. Comforted by Philosophy, even a death as horrible as his is put into perspective.

Impact of *The Consolation*

The Consolation inspired Dante, Chaucer, and Aquinas, and was rendered into English by both King Alfred (9th century) and Elizabeth I (16th century). At a general level, the book helped to inspire the piety and introspection that we now associate with the Middle Ages.

Boethius' desire to enlighten the broader public is expressed in the form in which *The Consolation* is written, through the interleaving of prose and poetry known as Menippean satire, which until then had been a popular and light-hearted literary style. The book was designed to seduce the reader into accepting its arguments through the provision of delight as much as solace, and this it does. P. S. Walsh's translation brilliantly captures the intent of the book.

Final comments

Though Boethius was one of the great intellects of his time, his book is above all a personal work that speaks directly to the reader in whatever age, offering instant advice, solace, and inspiration. Its central question of free will may at first seem too intellectual, but in fact it is pivotal to the whole self-help ethic, for being free of mind even when you are not physically free, which Boethius achieves, is the essence of maturity. *The Consolation* is one of the most in-depth discussions of the nature of happiness you are ever likely to read.

How Proust Can Change Your Life

1997

"Though Proust never liked it, and referred to it variously as 'unfortunate' [1914], 'misleading' [1915] and 'ugly' [1917], In Search of Lost Time had the advantage of pointing directly enough to a central theme of the novel: a search for the causes behind the dissipation and loss of time. Far from a memoir tracing the passage of a more lyrical age, it was a practical, universally applicable story about how to stop wasting and begin appreciating one's life."

"Though philosophers have traditionally been concerned with the pursuit of happiness, far greater wisdom would seem to lie in pursuing ways to be properly and productively unhappy. The stubborn recurrence of misery means that the development of a workable approach to it must surely outstrip the value of any utopian quest for happiness."

In a nutshell

Appreciate the rich experience of life, despite circumstances. Low expectations make for pleasant surprises.

In a similar vein

Thomas Moore, *Care of the Soul* (p242)

CHAPTER 7

Alain de Botton

The father of the Proust family was an esteemed professor of hygiene who wrote countless scholarly papers and traveled widely. The son also became a doctor, financially successful and fond of sports, so robust that he had once been run over by a cart and horses and lived.

Then there was the other son, a sickly aesthete who lived off his parents' money and could not even keep a simple library job. In his healthier times, he was to be seen at the Paris opera or giving dinner parties. Only after both his parents had died was he ready to make something of his life, and he was in his mid-30s by the time he settled down to write; it would then be years before he would receive any recognition. As Alain de Botton relates it, Proust expressed to his maid what must have seemed a forlorn hope: "Ah, Celeste, if I could be sure of doing as much with my books my father did for the sick."

Given the fame that we know would later greet Proust, it seems a little ridiculous to have held such low hopes. Yet in de Botton's eyes, the remark encapsulates the meaning of Proust's work: The writer did honestly seek to emulate his father's success, and also as a healer. De Botton's book goes beyond the literary merits of a masterpiece (*In Search of Lost Time*) to unveil its therapeutic power, making us see that it was by this that Proust would ultimately have wanted to be judged.

The purposes of pain

Proust was interested in putting suffering to good use; for him this was "the whole art of living." Noting that philosophers have traditionally been in pursuit of theories of happiness, in Proust de Botton finds a substantially more useful form of life advice: Instead of seeking to make our lives a sort of Disneyland of fulfilled aspirations, it is better to find ways in which we can be "productively unhappy."

Suffering always seems to surprise us, when maybe it shouldn't. Many of the characters in Proust's writing are bad sufferers, employing defense mechanisms against facing up to their "issues," making them insufferable people. The good sufferer sees the bitter logic in what he or she is feeling, knowing that matters inevitably lose their emotional intensity, leaving residues of wisdom.

The art of living, as Proust understood it, is not about a great lifestyle, but about locating worth and meaning despite your circumstances, rather than through them. Seen this way, productive unhappiness turns out to be quite a good way to approach life.

How to win friends . . . and still keep your place in history

Proust had lots of friends who loved him dearly and several wrote glowing memoirs of their time with him. De Botton shows us just how the writer came to enjoy such veneration.

First of all, he did not believe that friendship was an opportunity to bare one's soul to another, even if the other person was interested in hearing what you had to say. Indeed, to keep a friend and to get the most out of their personality, you had to let them do the talking. Proust was loved perhaps because he was such a great listener. Secondly, he believed that friendships should be light-hearted and non-intellectual— conversation was an opportunity to amuse the other person and to make them feel special.

All of this might be taken direct from the Dale Carnegie book of interpersonal relations, and in fact Proust's friends invented the verb Proustify, to give abundant attention and praise. However, there is more to it than this: De Botton insightfully shows how Proust deliberately excised "truth" and the intellect from the friendship equation, allowing him to express his laser-like powers of analysis in his writing—thereby keeping his friends.

The message we can glean from this master of friendship is to have lower expectations of your friends, and generally not to depend on other people for your happiness. Get a grip on your deeper passion or love (which is usually not a person but a thing that cries out for fulfillment or pursuit—in Proust's case, writing) and live according to it. The satisfaction this gives will put friendship and other relationships into their proper perspective.

How to get a life (that is not like anyone else's)

If the doctor told you that you had a week to live, the world would seem wonderful, a miracle. How is it that in the normal state of affairs we can so easily get depressed, bored, or completely fed up? Proust believed that these latter feelings, while quite normal, were a mistake in perception. The narrator in his book goes to the seaside hoping to see a stormy, dark coastline with wailing seabirds, but instead finds a regular resort town. Nevertheless his painter friend Elstir, by pointing out simple things like the whiteness of a woman's cotton dress in the sun, is able to retrieve the narrator's appreciation of beauty.

For many, the word "Proust" conjures up images of untouchable intellectuality and refinement, writing that can take us back to a Parisian golden age when life was somehow grander and richer. De Botton tells us how wrong this view is. The irony of his homage to Proust is that it contains a warning not to love the French writer too much. We should not bother to visit the town of Combray where he spent some of his childhood summers, trying to see what he saw; rather, the object of reading him is to come away with a heightened sense of perception that can be employed wherever you are and in whatever time you live. To wish we had lived in Proust's time, with its madeleine cakes, horse carriages, and banquets, is a crime committed against the possibilities of the present.

Time

At one level, Proust's work is about appreciating the moment, the tiny details of life. He wanted us to feel the luxury of time, to revel in it, and his writing style famously reflects his obsession. If a sentence could be understood to be a moment in words, he sought to prolong those moments; if something was worth writing about, it was worth doing so at length. De Botton refers us to one sentence that in standard font would run to four meters, or stretch around a bottle of wine 17 times!

At another level, Proust lived in quiet disregard of time. *A la recherche du temps perdu* has often been translated as *Remembrance of Things Past*, and indeed a popular picture of Proust's work is that it is a resurrection of the forgotten for sentiment's sake. The impression that De Botton gives us, however, is that this masterpiece is not "about" the past at all; rather, like all great novelists Proust used the past to describe a vision of how things are separate to time. Events are in the past, but the deep understanding of people, of love, and of life that Proust provides is not tied to time. De Botton was inspired to write his book because of this very timelessness in Proust.

Final comments

Does the seven-volume, million-and-a-quarter-word *In Search of Lost Time*, considered by many the greatest book of the twentieth century, really have anything to do with self-help? The suggestion that it does has enraged some Proust devotees, because Art is not to be cheapened by suggestions of practical therapeutic value. Though the book has an élitist and cultured image, Proust once said that the readers he sought were "the sort of people who buy a badly printed volume before catching a train." As De Botton has it, Proust did not write so that he could receive recognition as a literary maestro, but for his own redemption. If it had helped him, maybe it would help others.

How Proust Can Change Your Life is not merely a homage to a person but a tribute—even if intended ironically—to the ethic of self-help. Its great service is to have given those people who may never actually read the French genius his essential philosophy. A Proustian understanding of life, in all its complexity and subtlety, is now an option for readers who may never have bothered to look beyond the clear-cut, rosy answers of a Stephen Covey or an Anthony Robbins.

De Botton, and through him Proust, will have succeeded if the people who might normally read books about "time management" can be moved to consider the nature of time itself.

Alain de Botton

De Botton grew up in Switzerland, went to England's Harrow School, and has a degree from the University of Cambridge. Other books include Essays in Love *(1993),* The Romantic Movement *(1994),* The Art of Travel *(2002),* The Pleasures and Sorrows of Work *(2009), and* Religion for Athiests *(2012).* The Consolations of Philosophy *(2000) was adapted for a British Channel 4 television series, in which the author applied the thoughts of Socrates, Epicurus, Seneca, Montaigne, Schopenhauer, and Nietzsche to everyday problems.*

De Botton lives in London, where he oversees The School of Life, which provides seminars and coaching guided by philosophy.

Transitions: Making Sense of Life's Changes

1980

"Throughout nature, growth involves periodic accelerations and trans-formations: things go slowly for a time and nothing seems to happen—until suddenly the eggshell cracks, the branch blossoms, the tadpole's tail shrinks away, the leaf falls, the bird molts, the hibernation begins. With us it is the same. Although the signs are less clear than in the world of feather and leaf, the function of transition times are the same."

"Whether you chose your change or not, there are unlived potential-ities within you, interests and talents that you have not yet explored. Transitions clear the ground for new growth. They drop the curtain so the stage can be set for a new scene. What is it, at this point in your life, that is waiting quietly backstage for an entrance cue?"

In a nutshell

All life transitions have a pattern, which if acknowledged will make tough times more comprehensible.

In a similar vein
Robert Bly, *Iron John* (p28)
Joseph Campbell with Bill Moyers, *The Power of Myth* (p72)
Clarissa Pinkola Estés, *Women Who Run with the Wolves* (p156)
Thomas Moore, *Care of the Soul* (p242)

CHAPTER 8

William Bridges

Villiam Bridges only reluctantly started writing this book when he was going through a period of change himself and found that there were no guides to transition. To his surprise, *Transitions* found an immediate niche and has sold over a quarter of a million copies. It is quietly passed from one person to another.

The depth of the book is that it is not just a manual on "how to cope," but gets us to see that the process of disorganization, death, and renewal is fundamental to nature and a central theme in mythology. Rather than stability, this cycle is the natural state of affairs. We all intuitively know this, but Bridges says that admitting it to yourself, and looking more closely at the process, will make the inevitable times of change easier to deal with.

The way of transition

One of the interesting things about transition is the way it descends on us unexpectedly. Many women and couples have a hard time dealing with the loss of time and freedom that accompanies a newborn baby in their lives, for example. Before they can enjoy the marvel of the child, they have to deal with the ending of their old, less restricted life.

A man came to one of Bridges' group meetings on dealing with life transitions who had recently received a big promotion. His family were now getting everything they had wanted, but psychologically he was finding it hard to deal with. Why? We all have our patterns of living and in a way it doesn't really matter whether we were happy with them or not—when they change there is a loss. Even a musician toiling away in small clubs for years who suddenly finds herself a star or a lottery winner will need a time of adjustment.

The morale is: Focus less on whether an event is good or bad, but whether or not it involves an important change of life for you. And don't be worried if the event seems relatively inconsequential; it may merely be the most obvious symbol of change, when there are deeper rumblings in the psychological ground beneath.

The only constant is change

It can be useful to see transition within the context of a larger life journey. Many social scientists see age 30 as a key turning point, a moving from youth to real adulthood, where in the past this point was 21. Men come to Bridges and say, "I seem to be entering old age and have barely got out of adolescence!" The fact is that transitions happen throughout our life and don't necessarily correspond to a set age.

Bridges discusses the myth of Odysseus and his long journey home through many trials and tribulations. Though a great leader, Odysseus found that he had to unlearn many of the ways he had dealt with life in the past. One of the messages of transition is that we can't be the same person doing the same thing all our life. When you are young you imagine that from age 30 until death life is one unbroken plain of stability. However this is rarely so, and if life seems too settled you either choose to make changes or have them forced on you.

Following is a rough outline of Bridges' three stages of transition, which follow the "rites of passage" identified by anthropologists and evident in the most tribal rituals.

Endings

To have a new beginning you need to acknowledge an ending. It is universal practice among traditional peoples that when one of their number is about to undergo an inner transition they are taken out of their normal daily life. In our times of change we may feel this need for *disengagement* from our normal experience.

This can be followed by a sense of *disidentification*, when we don't know quite what know who we are any more. The old motivations are gone. Another stage is *disenchantment*, the point when we realize that how we saw the world was not a very good reflection of reality after all. This can be the first stage of transition, but also the last, as it flattens the ground for a new beginning and way of seeing the world.

We all have different styles when it comes to coping with an ending, but each ending may reawaken old hurts or feelings of shame. If you were made to feel unworthy as a child, each seeming failure in later life will bring acute pain as you are reminded of perceived unworthiness. Although they sometimes feel like it, endings are not the end of us. In tribal cultures they are ritualized so that the person sees an ending not as something final, but as a necessary stage to bring new life.

The neutral zone

We usually want to escape as quickly as possible from this uncomfortable time after the shock of an ending. It could, however, be one of the most valuable times in your life, when because you have been "broken open" you are also ready to consider other ways of being and doing. Bridges has some suggestions for your time in limbo:

1 Make sure that you find time to be alone. Welcome the emptiness. Go somewhere with few distractions where you can do literally nothing, but don't expect any great revelations. The point is to pay attention to your dreams and thoughts.
2 Keep a diary or log of your neutral-zone experiences, or write your autobiography. Give yourself the chance to "rewrite" your life story.
3 Try to discover what you really want, what your purpose for living may be. If your life ended today, what you do feel you should have done by now?

Many of the great figures of history (St. Paul, Mohammed, Dante, Buddha) saw the need to "go into the woods" or the desert. Your intention may not be to save the world, but be reassured that humans have been going into retreat, and needing to do so, for thousands of years.

New beginnings

How do we know when the neutral zone can be left behind? When do we make our great new start? Beginnings can often only be seen in retrospect—they don't seem impressive at the time. We meet someone who ends up being our spouse at a party we didn't want to go to, we happen to open a book at a friend's place that changes us for ever.

When we are ready to move on, opportunities will appear and it will be an exciting time. But be easy on yourself and maintain at least some form of continuity with your old life. Fresh with your insights from limbo time, don't be too disheartened if things don't move as quickly as you would like. Bridges recalls the Zen saying, "After enlightenment, the laundry."

Final comments

If you have experienced a significant transition, whether it be a divorce, going back to university, or starting a new career, a common feeling is that you are going "back to square one," that all the previous years have been wasted. You are likely to think, "Maybe I should have stayed doing what I was doing—it wasn't that bad, was it?"

Hopefully, Bridges' book can be a support and a motivator, because it shows us that transition is not the end of everything but a cyclical process whose ultimate reward is a sense of direction much clearer than you have had before. The author quotes Ralph Waldo Emerson, who said, "Not in his goals but in his transitions man is great." If you can become skilled at getting through difficult periods, you will feel much more confident to cope with life generally.

This classic may not seem attractive right now, but try to remember it when you next start to feel that a period of stability is coming to a close.

William Bridges

Born in 1933, Bridges grew up in New England. He studied English at Harvard, did an MA in history at Columbia University, and was awarded his PhD from Brown University. Formerly a professor of American Literature, Bridges shifted to the field of transition management in the mid-1970s. He worked as a consultant and lecturer, developing transition strategies for large companies such as Intel, Apple, and Shell.

Other books include the bestsellers Jobshift, Creating You & Co, *and* Managing Transitions. The Way of Transition *was written in response to the loss of his wife, Mondi. He lived in Mill Valley, California, and died in 2013.*

The Road to Character

2015

"Character is built in the course of your inner confrontation. Character is a set of dispositions, desires, and habits that are slowly engraved during the struggle against your own weakness. You become more disciplined, considerate, and loving through a thousand small acts of self-control, sharing, service, friendship, and refined enjoyment . . . If you don't develop a coherent character in this way, life will fall to pieces sooner or later. You will become a slave to your passions. But if you do behave with habitual self-discipline, you will become constant and dependable."

"People with character . . . are anchored by permanent attachments to important things. In the realm of the intellect, they have a set of permanent convictions about fundamental truths. In the realm of emotion, they are enmeshed in a web of unconditional loves. In the realm of action, they have a permanent commitment to tasks that cannot be completed in a single lifetime."

In a nutshell

Willingness to engage in moral struggle is more important than climbing the ladder of success.

In a similar vein
Boethius, *The Consolation of Philosophy* (p34)
Clayton Christensen, *How Will You Measure Your Life?* (p96)
Viktor Frankl, *Man's Search for Meaning* (p162)
James Hillman, *The Soul's Code* (p194)
M. Scott Peck, *The Road Less Traveled* (p260)

CHAPTER 9

David Brooks

As a pundit and columnist, David Brooks "was born with a natural disposition towards shallowness," he admits, and "paid to be a narcissistic blowhard" with big opinions.

He was keenly aware that people can become very successful "playing the game," while never exploring the deepest aspects of themselves, or even thinking it is important to have practices that refine and better the self. If people seem to like you, and your family loves you, then you must be good enough. "I have lived a life of vague moral aspiration," Brooks writes in the early pages of *The Road to Character*, "vaguely wanting to be good, vaguely wanting to serve some larger purpose, while lacking . . . a clear understanding of how to live a rich inner life." Researching it would provide him with an opportunity to study people who represented moral victory, who had made unshakeable commitments to things greater than themselves. One could be good at the strategy of life, Brooks realized, but have no strategy for the building of "eulogy" virtues, the ones talked about at your funeral: kindness, bravery, honesty, faithfulness.

Paradoxically, it is when we fail in worldly activity that we learn humility, and so win in a moral sense. We move ahead in a career by building on our strengths; we develop morally by dealing with our weaknesses. Building character is a conscious project, and the most important one of our lives.

Instead of pushing, be pulled

Brooks talks about the commencement addresses at American college graduation ceremonies, in which an outsider is invited to the college to spur on the graduates as they enter working life. These addresses abound with clichés about the need to discover one's passion and find one's purpose in life, so one can be fulfilled and happy. By this outlook, you are the master strategist of your life. First, you do an inventory of passions and gifts, then you set goals and set out to achieve them. Yet this whole outlook, Brooks says, begins and ends with the self.

There is another way: he profiles Frances Perkins, a young New

York woman of good standing who decided to make her life into a cause for better worker conditions, following the terrible Triangle Shirtwaist Factory fire of 1911. Like Perkins, we should be willing to be pulled by something, rather than always pushing. Instead of asking what we want from life, is it not more powerful to ask: *What does life want from me? What are my circumstances calling me to do?* We have been thrown by evolution or God into a particular space and time, and our task is to find out what we can do with it. The novelist Frederick Buechner asked, "At what point do my talents and deep gladness meet the world's deep need?"

You can choose a career, but generally a vocation chooses you, or as it says in the Jewish Mishnah: "It's not your obligation to complete the work, but neither are you free to desist from beginning it." A vocation is bigger than you, and therefore you will not "complete" anything before you die. You are a contributor to the unfolding of something, and can take joy in the effort. Frances Perkins, Brooks says, knew that "performing service is not something you do out of the goodness of your heart but as a debt you are repaying for the gift of life." This had been drummed into her at college. In her time, the object of college education was not so much to set you up for a career, but to develop self-control, character, and poise, to make one into a steady and balanced person. Students were taught that it was possible to be something heroic, but certainly not for one's own glory. Their weaknesses were clearly pointed out to them—quite the opposite of today when young people are taught to believe they are "awesome."

Today, doing some kind of community service, Brooks contends, is a patch over the fact that the inner life is weak. If we do profess to serve, it is in terms of asking how we can have the "biggest impact," or help the "greatest number." We ask, what justifies the employment of my great self, and who will be the lucky beneficiaries of my largesse? "Benevolence is the twin of pride," Nathaniel Hawthorne noted.

Perkins' work to improve industrial conditions and the lot of the working man led her to become industrial commissioner in the administration of Franklin D. Roosevelt, and she served in the role for his two terms. She was an important impetus behind the New Deal reforms, particularly the creation of Social Security and jobs programs, laws for overtime, a minimum wage, and unemployment insurance. At a time when there were hardly any women in government, it was a tough job and she was relentlessly criticized. But as Brooks notes: "A person with a deep vocation is not dependent on constant positive reinforcement. The job doesn't have to pay off every month, or every year. The person thus called is performing a task because it is intrinsically good, not for what it produces." How different this is from the "career advancement" of today.

Not about me

George Marshall was not considered smart as a boy, but his parents got him into Virginia Military Institute. Through hazing, strict rules, constant saluting, and harsh self-discipline, he was made into something he wasn't before. The boy became a young man who was "deliberately austere and undramatic," the essence of controlled power.

Yet like his contemporary Ike Eisenhower, Marshall was a late bloomer in the US military. At 39 he was still only a temporary lieutenant colonel, watching younger men get promoted ahead of him. He endured lots of undistinguished roles, in the absence of major wars becoming an expert on administration and logistics. When America got involved in the Great War, he organized the movement of thousands of men and supplies in the trenches of France. When the war ended, Marshall worked diligently for General Pershing, but got no promotions himself. It would take him another 18 years to get his first star. When appointed Chief of Staff for the US's entry into World War Two, he was almost 60.

These days, Brooks notes, nobody wants to be an Organization Man, giving themselves selflessly to the firm or the department or the battalion. Instead we chart careers based on what is best for us, for our self-fulfillment, going from one organization to another to improve our CV. We've forgotten what it means to truly commit, come what may, as Marshall did to the US Army; instead we venerate the start-up, the disruptors, the rebels, the NGO, and the social entrepreneur. This is all well and good, but one side effect is institutional decay; big institutions are seen as dinosaurs.

Yet all institutions are designed to make us grow and allow us a way to contribute to society. They were there before we were born, and will be there afterwards. Institutions "guide behavior gently along certain time-tested lines," making it easier for us to become good. Instead of seeking to cut a glorious swathe through an open field for ourselves, we can work to make an institution better. The army had made Marshall who he was, so he had a debt of service to it. He revolutionized army training, making everything simpler and more attuned to the reality of war. When Franklin Roosevelt put him in charge of the war effort, he was chosen purely on merit. Once in the job he had to implement a brutal cull of the officers, ending many careers. Yet Congress and the British held him in the highest esteem because they knew he was above politics, and only wanted to win the war.

Roosevelt decided to give the job of heading the Allied offensive against Germany in France to Eisenhower, but only because Marshall had not said that he wanted the job (although he privately did). Eisenhower became a great war hero, and Marshall less well known, simply because he had not tried to promote himself. Yet Churchill always said that it was Marshall who contributed the most, calling him "the organizer of victory."

After a distinguished career, Marshall was about to retire when President Truman asked him to become ambassador to China. He accepted without hesitation, even though he had just bought a retirement home for himself and his wife. It was in the subsequent post of Secretary of State that he enacted the famous Marshall Plan (officially the European Recovery Plan) in which the United States helped devastated European countries to rebuild.

Brooks' point: Marshall became great precisely because he never put himself first; whatever was done was in the service of army and country. In an age of everyone being urged to "think outside the box," such commitment to an institution sounds terribly old-fashioned. Yet institutions are the bedrock of society, and sometimes the most moral choice is to give ourselves to their preservation and refinement, so that they can continue to serve people we will never personally know.

The power of surrender

As a young man, Augustine was something of a rising star. His brains and talent, along with the pushiness of his ambitious mother Monica, led him from the fringes of the late Roman Empire to its heart. He crossed the Mediterranean to become a lecturer and rhetorician in the Imperial court in Milan.

But the higher he rose, it seemed, the unhappier he became. He had always believed that to be successful he had to be the captain of his own ship: to work harder, to have more willpower, or make better decisions. Yet this sense of self-sufficiency, of separateness from the world, did not bring peace to Augustine, only more anxiety. In contrast, the more he surrendered himself to something he believed to be vastly greater, God, the more power and peace seemed to come to him. As he would later write in his famous *Confessions*: "Our hearts are restless until we rest in Thee."

Augustine's famous conversion scene in a garden finally ends his belief in self-cultivation. He surrenders himself to God and is flooded with grace and a sense of purpose. Until this point he had resisted surrender because he was not willing to give up worldly pleasures, but his epiphany makes him see that nothing is as joyful as a life of devotion. Augustine found, Brooks says, that "as people become more dependent on God, their capacity for ambition and action increases. Dependency doesn't breed passivity: it breeds energy and accomplishment." The process of *kenosis* or self-emptying is about "Moving down to dependence to gain immeasurable height." Augustine had wanted to be great, and he became so, but not in the way he expected; he would use all his skills and energy in helping to make the modern Church. How much more significant this was than the life he might have lived, as a top lawyer or speaker who had done very well for *himself*.

Brooks tells Augustine's story as a contrast to the modern ethic of self-development. Self-help and motivational books claim to put us in the driving seat of our lives, yet they all depend on the conceit that we are in control. The only thing we can fashion and control is our character, which requires us to subsume our personal wishes, whether it is the Christian God, the Buddhist Mind, or some system of ethics that takes us beyond the self. Indeed, the longer you believe in control, Brooks writes, "the further you are taken away from truth . . . The mind is such a vast, unknown cosmos that you never know yourself by yourself." How could you, when your desires are infinite, your emotions change all the time, and your powers of self-deception are endless? To flourish and really be of use to the world, we must identify with that which does not change. "We did not make ourselves," Augustine wrote, "he who made us never passes away."

From moral struggle to achievement struggle

The moral climate of every society serves its circumstances, emphasizing one value over another. Some qualities are forgotten or considered old-fashioned, while others become more important. In the "moral realist" tradition, Brooks notes, societies emphasize reducing the role of the self, serving great institutions, and focusing on universal values. People brought up in the nineteenth century and the early part of the twentieth century had the virtues of self-effacement, reticence, self-restraint, and sacrifice drilled into them. The idea of "sin" was a part of everyday life, amid warnings of what could happen if people erred from certain moral standards.

A change in the moral environment seemed to occur after World War Two, when people wanted to shake off self-restraint, to relax and enjoy themselves. Writers such as Harry Overstreet (*The Mature Mind*, 1949) argued that the emphasis on sin had meant that people did not trust themselves and maligned themselves unnecessarily. Humanistic psychology taught that people need to love themselves and open up; we are basically good and trustworthy, therefore self-love, self-praise, and self-acceptance are part of the achievement of happiness. The self-esteem movement also had the effect of creating a "culture of authenticity" in which one should always trust one's feelings, follow one's inner voice, and not give in to a conformist or corrupting world. Sin is never inside you, only in society, in racism, oppression, or inequality, and big choices are made by what "feels right," rather than by objective moral standards.

The result is a "depoeticized and despiritualized" person—smart, achieving, but without much depth. The self becomes about talent, not character. The meritocratic culture requires you to become "a shrewd animal" who has "streamlined his inner humanity to make his ascent more aerodynamic," Brooks writes. It tells you *how* to achieve, but not *why* you are choosing one path over another. Every event, even a social one, is seen as an opportunity to advance yourself. People use commercial words to describe the private sphere: "quality" time, "human capital." Whereas character once mean selflessness, generosity, self-sacrifice (qualities that were probably not compatible with getting ahead), now character has come to mean the traits of grit, resilience, willpower, tenacity (traits that make worldly success more likely). Moral struggle is replaced by achievement struggle.

Yet at some point in life, or at some moment of crisis, we may come to see that the struggle for achievement was not as worth it as we thought. In place of narcissism and self-aggrandizement, there is a desire to find out who we are, what cause or purpose we can align ourselves with, what traits or virtues we need to develop to be of genuine service, not just to ourselves. We realize that we are not the center of the universe, that we are not as good as we had thought, that talents alone are not enough for a good life. Life is not so much about achievement, but making the soul more excellent, as the result of inner struggles and refinement of the self. We see that our biggest enemy was pride, which blinds us to our weaknesses and stops us from being vulnerable "before the people whose love we need." Pride allows cold-heartedness and even cruelty to happen, and "deludes us into thinking that we are the authors of our own lives."

Final comments
"I wrote this book not sure I could follow the road to character," Brooks writes, "but I wanted at least to know what the road looks like and how other people have trodden it."

The Road to Character was originally conceived as a book about "cognition and decision-making." It somehow became a much greater work, taking Brooks, and us the reader, beyond psychology to things that matter more. We are not simply a bundle of reflexes, emotions, or evolutionary impulses, but moral beings whose lives come down to consciously made decisions to better ourselves; this spotlight that Brooks shines on the inner life has never been more welcome.

Brooks' profiles are deeply fascinating. He has a genius for making historical figures come alive, from Eisenhower to Samuel Johnson, Montaigne to George Eliot, such that you feel you know them, in the moment, as if they were a friend or contemporary. How far this is from the dusty biographies that set the famous person in stone. Yet it is the wrestling with moral questions, more than their skills as orators or movement leaders, that made a Gandhi or a Martin Luther King great. *The Road to Character* reminds us that genuine leadership is always moral leadership.

David Brooks

Brooks was born in 1961 in Toronto but grew up in New York City and Philadelphia. His father was an English literature professor and his mother studied history. He completed a history degree at the University of Chicago, then worked as a police reporter. He became an intern at National Review, *William F. Buckley's conservative journal, worked at the Hoover Institution, and wrote movie reviews for* The Washington Times. *In 1986 he began working for the* Wall Street Journal, *first as a book and film reviewer, then as a columnist based in Brussels. In 2003 he was hired as a columnist at the* New York Times *to replace William Safire. He considers himself a conservative in the mould of Edmund Burke and Alexander Hamilton.*

Brooks has been a visiting professor at Duke and Yale Universities, and is on the Board of Trustees of the University of Chicago. Other books include Bobos in Paradise: The New Upper Class and How They Got There *(2000), and* The Social Animal: The Hidden Sources of Love, Character and Achievement *(2011).*

Daring Greatly

2012

"After doing this work for the past twelve years and watching scarcity ride roughshod over our families, organizations, and communities, I'd say the one thing we have in common is that we're sick of feeling afraid. We want to dare greatly."

"Armor makes us feel stronger even when we grow weary from dragging the extra weight around. The irony is that when we're standing across from someone who is hidden or shielded by masks and armor, we feel frustrated and disconnected. That's the paradox here: Vulnerability is the last thing I want you to see in me, but the first thing I look for in you."

"Vulnerability is not weakness, and the uncertainty, risk, and emotional exposure we face every day are not optional. Our only choice is a question of engagement."

"To love ourselves and support each other in the process of becoming real is perhaps the greatest single act of daring greatly."

In a nutshell

Not only is vulnerability not weakness, it can be the source of our power.

In a similar vein
David Brooks, *The Road to Character* (p50)
Louise Hay, *You Can Heal Your Life* (p190)
Susan Jeffers, *Feel the Fear and Do It Anyway* (p200)

CHAPTER 10
Brené Brown

"The credit belongs to the man who is actually in the arena, whose face is marred by dust and sweat and blood . . . who at the best knows in the end the triumph of high achievement, and who at the worst, if he fails, at least fails while daring greatly . . ."

Teddy Roosevelt gave his famous "Man in the arena speech" at the Sorbonne in Paris in 1910. It has since become a kind of anthem for anyone who considers themselves a doer as opposed to a critic, who is willing to bare their deficiencies in the pursuit of something they believe in. The "arena" could be a new relationship, a new job, an important conversation, or a creative process, but the point is that you can't wait until everything's perfect before you enter; you must walk in as you are. Deciding not to brings a cost: the wish for safety leads us to lose touch with our real selves.

Partly inspired by the speech, social scientist Brené Brown spent over a decade researching vulnerability, shame, and empathy. The people she got involved in her early research had "the fear of not being worthy of real connection." Thanks to various heartbreaks and betrayals they were keenly aware of their failings and perceived deficiencies, and struggled with their own worthiness. But she also investigated the opposite, people whom she called, in a nod to psychologist Karen Horney, "the Wholehearted," who possessed a willingness to be vulnerable, in work, relationships, and society.

A culture in which so many people believe they are not enough—not successful enough, thin enough, powerful enough, smart enough, extraordinary enough, or certain enough—is a "culture of scarcity," Brown writes in *Daring Greatly: How the Courage to Be Vulnerable Transforms the Way We Live, Love, Parent, and Lead.* They find it difficult to take risks, social, emotional, and professional. Yet "daring greatly," or daring anything at all, is the only way we become what we were meant to be.

59

Do vulnerability

Dictionary definitions of vulnerability include "open to attack and damage," or "capable of being wounded." This suggests weakness, yet real weakness, Brown suggests, stems from never being aware of, or admitting to, our tender spots. This makes us a more rigid, less empathic person who turns people away from us, causing much greater, unpredicted damage to our relationships in the future. Invulnerability is a deadly illusion.

A vulnerability can be: saying something that's unpopular; standing up for yourself; asking for help; saying no; starting your own business; initiating sex with your spouse; helping your spouse who has cancer write their will; calling a friend whose child has just died; getting pregnant after three miscarriages; exercising in public, when you don't look fit; asking to be forgiven; getting promoted and not knowing how you will do.

None of these things are weaknesses; all involve courage. All (you can insert your own) make your heart palpitate, hands go sweaty, stomach lurch, make you feel you are losing control, *naked*. Yet a good question to ask is: "What's worth doing even if I fail?" After Brown gave a TED talk at Long Beach, California, she felt that, even if it was poorly received, or a total flop, it was still really worth doing. No matter what people thought of her, she had got some of the research results on shame and vulnerability into the public, which was her aim. Often, she says, "the result of daring greatly isn't a victory march as much as it is a quiet sense of freedom mixed with a little battle fatigue."

As children we look to a time when we will no longer be small, and as adults we equate success with no longer being vulnerable, with attainment of a state in which we have surmounted all risk and uncertainty. But there is no "Get out of vulnerability free" card. In every domain of life, no matter how rich or famous or successful we are, we are continually presented with moments at which, to move forward, we have to risk something. Anyone who says they "don't do vulnerability" develops compensating behaviors and takes on psychological armor, both of which can end up being a lot more damaging than emotional exposure or living with uncertainty. Professions where you need to be aggressive and emotionally detached, and which involve win or lose situations (e.g. lawyer or soldier) have high emotional costs. Being required to be invulnerable equips you well for the court or the field of battle, Brown notes, but is terrible for normal life.

Naming the shame

Unless you are a sociopath, you will feel shame about something. We are communal creatures, and shame involves the fear of being disconnected from the community via something you have done, which makes you unworthy of being admired, loved, and accepted.

We can feel shame about appearance, level of wealth, quality of parenting, addiction, physical and mental health, our age, our religion, a past trauma. When in her research Brown asked people what sort of shame they had felt, answers included: being asked when I'm due, when I'm not pregnant; hiding the fact that I'm recovering from an addiction; being fired, and having to tell my pregnant wife; telling my fiancé my dad lives in France, when he's in prison; badly losing my temper with my kids; being made a bankrupt; not making partner; infertility; internet porn; flunking out of school; my parents' fighting. Whereas we are much more likely to be open about physical pain, there are some mental pains that we want to keep under wraps at all costs.

If guilt is the feeling, "I did something bad," shame is the feeling, "I *am* bad." While guilt about having acted in a way that doesn't match up with our values is constructive, because it can make us change our ways, shame is always destructive, because it assumes a fixed, bad self that can't be changed. It is shame that leads to addiction, violence, aggression, bullying, eating disorders, and depression. A person who feels shame will either want to engage in self-deadening or self-destructive behavior, or want to hurt or shame others. There is also a difference between shame and humiliation: people feel that their shame is deserved, but feel quite the opposite about being humiliated. "How dare they!" is the natural response to humiliation.

We can develop "shame resilience," Brown says, which involves converting our shame into its antidote, empathy. Shame cannot survive if it is communicated to someone who listens to us in an empathic way, who has done something similar before, or who can make us laugh at our actions. The key is to be reminded that you are not alone, not unique in your "badness." Shame cannot survive if we are compassionate with ourselves.

Women, men, and shame

Brown found that men and women experience shame equally, but what they feel shame about differs. Women tend to feel more shame about not looking "perfect," not being good mothers, not having children or being married, only having one child, not being a working mother, or only staying at home.

After her first TED video went viral, the self-confessed introvert Brown was horrified. She wanted to hack into the TED servers and delete it. Why? She realized that she had always wanted to keep her work small; fewer people knowing about it meant a lower likelihood of criticism, while having her work out there in the online world invited torrents of criticism and even abuse. And indeed, she got plenty of abuse in "Comments" sections about her weight, appearance, mental stability, and quality of motherhood. "Less research. More Botox" was one of the milder barbs. Instead of going after her arguments, people wanted to cut where they know it hurts for women. She realized that women still fall for the unspoken expectation that they should be "small, quiet, and pretty," and escaping this mental trap requires you to defy the traditional sources of female shame. The escape involves recognizing that every move a woman makes has consequences; you will never please everybody, so go ahead and act.

Brown spent the first few years of her research only interviewing women. She left her comfort zone and started investigating shame and vulnerability in men. For men, shame is most commonly experienced as a failure at work, in finances, in a marriage. Shame is a failure to be successful, of being proven wrong and ridiculed, of being seen to be soft, or weak, or fearful. One man told how, as a child, he loved to draw and paint. After his grandfather remarked to his dad, "What, you're raising a faggot artist now?" he was forbidden from taking any art classes, and never picked up a pencil again. Many men reported that their wives and daughters would not accept it if they lost their job or started to talk about their feelings. Some wives have very fixed ideas about what a man should be, which puts the man in a state of shame if they cannot live up to it.

In relationships, men and women feel shame differently: women feel it when they are not heard and not validated in their feelings. Men feel shame when their partner perceives them as inadequate— they never earn enough or do enough. When they feel accused like this, men get angry, or shut down, which makes women complain, prod, and poke even more.

The reason so many people, men and women, unravel or have crises or affairs at mid-life, Brown argues, is that they are sick of the expectations that make them feel shamed, and that stop them from realizing or being who they are. They are reduced to being a mom, or a breadwinner, and want to feel worthy as they are. Sometimes, it seems that only people outside the family provide this.

Shielding the soft spots: psychological armor

Brown identifies three kinds of psychological shielding against vulner-ability and shame.

Foreboding joy is when you worry about bad things that may happen so much that it reduces the quality of the present. Most of us are in much better material positions than our ancestors, but precisely because things are good we have dreadful fears of the next terror attack, natural disaster, school shooting, or *E. coli* outbreak. Brown was shocked when her research participants said the moments they felt most vulnerable were also moments of *joy*. As soon as they experi-enced a feeling of how much they loved their husband/kids/parents, there was an immediate follow-on thought that it couldn't last/some-thing will go wrong/they will die. Eighty percent of the parents she interviewed admitted that, at the very moment that they are looking at their child and thinking, "I love you so much I can barely breathe," they are also having images of bad things happening to the child. Brown herself used to imagine car wrecks and terrible phone conver-sations with police, and until she told participants about it, "constant disaster planning was my little secret."

Why do we do this? It's simple, Brown says: "We don't want to be blindsided by hurt. We don't want to be caught off-guard, so we literally practice being devastated . . ." Catastrophic images are our unconscious antidote to too much joy, and we are helped along by all the violent images we see on the news and in crime dramas. Brown's suggestion is to replace the moments of terror with grati-tude. Being deeply grateful for joyous moments allows you to fully enjoy them, while at the same time you are being open about the uncertainty of life. When you feel joy, and admit that you feel it, you are effectively saying that, *in this moment, I have everything*. If you're worried about the kids going on a school trip, or your husband taking them for a weekend away without you, admit your feeling of vulnerability, even say it out loud to your spouse. The alternative, making up reasons for the child not to go, is less about the real risks of the situation than about your irrational desire to control things.

A second kind of shielding is *Perfectionism*: if I can just do everything perfectly, shame will have no chance to exist in my life. Perfectionism is not about excellence or self-improvement, it's about trying to earn approval for ourselves, based on the feeling that we are deep-down unworthy; it's a defense against shame. Perfectionism becomes a vicious circle, because when we do experience failure, it's because we weren't perfect enough. The antidote to perfectionism is self-love. Yet self-compassion is not a one-off but a *practice* that perfectionists need to put into place, and which allows you to do a lot of things that are "good enough" or "better than nothing."

Numbing, a third kind of mental shielding, is the embrace of whatever reduces the feeling of shame or pain, or anxiety about the ability to cope with the demands of life. Being "crazy-busy" is a defense against really examining our lives, and truly being aware of how we are feeling. So is the numbing of our emotions through "taking the edge off" with a few glasses of wine. Each of these things, while perhaps quieting uncertainty or negative emotions, can stop us feeling love, joy, belonging, and creativity too. "We can't selectively numb emotion," Brown notes. "Numb the dark and you numb the light."

Brown goes through the various guises she had adopted in her life: good girl; clove-smoking poet; angry activist; career woman; party girl. Each, she realizes, were "suits of armor," that she thought protected her from becoming "too engaged and too vulnerable." Being "cool" is a response to vulnerability, and any person who uses the terms "lame," "stupid," or "loser" to describe others is betraying a fear of risking anything of themselves, and of being seen as weak if they care about something.

We can easily see other people's psychological armor, and it feels like a barrier between them and us, but it can be hard to see our own if we have worn it for so long. It becomes a second skin, and we can even forget what the real "me" is like, it has been covered up for so long. What is the way out of shields, armor, and masks? Mainly, to have the courage to say that we are "enough" as we are. Instead of disengaging, we show up, take risks, and let ourselves be seen. Instead of entertaining disaster, fully admitting our emotional dependence. In taking these small risks, which are often uncomfortable at first, the lives of Brown's subjects were often changed. Putting yourself out there is far more important than waiting until everything is perfect, a point that may never come.

Final comments

Don't be under any illusion. Walking into the arena and daring to do things, "you're going to get kicked around," Brown admits. But remember, when anyone is mean-spirited, hypercritical, or cynical about something we've created or a position we've taken, they are likely to be the type that considers vulnerability weak. Your daring holds up a mirror to their own fears and fixed-mindedness, and so they react by abusing you instead of examining their own lack of courage and willingness to embrace uncertainty. Fair criticism is helpful, Brown notes, but when cruelty is present, "vulnerability is likely to be the driver."

Anyone who puts "PhD, LMSW" after their name must have some worry about their credibility, and indeed Brown goes to some lengths to prove that her ideas are backed by academic research. Such things remind us that being vulnerable is hard, even for vulnerability researchers (Brown admits this in the book).

The fact that her books and videos have been such a hit tells us that our approval-seeking culture is not the one we really want, indeed that a "yearning for more courage" is universal.

Brené Brown

Born in San Antonio in 1965, Brown spent part of her childhood in New Orleans, where her father was posted for work. In her twenties she worked in a variety of jobs, and was almost 30 by the time she obtained a Bachelor's degree in social work at the University of Texas, Austin, followed by a Master's at the University of Houston. She got her PhD in social work in 2002, and is currently Research Professor at the University of Houston Graduate College of Social Work.

Brown's other books are Rising Strong *(2015),* The Gifts of Imperfection *(2010), and* I Thought It Was Just Me (but it isn't): Telling the Truth About Perfectionism, Inadequacy, and Power *(2007). She has published many scholarly articles on shame resilience theory. Her TED talk on "The Power of Vulnerability" has been viewed 29 million times.*

Brown's practice methodology to deal with shame and vulnerability, "The Daring Way," is used with individuals and organizations, and her online learning community, "CourageWorks," has courses on courage and leadership. She lives with her husband, a pediatrician, and their two children in Houston, Texas.

Feeling Good: The New Mood Therapy

1980

"You don't have to be seriously depressed to derive great benefits from these new methods. We can all benefit from a mental 'tune-up' from time to time. This book will show you exactly what to do when you feel down in the dumps."

"What is the key to releasing yourself from your emotional prison? Simply this: Your thoughts create your emotions; therefore, your emotions cannot prove that your thoughts are accurate. Unpleasant feelings merely indicate that you are thinking something negative and believing it. Your emotions follow your thoughts just as surely as baby ducks follow their mother."

In a nutshell

Feelings are not facts. Always question whether your emotions accurately reflect reality.

In a similar vein
Daniel Goleman, *Emotional Intelligence* (p178)
Martin Seligman, *Learned Optimism* (p278)

CHAPTER 11

David D. Burns

Feeling Good grew out of dissatisfaction with the conventional Freudian treatment of depression. Aaron T. Beck, David Burns' mentor, found that there was no empirical evidence for the success of psychoanalysis in treating depressed people; in fact, the patient is generally made to feel like a loser. Freud believed that if a patient admitted to deep faults, they were probably correct!

Beck's experience with the depressed showed a contradiction between their present opinion of themselves and their actual achievements; their protestations of "I am worthless" simply did not make sense to the observer. He concluded that depression was the result of wrong thinking. Negative or incorrect thoughts spiral a person into the full set of depressive symptoms, which then tend to compound the condition. This insight laid the basis for cognitive therapy, which gets patients to "talk themselves out of" depression, rebutting their own thoughts until they become free of distorted self-perceptions.

The research created a wave of interest that made the cognitive approach into a pillar of modern depression treatment, along with drugs and other forms of psychotherapy.

The *Feeling Good* story

David Burns was part of the team at Beck's Center for Cognitive Therapy at the University of Pennsylvania, and *Feeling Good* was the popular outcome of its clinical treatment and research. Though obviously not so new now, *Feeling Good* is still a superb introduction to the cognitive therapy way of beating the blues, and continues to be a bestseller.

If you want a more clinical approach to personal development and mood mastery than the average self-help book, it should not disappoint (US mental health professionals rated it No. 1 out of a list of 1,000 books for self-help depression treatment). The graphs, tables, and imaginary patient–doctor scripts might be a little off-putting to some readers, but it is easy to skip over these.

Feeling Good is not simply an anti-depression manual, however. It has sold three million copies because it also trains you to sail the more mundane seas of daily mood and emotion. Just as Seligman's classic *Learned Optimism* originated in research into learned helplessness, so the quest of Drs Beck and Burns to learn about the "black bile" of depression resulted in a book that shows you how to cultivate its opposite: joy, and the self-mastery that engineers it.

We look more closely below at some of the main points in the book.

Demystifying depression

❖ Throughout the history of psychiatry, depression has been an emotional disorder. The cognitive view is that an intellectual error creates or worsens the depressive illness. Depression is one illness that we do not have to have.

❖ Negative thoughts have a snowball effect. Just one can lead into a mild case of the blues, which in turn expands into a fog of general distorted perception, in which everything looks bad or lacks meaning. When someone is depressed their worthlessness, expressed in terms of the four "*D*s" of defeated, defective, deserted, and deprived, seems to be the absolute truth. Depressed patients actually lose the ability to think clearly, and the worse the depression, the greater the distortion. When thinking is clear and has a sense of perspective, it is impossible not to have a healthy level of self-esteem and confidence.

❖ Burns makes a distinction between genuine sadness and depression. The former is a part of being human, enlarges our experience of life, and brings self-knowledge. The latter suffocates us by closing our view of life's possibilities.

Feelings are not facts

❖ We tend to believe that our emotions reflect a self-evident truth that is beyond question. Emotions fool us into thinking that they are "right," and bad feelings about ourselves or our abilities seem unchallengeable. We are told to "trust our feelings." But if the thoughts feeding them are not rational, or are based on misconception or prejudice, trusting our feelings is a very risky thing to do.

❖ Burns employs this analogy: "Your emotions follow your thoughts just as surely as baby ducks follow their mother. But the fact that the baby ducks follow faithfully along doesn't prove that the mother knows where she is going." Emotions are almost the last thing we should trust, because "feelings are not facts."

❖ Does "feeling great" prove that you are a particularly worthy person? If the answer is no, then feeling bad does not, logically, say anything about your true worth. "Your feelings do not determine your worth, simply your relative state of comfort or discomfort," Burns says. Not surprisingly, he counsels never to label yourself with terms like "worthless" or "contemptible." We are not set things that can be judged like that; each person is an evolving, flowing phenomenon that defies easy judgments. Some aspect of our behavior might be no good, but it makes no logical sense to take an opinion about our behavior and turn it into a larger judgment about our basic self.

How to develop a low IQ ("Irritability Quotient")

❖ The two regular approaches to anger and irritability are turning anger inward, where it corrodes from inside and leads to depression and apathy; and expression, or "letting it all out."

❖ Expression can sometimes be effective, is simplistic, and may even get you into trouble. The cognitive approach transcends both by virtually eliminating the need to deal with anger, because there is very little of it around in the first place. However, first you must have the realization that it is "hot thoughts," rather than events, that create your anger. Even if something happens that by any normal standards is bad, you should still be able to choose your response, rather than being prey to automatic or uncontrollable reactions. If you are angry, it is because you have chosen to be.

❖ Would you like to overcome your fear of criticism? Even more, to be able to talk back when criticized, in a cool, non-defensive way? This ability would have a tremendous impact on your self-perception. Criticism may be right or wrong, or somewhere in between, but one way to find out clearly is to ask the critic questions. Be specific, even if what was said was harsh and personal. This will reveal either the truth in what has been said, giving you the opportunity to rectify your behavior, or that the person is talking out of anger, in which case you will know that the criticism was an expression of their own frustration rather than a real criticism of you. Either way, there is no need for a negative emotional reaction on your part. You are left in the position where you can either use the criticism or dismiss it and get on with things. You also defuse the wrath of the critic.

❖ Much anger is defensiveness against loss of self-esteem. However, by learning to control your angry feelings your self-esteem stays on an even keel, as you refuse to turn every situation into an emotional one. As Burns says: "You rarely need your anger in order to be human." Controlling your feelings does not turn you into a robot, but on the contrary gives you vastly more energy for living life and enjoying it.

Rest of the book

❖ There are excellent chapters on guilt, overcoming the "approval addiction" and the "love addiction," work ("Your work is not your worth"), the value of aiming low ("Dare to be average! Ways to overcome perfectionism"), and "How to beat 'do-nothingism.'"

❖ Perhaps surprisingly, the book's last chapter looks at the chemical treatment of depression (for example Prozac). Used simultaneously with cognitive therapy, drugs often work because they enable a person to think more rationally, and from that base cognitive therapy is likely to have more effect.

Final comments

You may believe that mood swings and self-defeating behavior are a natural part of being human. The amazing thing about *Feeling Good* is that it not only shatters this myth but shows how easily they can be prevented by deploying simple but effective principles and techniques. Most depression is usually only a case of having fallen into a rut and having forgotten the original purpose trigger. Where before you may have thought "These are important deep feelings I have to deal with," now you can see them for what they really are: a waste of your time.

Emotional mastery is not about turning yourself into a robot, but about increasing your humanity. The significance of *Feeling Good* is that it blazed a trail for successful titles like *Emotional Intelligence* and

Learned Optimism, which have collectively attempted to reinstall reason as the monarch that unites and rules over emotional territory.

David D. Burns

Born in 1992, Burns attended Amherst College and received his MD from Stanford University. He completed his psychiatric training at the University of Pennsylvania, where he was Acting Chief of Psychiatry of the Medical Center. He has been a Visiting Scholar at Harvard Medical School and is currently Adjunct Professor Emeritus of Psychiatry and Behavioral Sciences at Stanford University School of Medicine.

As well as the successful spin-off Feeling Good Handbook, *Burns has published* Love Is Never Enough *on relationships and* Ten Days to Self-Esteem.

The Power of Myth

1987

"*MOYERS: Do you ever have this sense when you are following your bliss, as I have at moments, of being helped by hidden hands? CAMPBELL: All the time. It is miraculous. I even have a superstition that has grown on me as the result of invisible hands coming all the time— namely, that if you do follow your bliss you put yourself on a kind of track that has been there all the while, waiting for you, and the life that you ought to be living is the one you are living. When you can see that, you begin to meet people who are in the field of your bliss, and they open the doors to you. I say, follow your bliss and don't be afraid, and doors will open where you didn't know they were going to be.*"

In a nutshell

Always do what you love and appreciate your life as a wonderful journey.

In a similar vein
Robert Bly, *Iron John* (p28)
James Hillman, *The Soul's Code* (p194)
Thomas Moore, *Care of the Soul* (p242)

CHAPTER 12

Joseph Campbell with Bill Moyers

This is a red-blooded book from a man who lived a very full life. Campbell was essentially a storyteller, spending his days uncovering and telling old stories and myths that he felt had the power to soak up the alienation of modern life. Though a respected academic mythologist, he also played a key role in the creation of a definitive modern tale, *Star Wars*. Director George Lucas said that Campbell's *The Hero with a Thousand Faces* (1949) was the catalyst in dreaming up the film, and that the inspiration for Yoda, the ancient and wise one, was Campbell himself.

Yet Campbell should not have been too ironic about his life taking on mythical proportions, since one of his key ideas was that everyone's life could resemble a great myth. His idea of the "hero's journey" has had a huge impact, launching many an unassuming person on a great trajectory.

The Power of Myth is a sort of campfire dialog between Campbell and writer/journalist Bill Moyers, covering the stories and symbols of civilization. Filmed for a television series at George Lucas's Skywalker ranch, the series caught the American public's imagination and the book became a bestseller. Campbell did not live very long after the taping, and *The Power of Myth* became a final snapshot of his wisdom and knowledge.

The power of myth

Campbell's big question was: "How can myth be powerful for a person living today?" Are our lives really comparable to the likes of Odysseus or the goddess Artemis?

He believed that mythical characters act as archetypes of human possibility: They are confronted with problems and their ensuing action gives us an idea about how life might be handled. To identify ourselves with, for instance, the young warrior Arjuna in The Bhagavad-Gita is not an inflation of our ego, but an acceptance that this figure has something to teach us. In mythology we could never really feel alone, for within it were guides for the human spirit belonging to everyone, providing a map for every cycle of life or experience through which we may go. He called mythology "the song of the universe," put into tune by a thousand different cultures and peoples. With myth, all experience can be empowering; without it, life can seem merely a meaningless series of ups and downs.

We don't look to myth to find the meaning of life, Campbell said, its purpose is to make us appreciate "the adventure of being alive." Without some sense of ourselves within a larger history of human imagination and experience, our life would inevitably lack romance and depth. The stories and imagery that we have in our heads are only a tiny fraction of what is available to us and, in increasing our knowledge of past culture and art, life is enriched immeasurably.

Following your bliss

In *The Power of Myth* Campbell talked about the medieval idea of the wheel of fortune, a metaphor for life that has had us in its thrall for millennia. The wheel has a hub, radiating out to its rim. As it turns through time, we hang on to its rim, either going up or down, experiencing the great highs and lows. In modern terms, chasing rewards like a higher salary or power or beautiful bodies is rim hanging. We hang on, sometimes for dear life, in this relentless cycle of pleasure and pain.

The wheel of fortune idea nevertheless contains its own solution: the possibility of learning to live at the hub, centered, focusing on what Campbell called one's "bliss." Our bliss is an activity, work, or passion with the power to fascinate endlessly. It is unique to us, yet may come as a total surprise, and we may resist it for years. In modern psychological phraseology, bliss is the state of "flow" (see Csikszentmihalyi) that we experience when we are doing what we are best at; time seems to stand still and we feel effortlessly creative. Here is joy, as distinct from merely pleasure.

Campbell portrayed bliss as the track that has always been waiting for you, with "hidden hands" seeming to help you attract the right circumstances for the fulfillment of your work. In mythological terms, bliss is represented by the cosmic mother, who guards an inexhaustible well offering solace, joy, and protection from mundane life.

In another book, *The Way of Myth*, Campbell talked about the people he had seen who had spent their lives climbing the "ladder of success," only to find that it was put up against the wrong wall. Kevin Spacey's character in the movie *American Beauty* is a portrayal of a man whose whole life has been dictated by other people's expectations, who then decides to do what he wants. He has had enough of rim life. The message of this film, and of the sum of Campbell's writings, is that the banality of your current life is always waiting to yield to a greater story.

The hero's journey

Campbell's voluminous reading was legendary. He came back from Europe to the United States just a few weeks before the Wall Street Crash and didn't have a job for five years. Nevertheless it was a rich time: "I didn't feel poor. I just felt that I didn't have any money." His bliss was basically reading every day, all day, in a shack rented for virtually nothing.

What began as a simple thirst for knowledge became a quest to find "the key to all mythologies." The more he read of the world's stories, the clearer it became that there was an underlying template that most followed: the "hero's journey," a sequence of experiences that both tests and proves the person-cum-hero.

Myths typically begin with the protagonist on home turf, living a quiet but unfulfilled life. Then something happens and he or she gets the "call" to leave on an adventure with some specific goal or quest. In Arthurian legend, Arthur begins a search for the grail; in *The Odyssey*, Odysseus simply tries to return home; in *Star Wars*, Luke Skywalker must rescue Princess Leia. Following numerous smaller trials, the hero endures a supreme ordeal in which all seems lost, followed by a triumph of some sort. The hero must then try to bring his "magic elixir" (some secret knowledge or thing) back home, to reality. There are many subtleties and variations to the pattern, but these are the basic stages.

What is the relevance of the hero's journey to our age? Or, as Moyers put it to Campbell, how is the hero different to the leader? The leader, Campbell said, is one who sees what can be done and accomplishes it, who is good at organizing a company or a country; a hero actually creates something new. (With today's business focus on innovation, personal journeys clearly become important.)

Final comments

Myths reveal to us the incredible potential for more life, in whatever form it comes. "I always feel uncomfortable when people speak about ordinary mortals because I've never met an ordinary man, woman or child," Campbell stated. Yet he acknowledged that too many accept the sadness and desperation of inauthentic lives, living without their bliss or not even knowing that it exists.

Campbell was a polymath, fascinated by everything. He noticed that the trend of western civilization was toward specialization, yet was proud of being a generalist, able to see the commonality of all human stories and life experience. His resurrection of the idea of the hero gave people a template on to which they could mount their own experiences and dreams; being present in all human myths, it knows no national boundaries. The idea involves no grasping or hurry (Campbell's life itself is a good example), but enjoyment of the richness of the moment. And significantly, it focuses on self-knowledge rather than aggrandizement of the ego.

The "human potential" movement of the 1960s and 1970s may have been important, but it took Campbell to remind us what myths have been saying for thousands of years: that everyone has the right to become a hero of some kind.

Joseph Campbell

Born in New York in 1904, as a boy Campbell loved Native American mythology. When he was 15 his family home burned down, killing his grandmother and destroying his collection of Indian books and relics. At Dartmouth College he studied biology and mathematics, later transferring to Columbia University where he wrote a Master's thesis on the Arthurian legends. He excelled as an athlete, setting the New York City record for the half-mile, and played saxophone in jazz bands.

In 1927 a scholarship took him to study old languages at the University of Paris, before transferring to the University of Munich to read Sanskrit literature and Indo-European philology. Back in the US he based himself at a shack near Woodstock for several years, and during this time also traveled to California, where he met John and Carol Steinbeck and their neighbor Ed Ricketts, immortalized in Steinbeck's Cannery Row.

Campbell's first real job was a modest post at the newly founded women's college, Sarah Lawrence, where he remained for 38 years, marrying former student and dancer Jean Erdman. He slowly increased his list of publications, including A Skeleton Key to Finnegan's Wake *(1944), and co-editing and translating* The Upanishads. The Hero with a Thousand Faces *was published in 1949.*

Campbell lectured to diverse audiences including the US State Department, the Soviet Academy of Sciences, and the Esalen Institute, and traveled widely. Notable later works include the series The Masks of God *(1969),* The Mythic Image *(1974), and* The Inner Reaches of Outer Space *(1986). He died in Honolulu in 1987.*

Don't Sweat the Small Stuff . . . and It's All Small Stuff

1997

"*So many people spend so much of their life energy 'sweating the small stuff' that they completely lose touch with the magic and beauty of life. When you commit to working towards this goal you will find that you have far more energy to be kinder and gentler.*"

"*One of the major reasons so many of us remain hurried, frightened and competitive, and continue to live life as if it were one giant emergency, is our fear that if we were to become more peaceful and loving, we would suddenly stop achieving our goals. We would become lazy and apathetic. You can put this fear to rest by realizing that the opposite is true. Fearful, frantic thinking takes an enormous amount of energy and drains the creativity and motivation from our lives.*"

In a nutshell

Put your little struggles into perspective; by doing this you can gain more enjoyment of other people and life generally.

In a similar vein

Marcus Aurelius, *Meditations* (p14)
Wayne Dyer, *Real Magic* (p144)
Norman Vincent Peale, *The Power of Positive Thinking* (p254)
Martin Seligman, *Learned Optimism* (p278)

CHAPTER 13

Richard Carlson

*D*on't Sweat the Small Stuff has been a massive international bestseller. The story of the title's genesis is recounted by the author in the introduction. Carlson was asked by a foreign publisher to get an endorsement for his book *You Can Feel Good Again* from bestselling author Wayne Dyer. As Dr. Dyer had provided a blurb for a previous book, Carlson said he would try and sent out a request. Time went by and nothing came back, and six months later Carlson's publishers sent him a copy of the foreign edition. To his extreme annoyance, the publisher had used Dyer's endorsement of the previous book for the current one! Carlson wrote a heartfelt apology to Dyer, explaining that he was trying to get the edition taken off the shelves. Some worried weeks later, Dyer wrote back with the following:

"Richard. There are two rules for living in harmony. #1) Don't sweat the small stuff and #2) It's all small stuff. Let the quote stand. Love, Wayne."

For Carlson, the graceful response inspired a super-practical guide that rests on an ethereal spiritual law: taking the path of least resistance. *Don't Sweat the Small Stuff* is no manual for self-perfection, simply a collection of ideas for avoiding struggle where possible. The 100 strategies, elaborated in short essays, apparently proved their worth among Carlson's clients and readers.

The way of perspective

The book has the quirky good-heartedness and love of people that you find in the likes of Dale Carnegie and Norman Vincent Peale, combined with an eastern conception of time and the value of stillness. However, the real value is in its awareness of the crushing demands of modern life and the culture in which we live. We might feel good about the meditation camp we went on or our weekend walk along the beach,

RICHARD CARLSON

but its effects soon wear off and by Tuesday morning we are again driving fast, getting angry, and hating our lack of time.

How do we bring that peace and perspective into the moment by moment of real life? This is Carlson's compelling question, and one of the refreshing things about *Don't Sweat the Small Stuff* is that it tells you not to worry about having bad feelings. Don't try to get rid of them, it says, but do try to put them into a larger context.

Many of Carlson's remedies are quite simple, others novel. Some of the interesting strategies among the 100 listed include the following.

Become an early riser
Getting up long before his wife and children gave Carlson a "golden hour" in which to read, meditate, or think about the day in peace and solitude. Many told him that this single act of becoming an early riser revolutionized their life.

Let go of the idea that gentle, relaxed people can't be superachievers
A frantic life of constant emergencies somehow seems to fit our idea of forceful, achieving individuals. Our idea of becoming more peaceful and loving seems to equate with a dreamy apathy. However, frantic thinking and constant movement leach motivation and real success from our lives. Carlson notes his good fortune at being surrounded by people who are gentle and relaxed, but who are outward success stories by any measure. If inner peace becomes your habit, there is ease in the way you achieve your goals and serve others.

Don't interrupt others or finish their sentences
This is a surprisingly easy way to become a more relaxed, loving person—try it.

Learn to live in the present moment
John Lennon said that "Life is what happens when we are busy making other plans." With attention to the present moment, fear—being associated mostly with an imaginary future—tends not to exist. You may be

80

amazed how easily tomorrow's troubles sort themselves out. Make this a habit of mind and see life subtly transformed.

Ask yourself the question, "Will this matter a year from now?"

With the frequent use of this question, Carlson finds himself actually laughing at things he used to worry about. The energy he once spent on getting angry and overwhelmed is now spent on his family and creative thought.

Allow yourself to be bored

Don't be afraid of the vacant moment. You are a human being, not a "human doing," so just be and consider your boredness. You may be surprised at how it clears the mind (after getting over the initial discomfort) and provides new thoughts.

Imagine yourself at your own funeral

This is a super-valuable way of reassessing your priorities now, when it matters. Not many people, looking back on their life, would be pleased by how much of it they spent being uptight, with all the "small stuff" over which they sweated. Ask yourself: What sort of person was I? Did I do the things I loved and did I really love and cherish those close to me every day?

Imagine the people in your life as tiny infants or as 100 years old

This nearly always provides perspective and compassion (as well as amusement).

Redefine a meaningful accomplishment

Instead of always thinking of an accomplishment as an external thing, ask yourself about the achievements you have made in terms of your self. This could include, for instance, staying centered in the face of adversity.

Be open to "what is"

The world is frequently not how you would like it to be. When someone disapproves of you, even someone close, or if at work there is some sort of failure, acknowledge to yourself that this is the case, rather than automatically becoming emotional about it. After some time, things that once bothered you so much slip by without damage. In many ways, you are free of them.

Other strategies include:

❖ Just for fun, agree with criticism directed toward you (then watch it go away).
❖ Be grateful when you're feeling good and graceful when you're feeling bad.
❖ Be happy where you are.
❖ Cut yourself some slack.

Final comments

If you are interested in self-help ideas but have no time to read books, *Don't Sweat the Small Stuff* may be the best compromise. Though it looks quite folksy and simplistic, the book is in fact grounded in cognitive therapy, which shows how closely feelings are the product of thoughts; by becoming more conscious of what you are thinking, you are in a position to change your thoughts and therefore your feelings. "Not sweating the small stuff" is not as cheesy as it sounds. The esteemed psychologist Abraham Maslow recognized it as a key feature of what he called the self-actualizing person, a person who has given up pettiness for an unusually wide view of the world and life.

The layout of the book is such that it can be grabbed when you have a moment and opened up at any random page for the perspective or inspiration you need. Free of lengthy argument or anecdote, it condenses what more learned writing has taken hundreds of pages to say. If only one or two of the strategies stays in your mind, it will have been worth reading.

Richard Carlson

Born in 1961, Carlson grew up in Piedmont, California. He studied the psychology of happiness for his PhD, graduating in 1986. This led to a popular newspaper serialization called "Prescriptions for Happiness," which launched his career as a happiness and stress-reduction expert.

Don't Sweat the Small Stuff has sold over ten million copies and been translated into many languages. It was the No. 1 selling book in the US for two consecutive years.

Carlson's 15 popular books include You Can Feel Good Again, Short Cut through Therapy, and, with Benjamin Shield, Handbook for the Soul and Handbook for the Heart. He has also written Don't Worry, Make Money, Slowing Down to the Speed of Life, Don't Sweat the Small Stuff in Love (with his wife Kristine), Don't Sweat the Small Stuff with Your Family, and For the Love of God: Handbook for the Spirit.

Carlson lived with his wife and two daughters in northern California. He was only 45 when, in 2006, he suffered a pulmonary embolism and died on a flight from San Francisco to New York.

How to Win Friends and Influence People

1936

"*Instead of condemning people, let's try to understand them. Let's try to figure out why they do what they do. That's a lot more profitable and intriguing than criticism; and it breeds sympathy, tolerance and kindness. 'To know all is to forgive all.'*"

"*Remember that the people you are talking to are a hundred times more interested in themselves and their wants and problems than they are in you and your problems. A person's toothache means more to that person than a famine in China which kills a million people. A boil on one's neck interests one more than forty earthquakes in Africa. Think of that the next time you start a conversation.*"

In a nutshell

Really try to see the world as another sees it. The appreciation he or she feels means that whatever you have to say will be truly heard.

In a similar vein
Stephen Covey, *The 7 Habits of Highly Effective People* (p110)
Norman Vincent Peale, *The Power of Positive Thinking* (p254)

CHAPTER 14

Dale Carnegie

The title *How to Win Friends and Influence People* reeks of insincerity. How many people would boast of "winning" a friend and influencing them for their own personal gain? It just doesn't sound nice. To a modern reader, the book conjures up mental trickery for a dog-eat-dog world, a shonky product hawked by a Depression-era salesman. In this case, judging a book by its cover would seem a very reasonable thing to do. Yet the reader should consider some points in the book's defense.

Reasons to read and like Carnegie

1   There is a strange inconsistency between the brazenness of the title and much of what is actually in the book. When read carefully, it is not at all a manual for manipulation, in the manner of Machiavelli's *The Prince*. Carnegie genuinely despised "winning friends" for a purpose: "If we merely try to impress people and get people interested in us, we will never have many true, sincere friends. Friends, real friends, are not made that way." The energy that makes the book a great read comes from a love of people. Maybe it is still bought by shallow egomaniacs—current editions are marketed as tools to gain popularity, for instance—but it is about time Carnegie's classic was seen in a kinder, truer light.

2   Carnegie wrote the book in the America of the 1930s. The country was still clawing itself out of the Great Depression, and opportunities, particularly for people with limited education, were scarce. Carnegie offered a way to get ahead, taking advantage of the one thing you owned outright—your personality. By modern standards, the claims made in *How to Win Friends* do not seem too wild; motivational psychology is now well established. But try to imagine its impact in 1937, before the great prosperity of the post-Second World War period. To many people it would have seemed like gold. For many today, it still is.

3 *How to Win Friends* is a self-confessed manual of action, "letting the reader in on a secret." No theory, just a set of rules that work "like magic." Carnegie's conversational style was a breath of fresh air to those who had tried to read academic psychology, and even more attractive to those who didn't read books at all. Labor-saving ideas are a hallmark of American culture, so a book promising a transformed life without years of toil and character building was bound to get a good reception.

4 The book was not written with an eye to bestseller glory, but as a textbook for Carnegie's courses on Effective Speaking and Human Relations (the "How to" part of the title is a giveaway to its course origin). The initial print run was only 5,000 copies. Rather than being devised as part of some master plan to profit from people's baser instincts, the aim was to bring the messages of the Carnegie courses to a reading audience.

The *How To Win Friends* phenomenon

Nevertheless, initially no doubt due to the title alone, the book caused a sensation. It is one of the biggest-selling books ever (over 15 million copies, in all the world's main languages) and is still the biggest overall seller in the self-improvement field. In her preface to the 1981 edition, Dorothy Carnegie noted how her husband's ideas filled a real need that was "more than a faddish phenomenon of post-Depression days."

Indeed, *How to Win Friends* is written up in compendiums like *Most Significant Books of the 20th Century*, and takes its place in Crainer & Hamel's *Ultimate Business Library: 50 Books that Made Management*, among titles by Henry Ford, Adam Smith, Max Weber, and Peter Drucker.

The message: Education, not manipulation

The success of Carnegie's adult courses revealed a deep desire for education in the "soft skills" of leading people, expressing ideas, and creating enthusiasm. That technical knowledge or raw intelligence alone does not bring career success is now a given, but in Carnegie's time the idea that success was composed of many elements was only just starting to be researched. In seeing that people skills could make all the difference, Carnegie effectively popularized the idea of emotional intelligence, decades before it was established as fact in academic psychology.

He had kept in his mind a statement by John D. Rockefeller (the Bill Gates of his age) that the ability to handle people well was more valuable than all others put together, yet astonishingly he could find no book written on the subject. Carnegie and his researcher hungrily read everything they could find on human relations, including philosophy, family court judgments, magazine articles, classical texts, the latest work in psychology, and biography, specifically the lives of those recognized for superb leadership. Carnegie apparently interviewed two of the most important inventors of the century, Marconi and Edison, as well as Franklin D. Roosevelt and even the movie stars Clark Gable and Mary Pickford.

A set of basic ideas emerged from these researches. Originally written as a short lecture, they were relentlessly tested on the "human laboratory" of his course attendees before emerging, 15 years later, as the "principles" in *How to Win Friends and Influence People*. Whatever might be said about the book, it was not written on a whim.

Carnegie's principles

Did the principles work? At the start of the book Carnegie gave the example of a man who had driven his 300+ employees mercilessly, apparently the epitome of a bastard boss who was incapable of saying anything positive about his own people. However, after taking a Carnegie course and applying the principle "Never criticize, condemn, or complain," he was able to turn "314 enemies into 314 friends," inspire a previously non-existent loyalty, and, to top it off, increase profits. There's more, Carnegie told us: His family liked him more, he had more time for leisure, and he found his outlook on life "sharply altered."

What excited Carnegie most were not stories of the beneficial career or financial effects of his courses, but how they made people open their eyes and reshape their lives. They started to see that there could be more lightness in their life, which was no longer seen as a struggle or a power game.

The book's second chapter gets underway with a quote from the American philosopher John Dewey, that the deepest urge in human nature is the desire to be important. Freud's belief, Carnegie also noted, was that apart from sex, the chief desire was to be great; Lincoln said that it was the craving to be appreciated.

The person who really understands this craving for appreciation, Carnegie said, will also know how to make people happy—"even the undertaker will be sorry when he dies." Such a person will also know how to draw the best out of others. Carnegie loved telling the success stories of the great industrialists of his day. Charles Schwab was the first person to earn $1 million a year by running Andrew Carnegie's United States Steel Company. He confided that his secret of success was being "hearty in my approbation, and lavish in my praise" to the people under him. Valuing your employees, making them feel special in the scheme of things, is now accepted wisdom in management circles, but in the era of Andrew and Dale Carnegie it wasn't.

At the same time, Carnegie was against flattery. That simply involved mimicking the vanities of its receiver, whereas sincere appreciation of someone's good points is an act of gratitude that requires you really to see that person, maybe for the first time. One effect is that you seem more valuable to them, the expression of value only increasing your own. You get the priceless pleasure of seeing a face light up and, in the workplace, are an amazed witness as excited cooperation grows out of boredom or mistrust. Carnegie's principle "Give honest and sincere appreciation" is ultimately to do with seeing the beauty of people.

The book lists 27 principles, but most follow the logic of these first couple. They include:

❖ Arouse in the other person an eager want.
❖ Become genuinely interested in other people.
❖ The only way to get the best of an argument is to avoid it.
❖ Show respect for the other person's opinions. Never say "you're wrong."
❖ If you are wrong, admit it quickly and emphatically.
❖ Begin in a friendly way.
❖ Let the other person do a great deal of the talking.
❖ Appeal to the nobler motives.
❖ Give the other person a fine reputation to live up to.

Final comments

Though easy to parody, the book itself is genuinely funny—quite a rare event in personal development writing. It took Carnegie's log cabin sense of humor to make it a text that really pulls you in. One of its famous principles is: "Remember that a person's name is to that person the sweetest and most important sound in any language."

How to Win Friends and Influence People will be read another 50 years from now because it is essentially about people, a subject we assume we know a lot about but invariably don't. Before books like this, it was thought that dealing with people was a natural ability—you either had it or you didn't. *How to Win Friends* put firmly into the public's mind the fact that human relations are more understandable than we think, and that people skills can be systematically learned. It also carried the proposition, in direct opposition to the book's reputation, that we don't really influence a person until we truly like and respect them.

Dale Carnegie

Born in 1888 in Maryville, Missouri, Carnegie was the son of a poor farmer and apparently didn't see a train until he was 12 years old. In his teens, though he still had to get up at 3 am every day to milk his parents' cows, he managed to get educated at the State Teacher's College in Warrensburg. His first job after college was selling correspondence courses to ranchers, then he moved on to selling bacon, soap, and lard for Armor & Company. He was successful to the point of making his sales territory, south Omaha, the national leader for the firm.

A desire to be an actor led Carnegie to the American Academy of Dramatic Arts in New York, and after touring the country as Dr. Hartley in Polly of the Circus, *he returned to the sales fold, selling Packard cars. He persuaded the YMCA to let him run public speaking courses for business people, which were a great success, and his first book,* Public Speaking and Influencing Men in Business, *was written as an aid to teaching. Other books include* How to Stop Worrying and Start Living *and* Lincoln the Unknown. *Carnegie training courses are now run all over the world. Carnegie died in 1955.*

The Seven Spiritual Laws of Success

1994

"When we understand these laws and apply them in our lives, anything we want can be created, because the same laws that nature uses to create a forest, or a galaxy, or a star, or a human body can also bring about the fulfillment of our deepest desires."

"The best way to put the Law of Giving into operation . . . is to make a decision that at any time you come into contact with anyone, you will give them something. It doesn't have to be in the form of material things; it could be a flower, a compliment, or a prayer . . . The gifts of caring, attention, affection, appreciation, and love are some of the most precious gifts you can give, and they don't cost you anything."

"The fourth spiritual law of success is the Law of Least Effort. This law is based on the fact that nature's intelligence functions with effortless ease and abandoned carefreeness. This is the principle of least action, of no resistance . . . When we learn this lesson from nature, we easily fulfill our desires."

In a nutshell

There is an easier way to get what you want from life, involving attunement with nature and the universe.

In a similar vein
The Bhagavad-Gita (p18)
Florence Scovell Shinn, *The Game of Life and How to Play It* (p272)

CHAPTER 15

Deepak Chopra

With an effortless power and simplicity, *The Seven Spiritual Laws of Success* is a supreme example of contemporary self-help writing. You could throw away all other self-help books and live by this one alone.

The emphasis on success and prosperity may not seem "spiritual" enough for some, but this is the very point of the book. Unless you are a self-sufficient hermit, you are an economic actor who must be able to reconcile wealth generation with the spirit. In being both a devotional tract and a prosperity manual, *The Seven Spiritual Laws* acknowledges this and is therefore an emblematic work of our times.

Identifying immutable laws of success is the great challenge of the self-help literature. *Karma* (cause and effect) and *dharma* (purpose in life) have been with us for eons, and they form two of Chopra's seven laws. Here we look briefly at his other five.

The law of pure potentiality

The field of pure potentiality is the silent realm from which all things flow, from which "the unmanifest is made manifest." In this state of pure consciousness, we have pure knowledge, perfect balance, invincibility, and bliss. When accessing the field, we experience our higher, pure selves, and are able to see the futility and waste of living through the ego. While the ego is based in fear, the higher self exists in loving security:

"It is immune to criticism, it is unfearful of any challenge, and it feels beneath no one. And yet, it is also humble and feels superior to no one, because it recognizes that everyone else is the same Self, the same spirit in different guises."

When the veil of the ego drops, knowledge is revealed and great insights are normal. Chopra refers to Carlos Castaneda's remark that if we

91

could stop trying to uphold our own importance, we would start to see the grandeur of the universe. We can access the field of pure potentiality primarily through meditation and silence, but also through the practice of non-judgment and appreciation of nature. Once you know the field, you can always retreat to it and be independent of situations, feelings, people, and things. All affluence and creativity flow out of the field.

The law of giving

Have you ever noticed that the more you give, the more you receive? Why does this seem infallible? Chopra says it happens because our minds and bodies are in a constant state of giving and receiving with the universe. To create, to love, to grow keeps the flow going; not to give stops the flow and, like blood, it clots. The more we give, the more we are involved in the circulation of the universe's energy, and the more of it we will receive back, in the form of love, material things, serendipitous experiences. Money does makes the world go around, but only if it is given as much as it is received.

If you give, give joyfully. If you want to be blessed, silently bless people by sending them a bundle of positive thoughts. If you have no money, provide a service. We are never limited in what we can give because the true nature of humankind is affluence and abundance. Nature provides everything we need, and the field of pure potentiality provides the intelligence and creativity to produce even more.

The law of least effort

Just as it is the nature of fish to swim and the sun to shine, it is human nature to turn our dreams into reality, with ease. The Vedic principle of economy of effort says "do less and accomplish more." Is such a concept revolutionary—or crazy? Are hard work, planning, and striving a waste of time?

Chopra suggests that when our actions are motivated by love, not by the desires of the ego, we generate excess energy that can be used to create anything we want. In contrast, seeking power over others or trying to get their approval consumes a great deal of energy. We are trying to prove something, whereas if we are acting from the higher self, we simply make choices about how and where we will affect evolution and bring abundance.

The first step is to practice acceptance. We cannot hope to channel the universe's effortless power if we are fighting against it. Say to yourself, even in very difficult situations, "This moment is as it should be." Secondly, practice defenselessness. If we are continually defending our point of view or blaming others, we can't really be open to the perfect alternative that waits in the wings.

The law of intention and desire

This is the most complex law, and of course the most alluring. Chopra notes that while a tree is locked into a single purpose (to put down roots, grow, photosynthesize), the intelligence of the human nervous system allows us actually to shape the mind and the laws of nature to bring about the achievement of a freely imagined desire. This occurs through the process of attention and intention.

While attention on something will energize it and make it expand, intention triggers energy and information and "organizes its own fulfillment." How does this happen? The author uses the analogy of a still pond. If our mind is still, we can toss into it a pebble of intention, creating ripples that move through space and time. If the mind is like a turbulent sea, we could throw a skyscraper into it and there would be no effect. Once the intention is introduced, in this receptive stillness we can depend on the infinite organizing power of the universe to make it manifest. We "let the universe handle the details."

The law of detachment

Though you may have an intention, you must give up your attachment to its realization before it can manifest itself. We can have a one-pointed focus on something, but if we are attached to a specific outcome it will produce fear and insecurity at the possibility of its not happening. A person who is attuned to their higher self will have intentions and desires, but their sense of self is not riding on the outcome; there is a part of them that cannot be affected.

In Chopra's words:

"Only from detached involvement can one have joy and laughter. Then the symbols of wealth are created spontaneously and effortlessly. Without detachment we are prisoners of helplessness, hopelessness,

*mundane needs, trivial concerns, quiet desperation, and seriousness—
the distinctive features of everyday mediocre existence and poverty
consciousness."*

Without detachment we feel we must force solutions on problems; with
detachment, we are free to witness the perfect solutions that spontaneously emerge from chaos.

Don't let this outline suffice. For the detail and rich prose that
makes Chopra a delight to read, buy the book. It may take a while to
get on to his wavelength and understand his terms, but persevere—the
laws can have a real effect. On subsequent readings you may find yourself discovering new meanings in the text, the familiar mark of a
classic.

Final comments

The genius, intended or not, of the last century's self-help writing is
that spiritual messages have been delivered through instructions of a
more material kind. We buy a book about prosperity and find it telling
us about the universe's benign and perfect intelligence; we find another
that promises the laws of success and are surprised to see that the
answer involves maintaining good *karma* in our actions and detaching
ourselves from the fruits of success. Chopra is often accused of promoting spiritual values as the means to becoming wealthier. That is true,
but it is nothing to be ashamed of: When the nature of the universe
itself is abundant, a life lived in poverty consciousness is a wasted life.

The motif of the book is the unity of everything in the universe.
Though it is overtly concerned with "success," perhaps the real theme
is power. By becoming more open to that unity and perfection we
assume more of its power, while the illusion of separateness pits us
against the world, making us weaker in the process. The best personal
development writing, exemplified by *The Seven Spiritual Laws of
Success*, is transforming the genre's idea of success from being "master
of the universe" to achieving oneness with it.

Deepak Chopra

Born in 1946 in New Delhi, the son of a prominent cardiologist, Chopra studied medicine before moving to the US in 1970. In Boston he established himself as an endocrinologist, then taught at Boston University and Tufts medical schools. He was Chief of Staff at the New England Memorial Hospital.

The transformation from specialist to guru was assisted by meeting the Maharishi Mahesh Yogi, a holy man who came to America in the 1960s to popularize meditation. Chopra's subsequent involvement in the transcendental meditation movement was matched by a renewed interest in the Hindu healing philosophy Ayurveda, and he founded the American Association of Ayurvedic Medicine.

In 1999, Time *magazine included Chopra as one of the "Top 100 Icons and Heroes of the Century," a "poet-prophet of alternative medicine." He has spoken at the UN, the World Health Organisation, and the Soviet Academy of Sciences, and his 25-plus books—including* Quantum Healing *(1986),* Ageless Body, Timeless Mind *(1993),* Creating Affluence *(1993),* How to Know God *(2000), and* You Are the Universe: Discovering Your Cosmic Self and Why It Matters *(2017)— have been translated into over 35 languages. He has edited a collection of Rabindranath Tagore's poetry and written a novel,* The Lords of Light.

In 1996, Chopra co-founded the Chopra Center for Well Being runs courses and events. He currently lives in New York City.

How Will You Measure Your Life?

2012

"I came to understand that that while many of us might default to measuring our lives by summary statistics, such as number of people presided over, number of awards, or dollars accumulated in a bank, and so on, the only metrics that will truly matter to my life are the individuals whom I have been able to help, one by one, to become better people. When I have my interview with God, our conversation will focus on the individuals whose self-esteem I was able to strengthen, whose faith I was able to reinforce, and whose discomfort I was able to assuage—a doer of good, regardless of what assignment I had. These are the metrics that matter in measuring my life."

"Many of us have convinced ourselves that we are able to break our own personal rules 'just this once.' In our minds, we can justify these small choices . . . the marginal costs are always low. But each of those decisions can roll up into a much bigger picture, turning you into the kind of person you never wanted to be."

In a nutshell

We all want to get ahead and do well, but genuine success comes from commitment to values—standing for something—and thinking for the long term.

In a similar vein
David Brooks, *The Road to Character* (p50)
Stephen Covey, *The 7 Habits of Highly Effective People* (p110)

CHAPTER 16

Clayton Christensen

arvard Business School professor Clayton Christensen is well known for his work on "disruptive innovation." The *Economist* named *The Innovator's Dilemma* (1997) as one of the six most influential business books ever written.

In *How Will You Measure Your Life?*, Christensen sought to bring the same clarity, originality, and rigor to questions of life itself. The book's genesis was a speech Christensen gave to graduating Harvard students on how they might chart their lives and avoid big mistakes. This had particular meaning, as Christensen was suffering from cancer at the time. Karen Dillon, editor of *Harvard Business Review*, convinced Christensen he should turn it into a book, which he co-wrote with her and Harvard student James Allworth.

Before reading this book you may imagine the application of business theories to personal life to be a bit crass or hollow. Compared to something as nuts and bolts as business strategy, our lives seem too fluid and uncertain, too shaped by happenstance to be guided by deliberate aims. But Christensen's credible argument is that, over the long term, certain inputs inexorably lead to certain outcomes, whether good or bad. The book's subtitle is *Finding Fulfilment Using Lessons From Some of the World's Greatest Businesses*, and he writes:

> *"if you study the root causes of business disasters,*
> *over and over you'll find a predisposition toward endeavors*
> *that offer immediate gratification over endeavors that result*
> *in long-term success."*

What is true for businesses is true for our lives. A commitment to a purpose naturally makes us think long term, shaping our actions and decisions in the present. With a picture in our heads of the person we would like to be, we are forced to ask the crucial question, "What do I need to do now for that picture to be proved correct?"

Staying out of jail

Christensen begins by recalling his Harvard Business School reunions, and his surprise at the number of former classmates—who had all been good people with high hopes for their lives—who had gone off the rails. He was not talking simply of divorces, unhappy marriages, or estranged children, but classmates like Jeffrey Skilling who had headed the disgraced energy firm Enron. It wasn't just his Harvard classmates either: he had been a Rhodes Scholar, and observed the same pattern among his contemporaries while at Oxford. Christensen believes that none of these people intended to make a mess of things, yet their trajectories were not the result of blind luck or fate either. The outcomes they experienced were due to the life *strategies* they adopted, whether they were aware of them or not.

Christensen asks his students: "How can I ensure I will be successful and happy in my career, that my relationships with family and friends become an enduring source of happiness, and that I live a life of integrity?" These questions may seem too simple, he notes, but they are ones "so many of my classmates never asked, or had asked but lost track of what they learned." By becoming more conscious of our strategies, we can ensure that we have a useful, impactful life—and stay out of jail.

What were you thinking?

There are thousands of self-help books that can offer advice about how to live successfully. Yet when Christensen is asked for advice he doesn't give it. Instead he runs the questioner's dilemma through a *theory* which can result in a good answer.

People originally thought they would be able to fly if they strapped big enough feathers to their bodies, because they had seen that birds had feathers. But feathers themselves do not cause flight, and mankind had to wait for Daniel Bernoulli's theory of lift to explain what actually enables something (a bird or an airplane) to stay in the air. Christensen's point is that our theories in relation to success and happiness are frequently wrong, and it is worth spending the time to find out the actual causes of each.

Understanding what motivates us, for instance, is crucial to life and career satisfaction, and Christensen notes his debt to Frederick Herzberg's motivational theory, which distinguished between "hygiene" factors in work happiness, and "motivation" factors. Hygiene factors include status, pay, job security, workplace and company conditions, and worker–boss relations. These can make us satisfied or dissatisfied at work, but they are not genuine motivators. However high our pay may be, for instance, it can never make us love the work we do. If you love your job it is because of *motivation* factors including challenging and interesting tasks, personal growth, recognition, and responsibility. We love the work itself, and will want to keep doing it even if the hygiene factors in the job itself are not to our satisfaction. You might not earn a huge amount in a charity or in the military, for instance, but you stay for reasons other than money.

Who do people end up in jobs they hate? Christensen suggests that they were attracted more by the hygiene factors of the position such as pay or status than by the motivation factors. They found themselves adjusted to a certain standard of living provided by their job, but with little motivation for the work itself. Choosing a high-paying job after graduation is fair enough if you have big loans to pay off, and many young people believe they will just do the job for a few years and then do something they *really* like. But this tends not to happen, and they get stuck in what they are doing.

To avoid this, he suggests, instead of asking yourself how much a job will pay, ask: "Will it give me a chance to grow, develop, and be recognized? Will the work be interesting enough and will I learn new things? Will I be given responsibility?" Christensen quotes Apple's Steve Jobs: "The only way to be truly satisfied is to do what you believe is great work. And the only way to do great work is to love what you do."

The best strategy

Have you ever been caught between the need to chart a particular course in life, and wanting to explore or take up opportunities as they arise? This is the difference between a *deliberate* strategy and an *emergent* one. Life is about this balance between "calculation and serendipity," Christensen says.

If you are in a line of work that has "good enough" money and conditions, and which motivates you, then you should stick to it and map your career for the long term, Christensen argues, seeking to grow and prosper in it. But if you have yet to find work that satisfies you or that you love, it makes much more sense to be open to any kind of opportunity. A deliberate strategy can actually blind us to "distractions" and opportunities which can in fact turn out to be the source of future growth. He gives the example of Walmart founder Sam Walton. Walton wanted to change retailing with his low-cost model (deliberate strategy), but his actual success happened more by happenstance than design. His first store was built in a small town, and he wanted his second one to be in a big city. This seemed like the obvious path to getting bigger and growing the business. But his wife refused to move to a city, so the second store was also built in a small town. This "problem" or limitation was the seed of Walmart's success: its focus on underserviced towns rather than cities saw it enjoy phenomenal growth, because it didn't have much competition from other retailers.

In reality, Christensen notes, "Strategy almost always emerges from a combination of deliberate and unanticipated opportunities." With awareness of the distinction between the two, we are more likely to make good calls in terms of when to stay the course, or when to pursue a new direction or opportunity. Incidentally, Christensen himself has had three careers (consultant, entrepreneur and manager, college professor), and planned none of them. His deliberate strategy when he left college was to be editor of the *Wall Street Journal*, and he is still waiting for that offer!

What would have to be true for it to work?

But how do you actually choose between opportunities? What if several arise at once?

Christensen favors a tool developed by Ian MacMillan and Rita McGrath called "discovery-driven planning," which can be boiled down to a single question you can ask yourself at moments of decision: "What would have to prove true for this to work?"

In the business world, doing this simply means testing all the assumptions that are being made for a product or service to turn out as successfully as the proponents would like. What usually happens is that people get an idea of something they would like to do, then run projections and come up with numbers showing why it would work, without ever really testing the idea in reality. Because the numbers are done by people keen on the idea, naturally they look promising. So resources are allocated, only to find—when it is too late—that there was some fatal flaw in the plan. Yet the model could have been tested at small expense earlier. Christensen does not use the words "lean startup," but the principle of small, early, quick, and inexpensive tests to avoid later waste is what he is talking about.

His own example is Disney's near-disastrous assumption when it built the Euro Disney theme park outside Paris. It assumed that visitors would stay two or three days, like they did in other parks in the US and Japan. But it only built 15 rides, not the normal 45, so people on average only visited for a day, with a resulting huge discrepancy between forecast and actual revenue. Disney could have avoided this by doing things in reverse, asking, "What would have to be true for our revenue forecasts to eventuate?" This simple question could have made it obvious that it needed more rides.

We can also apply this question to our personal career choices, asking, "What would have to prove true about this position/job/role for me to be happy in it?" Christiansen mentions a former student who was keen to work in developing countries and took a job with a company that said it was doing developing nation projects. It turned out that it was doing almost no work in this area, which made her feel she had been led up the garden path. But asking the question above could have led her to examine the company's actual resource allocation for this area, which was almost zero. Answering, "What would need to be proved true?" may have led her to say no to the position at the outset, saving her a lot of angst. Use this question in any area of your life and you may be amazed at how it saves you time and resources, and delivers the results you want.

What's the job?

We don't so much buy products, Christensen says, we "hire them to get the job done." For instance, the job that many people have to do that IKEA performs is to furnish a whole flat or house in a hurry. Not only does it do this, having everything you could possibly need in one place, but you can leave your kids in the play area and have a meal in the café at the same time. It does several jobs for you at once. The V8 vegetable drink had been sold as an alternative to a range of other drinks, but it quadrupled sales when it was marketed as an easy way of consuming the advised daily intake of vegetables, but in a fraction of the time. People had an important job to do of getting their veggies, the makers realized, and in this mental category V8 could be sold as the perfect "job done" product. Scores of "interesting" products have been devised, Christensen notes, but if the product doesn't take account of the job a person is trying to accomplish, "it will struggle to succeed."

The principle applies to our relationships too. What we think our spouse needs or wants might be very different to the jobs they actually want us to do. Christensen's example is a father coming home from work to his frazzled wife and their young children. Assessing the scene, he might think that what she wants is for him to help clean up and make the dinner. That might indeed be useful, but what she *really* wants is some adult conversation after eight hours spent with needy toddlers.

We easily go wrong in relationships when we assume things. Work

101

out the jobs that your partner actually needs doing (mental, physical, practical) not simply what might give us a good feeling. It sounds old-fashioned, but Christensen notes the truth that sacrifice toward someone deepens the commitment. To stay in love, keep asking, "What job does my partner most need me to do?" What is the job they need me to perform?

Family is the greatest investment

According to Christensen, the reason why some of his classmates did not turn out well was not so much a moral failing but a simple problem of resource misallocation. At work, they chased a big promotion or a bonus because these provided the most immediate, obvious payoff. Meanwhile they were under-allocating resources in things that had a more long-term return, such as raising good children and spending time with their spouse. At some point down the line, they are surprised when their partner leaves them or they realize their kids have gone astray. Like everyone, their intention was to raise a good family and provide for them, but the actual way they spent their hours over the years meant that the money was there but the time for their loved ones was not. "With every moment of your time," Christensen says, "every decision about how you spend your energy and your money, you are making a statement about what really matters to you."

He admits that work can bring great fulfillment, yet it still pales in relation to the deep happiness you get from having cultivated relationships with family and friends over a long period. Many high-achievers make the mistake of outsourcing the raising of kids to others, or think their spouse won't mind all the late nights at work. But it is precisely the time when we think that attending to these relationships isn't necessary, that they truly are. When we realize this, it is often too late. Never take people for granted; they are not a means to your end.

The dangers of marginal thinking

The video rental company Blockbuster was doing so well that it felt it could afford to dismiss DVD rental-by-mail outfits like Netflix. What Netflix was doing seemed such a small part of the total video rental industry that the people at Blockbuster felt it wasn't worth disrupting their own model. Besides, if they got into the new field surely they would be cannibalizing their own business?

As we know now, this thinking sent Blockbuster into bankruptcy. It was so focused on protecting its existing model that it couldn't imagine that an upstart could bring dramatic change to the industry. What was happening at the margins didn't seem important. Christensen describes the dangers of this "marginal thinking": "You can see the immediate costs of investing, but it's really hard to accurately see the costs of *not* investing. When you decide that the upside of investing in the new product isn't substantial enough while you still have a perfectly acceptable existing product, you aren't taking into account a future in which somebody else brings the new product to market."

Marginal thinking is dangerous in private life too. The "marginal cost" of doing one small thing that is not in line with your integrity seems very low, so you think it's OK. But it can quickly lead you into a spiral (think of trader Nick Leeson's first small mistake that led to the downfall of Barings Bank, or an athlete's "one-time" use of drugs to give them an edge, which ties them into long-term usage and ruins their career). "The safest road to Hell," C. S. Lewis said, are the small, gradual, unnoticed decisions that slowly lead us into the wilderness.

While at Oxford Christensen (who is 6 feet 8 inches) was a key player in a basketball team coming up to its final championship game. But there was a problem: the game was scheduled for a Sunday, and his Mormon faith forbade activity like sports on Sundays. Christensen wrestled with the decision, before deciding that if he was committed to his religion at all, he must be committed totally. When he told his coach of his decision, the coach was astonished. In the end, the team won anyway. "It's easier to hold to your principles 100 percent of the time," Christensen notes, "than it is to hold to them 98 percent of the time . . . Decide what you stand for. And then stand for it all the time."

The marginal costs of a decision always seem low. We can do something "just this once" and will get away with it. But the terrible danger of being a "98 percent person" is that "each of those decisions can roll up into a much bigger picture, turning you into the kind of person you never wanted to be."

What's your purpose?

"I promise my students," Christensen writes, "that if they take the time to figure out their life's purpose, they'll look back on it as the most important thing they will ever have discovered."

A purpose is something freely chosen which is then committed to. A company or a person needs three things to achieve their purpose: a likeness (a picture of what you want to become); a commitment (to achieving that picture); and a metric (something by which to measure progress).

You might be thinking that a personal metric is a career goal achieved or assets accrued, but Christensen insists that the ultimate purpose of one's life is always non-material. "The only metrics that will truly matter to my life," he says, "are the individuals whom I have been able to help, one by one, to become better people." Whether this is raising someone's self-esteem, helping comfort another, or buttressing the faith of a fellow believer, this is what ultimately matters to him and how he feels he will be judged.

Echoing Rick Warren's opening words in *The Purpose-Driven Life* ("It's not about you"), this shift in thinking from what we think would be good for *us*, to how we can help one individual at a time in the best way possible, can bring a revolution in our lives. We can go from being "successful" in surface terms, to having a genuine positive impact on the people around us. While the exact nature of your purpose will be different to someone else's, the very fact that you are seeking to know what it is will lift you on to a path of real effectiveness.

Final comments
While experience can be a good teacher, Christensen notes, there are some insights that we just can't afford to learn while on the job: "You don't want to have to go through multiple marriages to learn how to be a good spouse," he says, "or wait until your last child has grown to master parenthood." His book offers a vital chance to get wise about life—*before* the bulk of it is lived. It is a potential life-changer, capable of disrupting your self-satisfied views and inspiring you to raise your standards.

Clayton Christensen

Born in Salt Lake City, Utah, in 1952 in a family of eight children, Christensen gained a degree in economics from Brigham Young University before becoming a Rhodes Scholar at Oxford University, where he took an M. Phil in econometrics and economics, focused on developing countries.

Between 1979 and 1984 he worked as a management consultant for Boston Consulting Group in manufacturing strategy, taking a leave of absence in 1982–3 to be a transport adviser in the Reagan administration. In 1984 he helped launched CPS, a ceramics engineering firm, which had a public floatation just before the stock market crash of 1987. After the share price dropped from $12 to $2 and Christensen was ejected as its head, he enrolled at Harvard as a PhD student. His dissertation on why big companies fail because the market they are operating in is disrupted by upstarts with new, cheaper technologies became The Innovator's Dilemma. *Christensen joined the faculty of Harvard Business School in 1992, and remains the Kim B. Clark Professor of Business Administration. Other books include* The Innovator's Solution *(2003);* Disrupting Class: How Disruptive Innovation Will Change the Way the World Learns *(2008);* The Innovator's Prescription: A Disruptive Solution for Healthcare *(2008); and* Competing Against Luck: The Story of Innovation and Customer Choice *(2016).*

As a young Mormon, Christensen did his compulsory two-year missionary stint in Korea, and speaks fluent Korean. He and his wife Christine have five children and live in Massachusetts.

The Alchemist

1993

"He had studied Latin, Spanish and theology. But ever since he had been a child, he had wanted to know the world, and this was much more important to him than knowing God and learning about man's sins. One afternoon, on a visit to his family, he had summoned up the courage to tell his father that he didn't want to become a priest. That he wanted to travel."

"'It's a force that appears to be negative, but actually shows you how to realize your destiny. It prepares your spirit and your will, because there is one great truth on this planet: whoever you are, or whatever it is that you do, when you really want something, it's because that desire originated in the soul of the universe. It's your mission on earth.'
'Even when all you want to do is travel? Or marry the daughter of a textile merchant?'"

In a nutshell

We too easily give up on our dreams, yet the universe is always ready to help us fulfill them.

In a similar vein
Joseph Campbell with Bill Moyers, *The Power of Myth* (p72)

CHAPTER 17

Paulo Coelho

Santiago is a shepherd. He loves his flock, though he can't help but notice the limited nature of the sheep's existence. Seeking only food and water, they never lift their heads to admire the green hills or the sunsets. Santiago's parents have continually struggled for the basics of life and have smothered their own ambitions accordingly. They live in beautiful Andalucia, which attracts tourists to its quaint villages and rolling hills, but for them it is no place of dreams.

Santiago, on the other hand, can read and wants to travel. He goes into town one day to sell some of his flock and encounters a tramp-king and a gypsy woman. They urge him to "follow his omens" and leave the world he knows. The gypsy points him toward the Pyramids of Egypt, where she says he will find treasure.

Crazily, he believes her. He sells his flock and sets sail. Sure enough, disaster is met early on when a thief in Tangier robs him of his savings. So much hard work and discipline for a little adventure! But strangely, Santiago is not devastated, apprehending a greater feeling—the security of knowing that he is on the right path. He is now living a different life, in which every day is new and satisfying. He keeps reminding himself of what he was told in the market before he left: "When you want something, all the universe conspires in helping you to achieve it."

Following the dream

This belief is a marvelous one, a support for anyone embarking on a major project. Nevertheless, is it a hope based on nothing? If you think about the energy you put into something once you are committed to it, probably not. The "universe conspiring" to give you what you want is, more precisely, a reflection of your determination to make something happen. In reading *The Alchemist*, we are reminded of Goethe's demand: "Whatever you can do, or dream you can, begin it—boldness has genius, power and magic in it."

The book does not get away from the fact that dreams have a price, but, as Coelho has noted in interviews, not living your dreams also has a price. For the same money, he said, you can either buy a horrible jacket that doesn't fit or one that suits you and looks right. There will be difficulties in whatever you do in life, but it is better to have problems that make sense because they are part of what you are trying to achieve. Otherwise difficulties merely seem insidious, one terrible setback after another. Dream followers have a greater responsibility, that of handling their own freedom. That may not seem like such a price, but it does require a level of awareness that we are maybe not used to.

The old man that Santiago meets in the town square tells him not to believe "the biggest lie," that you can't control your destiny. You can, he says, but you must "read the omens," which becomes possible when you start to see the world as one. The world can be read like a book, but we will never be able to understand it if we have a closed type of existence, complacent with our lot and unwilling to risk anything.

Love

The Alchemist is remarkable for being a love story that renounces the idea that romantic love must be the central thing in your life. Each person has a destiny to pursue that exists independently of other people. It is the thing that you would do, or be, even if you had all the love and money you want. The treasure that Santiago seeks is of course the symbol of the personal dream or destiny, but he is happy to give up on it when he finds the woman of his dreams in a desert oasis. Yet the alchemist he meets in the desert tells him that the love of his oasis girlfriend will only be proved real if she is willing to support his search for treasure.

Santiago's dilemma is about the conflict between love and personal dreams. Too often we see a love relationship as the meaning of our life, but the obsession with romantic coupling can cut us off from a life more connected with the rest of the world. But surely the heart has needs? Live your life around the dream, Coelho says, and their will be more "heart" in your life than you can now comprehend:

". . . no heart has ever suffered when it goes in search of its dreams, because every second of the search is a second's encounter with God and with eternity."

Romantic love is important, but it is not your duty—that is to pursue your dream. Only through devotion to the dream is the "soul of the world" revealed to us, the knowledge that destroys loneliness and gives power.

Final comments

So much of the self-help literature is about pursuing our destiny, but dreams do not always pull us along by their own force; they speak persistently but quietly, and it does not take too much effort to smother the inner voices. Who is willing to risk comfort, routine, security, and existing relationships to follow something that to others looks like a mirage? It takes courage, and dog-eared, stained copies of Coelho's classic have become the constant companion of people who need to make fearless decisions daily in order to keep true to a larger vision.

Paulo Coelho

Coelho grew up in a middle-class family in Rio de Janeiro, Brazil. His father wanted him to follow in his footsteps and become an engineer, but after stating his wish to be a writer Coelho was put in and out of mental institutions for three years. He became a hippie traveler, joined a cult in Italy for a while, and was held and tortured by the Brazilian police after a stint writing "subversive" lyrics for a rock band.

The Alchemist, which was inspired by a tale in The Thousand and One Nights, *has sold 20 million copies (his first publisher dropped it after selling fewer than 1,000 copies, but Coelho managed to find another one).*

Coelho is a Catholic and has a particular interest in pilgrim routes. Santiago de Compostela in Spain provides the setting for both The Pilgrimage *and* Diary of a Magus. *Other books include* The Valkyries: An Encounter with Angels, By the River Piedra I Sat Down and Wept, Veronika Decides to Die, *and* The Supreme. *He lives with his wife Christina Oiticica, a painter, in Geneva.*

The 7 Habits of Highly Effective People

1989

"The Character Ethic is based on the fundamental idea that there are principles that govern human effectiveness—natural laws in the human dimension that are just as real, just as unchanging and unarguably 'there' as laws such as gravity are in the physical dimension."

"People can't live with change if there's not a changeless core inside them. The key to the ability to change is a changeless sense of who you are, what you are about and what you value."

"Most people tend to think in terms of dichotomies: strong or weak, hardball or softball, win or lose. But that kind of thinking is fundamentally flawed. It's based on power and position rather than on principle. Win/Win is based on the paradigm that there is plenty for everybody, that one person's success is not achieved at the expense of exclusion of the success of others."

In a nutshell

Real effectiveness comes from clarity about your principles, values, and vision.
Change is only real if it has become habitual.

In a similar vein
David Brooks, *The Road to Character* (p50)
Viktor Frankl, *Man's Search for Meaning* (p162)
Benjamin Franklin, *Autobiography* (p168)

CHAPTER 18

Stephen Covey

Stephen Covey's book is one of the phenomena of modern personal development writing. It has sold over 15 million copies, has been translated into 32 languages, and forms the intellectual basis of a large corporation. It took Dale Carnegie's *How To Win Friends and Influence People* 60 years to have the same sort of impact.

What was it that lifted it above the mass of books claiming the secret to a better existence?

Inside-out success

First, it was timing. *The 7 Habits* came out just as we entered the 1990s. Suddenly, aspiring to be a "master of the universe" in a shoulder-padded world did not seem to satisfy, and people were ready for a different prescription for getting what they really wanted out of life. Covey's message of "restoring the character ethic" was so old-fashioned that it seemed revolutionary.

Having studied the success literature of the last 200 years for a doctoral dissertation, Covey was able to draw a distinction between what he termed the "personality ethic"—the quick-fix solutions and human relations techniques that had pervaded much of the writing in the twentieth century—and the "character ethic"—which revolved around unchanging personal principles. Covey believed that outward success was not success at all if it was not the manifestation of inner mastery. Or, in his terminology, "private victory" must precede "public victory."

A business plan for personal life

The second, more practical reason for the book's success is that it is a compelling read, both as a self-help book and as a leadership/management manual. This crossover status effectively doubled its market. It also means that the reader interested only in personal development

may not like the management terms, diagrams, and business anecdotes that fill it. For a book that is so much about changing para-
digms, it is remarkably representative of the paradigm of business
thinking.

But this should be a small price to pay for what is a brilliant guide
to reengineering your life, enlivened by Covey's personal and family
experiences. Covey may be Dale Carnegie's heir in many ways, but his
classic is more systematic, comprehensive, and life-expanding than any
of the modern self-help titles that came before it.

Habits: The building blocks of change

The emphasis on habits as the basic units of change has also been
important in the book's success. Covey saw that real greatness was the
result of the slow development of character over time; it is our daily
habits of thinking and acting that are the ground on which that greatness is built. *The 7 Habits* promises a life revolution, not as a big bang,
but as the cumulative result of thousands of small, evolutionary changes.
The English novelist Charles Reade summarized what Covey is
referring to:

*"Sow a thought, and you reap an action; sow an action, and you reap a
habit; sow a habit, and you reap a character; sow a character, and you
reap a destiny."*

Effective vs. efficient

Finally, the success of the book owes much to the use of "effective" in
the title. By the late 1980s, western culture had had decades of management theory about efficiency. The concept of time management, a
product of a machine-obsessed culture, had spilled over into the personal domain, and we could have been forgiven for thinking that any
problems in our lives were the result of "inefficient allocation of
resources." However, Covey took a different perspective, and he had
this message: Think about what is most important to you and see if it
is the center around which your life revolves. Don't worry about efficiency. There is no use being "efficient" if what you are doing lacks
meaning or an essential good.

The 7 Habits puts effectiveness at a higher level than achievement.

Achievement is hollow unless what you achieve is actually worthwhile, both in terms of your highest aims and service to others. Covey's view is that the personality ethic of twentieth-century self-help had helped to create a high-achieving society that also did not happen to know where it was going.

The habit of responsibility

The seven habits are predicated on a willingness to see the world anew, to have the courage to take life seriously. The book struck a nerve because it showed many of us, perhaps for the first time, what genuine responsibility was about. To blame "the economy" or "my terrible employer" or "my family" for our troubles was useless. To have fulfillment and personal power, we had to decide what we would take responsibility for, what was in our "circle of concern." Only by working on ourselves could we hope to expand our "circle of influence."

To review the seven habits briefly:

1 *Be proactive*. We always have the freedom to choose our reactions to stimuli, even if everything else is taken away. With that ability also comes the knowledge that we do not have to live by the scripts that family or society has given us. Instead of "being lived," we accept full responsibility for our life the way conscience tells us that it was meant to be lived. We are no longer a reactive machine but a proactive person.

2 *Begin with the end in mind*. What do I want people to say about me at my funeral? By writing our own eulogy or creating a personal mission statement, we create the ultimate objective or person first, and work backward from there. We have a self-guidance system that gives us the wisdom to make the right choice, so that whatever we do today is in line with the image created of ourselves at the end.

3 *Put first things first*. Habit 3 puts into daily action the far-sightedness of habit 2. Having that ultimate picture in our mind, we can plan our days for maximum effectiveness and enjoyment. Our time is spent with the people and the things that really matter.

4 *Think Win/Win*. One person's success doesn't need to be achieved at the expense of the success of others. In seeking Win/Win, we never endanger our own principles. The result is a better relationship — "not your way or my way, a better way" — created by truly seeing

from the other person's perspective.

5 *Seek to understand, then to be understood.* Without empathy, there is no influence. Without deposits in the emotional bank account of relationships, there is no trust. Genuine listening gives precious psychological air to the other person, and opens a window on to their soul.

6 *Synergize.* Synergy results from the exercise of all the other habits. It brings forth "third alternatives" or perfect outcomes that cannot be predicted from adding up the sum of the parts.

7 *Sharpen the saw.* We need to balance the physical, spiritual, mental, and social dimensions of life. "Sharpening the saw" to increase productivity involves taking the time to regularly renew ourselves in these areas.

Final comments

The author's heroes are a guide to his philosophy. Benjamin Franklin is put forward as a perfect example of the character ethic in action, "the story of one man's effort to integrate certain principles and habits deep within his nature." Anwar Sadat, the Egyptian leader who originated the Middle East peace accords, also ranks highly in Covey's mind as a person who successfully "rescripted" himself. Covey uses the story of concentration camp survivor Viktor Frankl (see *Man's Search For Meaning*) to support his personal responsibility ethic, and Henry David Thoreau (see *Walden*) to illustrate the independent mind.

It has been said that Covey's seven habits are merely common sense. On their own they may be, but put together in the one package, in that sequence, and with the philosophy of principle-centeredness to support them, they can produce the synergy that Covey celebrates.

A common criticism of self-help is that a seminar or a book can inspire us enormously, then we forget about it. Through its use of habits as the units of action and change, *The 7 Habits* gives readers the momentum to incorporate its teachings into daily life. We are given the means for changing the little, in order to transform the big.

Stephen Covey

Born in 1932, Covey had a Harvard MBA and spent most of his career at Utah's Brigham Young University, where he was a professor of organizational behavior and business management.

In 1984 he founded the Covey Leadership Center, which 13 years later merged with the Franklin Quest company to form Franklin Covey, a company that sells learning and performance tools in the areas of leadership and productivity. Covey's other books include Principle-Centered Leadership, First Things First, The 7 Habits of Highly Effective Families, and The 8th Habit.

Covey has several honorary doctorates and was voted one of Time magazine's 25 most influential Americans. He lived with his wife Sandra in Provo, Utah. They had nine grown children and 52 grandchildren.

Covey died in 2012, three months after a serious bicycle accident.

Flow: The Psychology of Optimal Experience

1990

"*Whether we are happy depends on inner harmony, not on the controls we are able to exert over the great forces of the universe. Certainly we should keep on learning how to master the external environment, because our physical survival may depend upon it. But such mastery is not going to add one jot to how we as individuals feel, or reduce the chaos of the world as we experience it. To do that we must learn to achieve mastery over consciousness itself.*"

"*Flow helps to integrate the self because in that state of deep concentration consciousness is unusually well ordered. Thoughts, intentions, feelings, and all the senses are focused on the same goal. Experience is in harmony. And when the flow episode is over, one feels more 'together' than before, not only internally but with respect to other people and the world in general.*"

In a nutshell

Rather than being idle, doing what you love is a pathway to greater meaning, happiness, and a self of higher complexity.

In a similar vein

The Dalai Lama & Howard C. Cutler, *The Art of Happiness* (p122)
Daniel Goleman, *Emotional Intelligence* (p178)
Richard Koch, *The 80/20 Principle* (p206)

CHAPTER 19

Mihaly Csikszentmihalyi

"**W**hy is it so difficult to be happy?" "What is the meaning of life?" Whether in idleness or frustration, we all mull over these big questions. Not many dare to provide answers, and fewer again are equipped to try. But in devoting his life to answering the first, Mihaly Csikszentmihalyi (pronounced "Me-hi Chicksent-me-hiee") found that it could not be divorced from the second. The linking of the two is the essence of his theory of "flow."

At a general level, the author's answer to the first question is surprisingly obvious: It is difficult to be happy because the universe was simply not built for our happiness. While religions and mythologies have been created to provide some security against this fact, first-hand knowledge cruelly reveals its truth again and again. Csikszentmihalyi says that it is best to think about the universe in terms of order and chaos (entropy). That healthy human beings find order pleasing is a clue to its intrinsic value, and to its role in the creation of happiness.

The bringing of order to consciousness, "control of the mind," is therefore the key to happiness. However, what gives us this control?

Happiness and flow

Csikszentmihalyi's research began not by looking at the nature of happiness *per se*, but by asking the question: "When are people most happy?" That is, what exactly are we doing when we feel enjoyment or fulfillment? Finding this out included buzzing people on a pager at random points through a week. They were required to write down exactly what they were doing and the feelings that the activity produced. The discovery was that the best moments did not happen by chance, according to the whim of external events, but could reasonably be predicted to occur when a specific activity was undertaken. The activities described as being of highest value, which when undertaken banished worry or thoughts of other things, were dubbed "optimal experiences," or simply "flow."

People in a state of flow feel that they are engaged in a creative unfolding of something larger; athletes call it "being in the zone," mystics have described it as "ecstasy," and artists term it "rapture." You and I may recognize our flow experiences as simply those that seem to make time stand still. The book's best definition of flow comes from the ancient Taoist scholar Chuang Tzu. In a parable Ting, the esteemed court butcher of Lord Wen-hui, describes his way of working: "Perception and understanding have come to a stop and spirit moves where it wants." You stop thinking and just do.

One of the key distinctions the author makes is between enjoyment and pleasure. While challenging tasks that require all our attention are enjoyed, mere pleasure does not have to engage us—it is passive. Television, drugs, and sleep can all be pleasurable, but involve little conscious will and therefore do not really assist our growth. The lesson of optimal experience is that we are genuinely happy when we are in control. Optimal experience is that which is directed by us and gives us a sense of mastery. This is why goals are so enjoyable to pursue: They bring "order in awareness," irrespective of the feeling one may get in seeing a goal actually achieved. An ordered mind itself is a source of happiness.

Flow: Complexity and meaning

To avoid meaninglessness, we can either devote our lives to pleasure, which usually ends in ruin or mental entropy, or sit back on autopilot and try not to think about all our possible choices in life. This last possibility amounts to a surrender to whatever happen to be the societal values of the day, letting ourselves be defined more as a consumer than as a person.

Csikszentmihalyi finds Freud to be particularly relevant here. Freud's "id" was a representation of the instinctual drives of the body, while his "superego" represented the external world to which our sense of self may be shaped. Freud's third element in consciousness, the ego, is that part of ourselves that has managed to gain an autonomous sense of self in spite of our bodily urges or environment. It is here, leaving behind the animal and the robotic, where humanity is to be found. A person living within this consciousness is doing so by will, and since the universe never makes things easy for us, this person must become increasingly complex (not in terms of confusion but higher order).

Csikszentmihalyi's research established a fascinating point about the flow experience: After each instance, a person is more than the person they were before. Each piece of knowledge absorbed, each new refinement of a skill, enlarges the self and makes it more highly ordered, forming, in his words, "an increasingly extraordinary individual."

This is why opportunities to create flow can be addictive—life without them feels static, boring, and meaningless. Happiness and a sense of meaning can therefore be increased, the author says, simply by doing more of what we love doing. The question of "the meaning of life" may not be answered in its most esoteric sense (that is, why does anything exist), but can be answered at a subjective, personal level: The meaning of life is whatever is meaningful to me. The experience of flow does not need an explanation for those who enjoy it; we are simply aware that it gives us the two things vital to happiness: a sense of purpose and self-knowledge.

A flow-centered culture?

Flow makes you feel more alive, certainly, but it has another, perhaps surprising effect: The growth in complexity entails both awareness of your uniqueness simultaneously with renewed understanding of how you fit into your world and your relationships with other people. Flow reconnects you to the world as well as making you more unique.

This double effect has tremendous implications for the rejuvenation of communities and nations. The author suggests that the most successful nations and societies of the twenty-first century will be those that make sure people have the maximum opportunities to be involved in flow-inducing activity. He refers to the inclusion of "the pursuit of happiness" in the American Declaration of Independence, a far-sighted aspiration that unfortunately metamorphosed into an expectation that it is government's role to provide happiness.

Whereas goal seeking (or living for the future) is a major part of contemporary western culture, a flow-centered culture would restore the present-centeredness that was the hallmark of hunter-gatherer societies, freeing us from the clock's tyranny. With increasing prosperity, if more of the population is engaged in doing what they love, the whole attitude to time would change. Time would cease to be framed by the work patterns of an industrial culture, with its sharp divisions between "work" and "leisure." Instead, time would be determined by individuals' subjective attitude to the activity in which they are engaged, that is, whether the activity is flow inducing or not.

It is said that contemporary western and particularly American culture is youth obsessed, one consequence being the terrible fear of aging. Yet the pressure of passing time is relieved if you are truly living and enjoying yourself in the moment, in other words, in a state of flow. As the German philosopher Nietzsche put it, maturity is "the rediscovery of the seriousness we had as a child—at play."

Final comments

The flow theory has had an extensive impact since it surfaced in academic journals 40 years ago because it is a meta-theory, applicable to pretty well any type of human activity. Csikszentmihalyi relates it to sex, work, friendship, loneliness, and lifelong learning. Yet flow experiences cannot be forced on people. As ever, it will be those individuals who can generate their own flow experiences who will tend to be happier.

Nietzsche believed that a "will to power" was the root of human action, but the implication of the flow theory is that a will to order is what feeds this and other motivations. Any activity that creates an ordered sense of self provides us with both a sense of meaning and a degree of happiness. As the possibilities for how we can live our lives have dramatically opened out, a need has arisen that seemingly takes us in the opposite direction: the need to create focus, order, and discipline in how we approach life and what we choose to do in it. The connection is not obvious, and in drawing attention to it *Flow* is a justifiably celebrated work.

Mihaly Csikszentmihalyi

Csikszentmihalyi was born in 1934 and emigrated to the United States from Yugoslavia in his early twenties. He is a professor of psychology and management at the Drucker School of Management at Claremont Graduate University in California, having been chairman of the Psychology Department at the University of Chicago. He is a fellow of the American Academy of Arts and Sciences, and has had articles published in the New York Times, Washington Post, Wired, Fast Company, *and* Newsweek. *Bill Clinton named him as a favorite author.*

Other books include Optimal Experience: Psychological Studies of Flow in Consciousness *(scholarly essays that were the forerunner to* Flow*) co-edited with his wife Isabella (1988),* The Evolving Self: A Psychology for the Third Millennium *(1993),* Living Well *(1997), and* Creativity: Flow and the Psychology of Discovery and Invention *(1996). He has also written books on flow as it applies to business and to running, and articles on the philosophy of Teilhard de Chardin as it relates to evolution and human progress.*

The Art of Happiness: A Handbook for Living

1998

The Dalai Lama:
"We each have a physical structure, a mind, emotions. We are all born in the same way, and we all die. All of us want happiness and do not want to suffer."

"I believe that the proper utilization of time is this: if you can, serve other people, other sentient beings. If not, at least refrain from harming them. I think that is the whole basis of my philosophy."

Howard Cutler:
"Over time I became convinced that the Dalai Lama had learned how to live with a sense of fulfillment and a degree of serenity that I had never seen in other people . . . Although he is a Buddhist monk . . . I began to wonder if one could identify a set of his beliefs or practices that could be utilized by non-Buddhists as well—practices that could be directly applied to our lives to simply help us become happier, stronger, perhaps less afraid."

In a nutshell

Achieving happiness does not have to depend on events. Through mental practice we can form the ability to be happy most of the time.

In a similar vein
The Dhammapada (p128)
Wayne Dyer, *Real Magic* (p144)

CHAPTER 20

The Dalai Lama & Howard C. Cutler

H ave you heard the one about the psychiatrist who met the Buddhist monk? Normally this would be the beginning of a good joke, perhaps involving a couch and a begging bowl. In this instance it forms the basis of a book.

The Art of Happiness is the result of collaboration between Howard Cutler, a respected psychiatrist, and His Holiness the Dalai Lama. It is a blend of the Dalai Lama's thoughts on various issues and Howard Cutler's personal and scientific reflections on them.

Many people have objected to the fact that the Dalai Lama is presented as "co-author" when he did not actually write anything, but it doesn't matter when you consider the result: an unusually strong happiness manual based on questions any of us might ask if we had a few hours with the man himself.

The nature and sources of happiness

Cutler began working on this book with certain beliefs derived from his western scientific background, such as that happiness is a mystery and that the most we can really hope for is the avoidance of misery. Over the course of many conversations, the Dalai Lama convinced him that happiness is not a luxury but the purpose of our existence—not only that, but there is a definite path leading toward it. First we have to identify the factors that invariably lead to suffering and those that lead to happiness. Then we must begin eliminating the suffering-causing factors and cultivate the happiness-causing ones.

Perhaps the most surprising point about happiness is that its achievement is "scientific" and requires discipline. As Cutler puts it:

"I realized that right from the beginning our interviews had taken on a clinical tone, as if I were asking him about human anatomy, only in this case, it was the anatomy of the human mind and spirit."

Below are some points from the book:

❖ Happiness has many levels. In Buddhism there are four factors—wealth, worldly satisfaction, spirituality, and enlightenment—which create "the totality of an individual's quest for happiness." Good health and a close circle of friends are also important, but the door into all these things is your state of mind. This not only works to create the experiences in your life, but is the filter through which you view them. Without a disciplined mind you are not really in control of what you are doing, nor can you be independent of events if you wish to be. The real source of happiness is control of your consciousness. A calm mind, for instance, or one engaged in meaningful work equates to happiness.

❖ A basic way to happiness is to cultivate affection and connection with other human beings. Even if you lose everything you will have this. The Dalai Lama notes that while he lost his country, he in a way gained the whole world, because he had the ability to bond with others quickly. Always look for what you have in common with others and you will never really be lonely.

❖ No matter how powerful they seem, negative emotions and states of mind have no foundation in reality. They are distortions, stopping us from seeing things as they really are. We only have to experience shame or embarrassment once after losing our temper to appreciate this. When we experience positive states, however, we are generally closer to the true nature of the universe and how we could be all the time. All emotions, if practiced regularly, grow in size. The Dalai Lama continually suggests that we cultivate the positive—like any good habit you start off small, but the end benefits are great.

❖ A positive state of mind is not merely good for you, it benefits everyone with whom you come into contact, literally changing the world. No matter how difficult it is, reduce your negative states of mind and increase your positive ones.

❖ Having "wholesome" actions as opposed to "unwholesome" actions is not a matter of morality or religion, it is the practical difference between happiness and unhappiness. Through self-training, you can develop a "good heart" that lessens the chances that you will act in an unproductive way.

❖ Don't confuse happiness with pleasure. Pleasure is of the senses and can seem like happiness, but lacks meaning. Happiness, in contrast, rests on meaning and is often felt despite negative external conditions. It is stable and persistent. While pleasures are a bonus in life, happiness is a must.

❖ Happiness is something to be developed over time. Make a decision to apply the same effort and determination that you devote to worldly success to studying and practicing happiness. Systematic seeking after the causes and ways to happiness can be one of our most important life decisions, like deciding to get married or embarking on a career, Cutler says. The alternative is drifting in and out of happiness by chance, vulnerable to unexpected attacks of unhappiness. The student of happiness will experience ups and downs, but will be better equipped to get back to a positive state more quickly, or to raise their "normal" mental state to a significantly higher level.

❖ Over time you must try to cancel out negative emotions, particularly anger and hatred, and replace them with tolerance and patience. The Dalai Lama's idea of countering negative thoughts with positive ones has been validated by the rise and success of cognitive therapy (see *Feeling Good*), which gets people to replace distorted modes of thinking (e.g., "my life is a mess") with more accurate ones ("this part of my life isn't good, a lot else is").

Compassion and connection

❖ The fundamental nature of human beings, the Dalai Lama suggests, is gentleness. Science and philosophy like to portray humans as self-interested, but many studies show that people like to be altruistic if they get a chance (e.g., in disaster relief efforts). We may think of a baby as the perfect example of humanity living only for its own physiological needs, but another way to look at it is in terms of the joy that babies give to those around them. When we see the world not as aggressive but as basically compassionate, it is easy to see the evidence.

❖ Compassion is useful. Rather than being sentimental, it is the basis of communicating well between people. Echoing Dale Carnegie, the

Dalai Lama says that only by really seeing and feeling things from another's point of view will you truly be able to bond with them. Compassion is not "feeling sorry for someone" but a recognition of commonality—what someone else feels today might be what you will be feeling next week.

❖ The Dalai Lama is "never lonely." The antidote to loneliness is to be prepared to connect with anyone. Most people who consider themselves lonely are surrounded by family and friends, yet they put all their longings into the hope of finding that "special someone." Open your eyes to the wealth of people, he says, and loneliness can be a thing of the past.

❖ Distinguish between love based on attachment and love based on compassion. All human beings want to be happy and avoid suffering; instead of loving a person just so that they will love you back, begin with seeing the commonality of the human condition and what you can do to increase this particular person's happiness.

❖ If you fail to cultivate compassion, or the ability to feel the suffering of others, you lose the sense of belonging to the human race that is the source of warmth and inspiration. While feeling another's pain may not seem appealing, without it we set ourselves up for isolation. While the ruthless person can never properly relax, the compassionate person experiences freedom of mind and a rare peace.

Final comments

An effect of reading *The Art of Happiness* is that you find yourself asking: "How would the Dalai Lama deal with this situation?" He gives off a sense of the lightness of life, despite all the negative things, and this is a person who has lost his whole country.

In the face of Cutler's probing questions it is surprising how often the Dalai Lama says "I don't know," particularly when addressing the case of individuals. People are complex, he says, but the western way is always to find the causes of things, which can lead to a kind of agony if we don't find an answer. We will not necessarily understand why life plays out the way it does within the scope of our lifetime.

This view partly comes from his belief in reincarnation and *karma*, but can be appreciated separately to Buddhist doctrine. Precisely because we may not understand everything about our existence, it is all the more important to be good to other beings and to leave the world a slightly better place. With this simple command we know that we can't go wrong.

The Dhammapada

*"There is the perfume of sandalwood, of rose-bay, of
the blue lotus and jasmine; but far above the perfume
of those flowers the perfume of virtue is supreme."*

*"Come and look at this world. It is like a royal
painted chariot wherein fools sink. The wise are not
imprisoned in the chariot."*

*"He who in early days was unwise but later found
Wisdom, he sheds a light over the world like that of
the moon when free from clouds."*

*"Better than a hundred years not seeing the Path supreme
is one single day of life if one sees the Path supreme."*

In a nutshell

**Refine and improve the quality of your thoughts and you will have
little to fear from the world.**

In a similar vein
The Dalai Lama & Howard C. Cutler, *The Art of Happiness* (p122)
Lao Tzu, *Tao Te Ching* (p226)

CHAPTER 21

Buddha's teachings

Tired of modern self-help books? The Dhammapada is an ancient source of wisdom and one of the truly great works of spiritual literature. It is also the perfect introduction to Buddhist thought, being an inspirational compendium of all the major themes in the sacred canon of Theravada Buddhism.

The title comes from the Sanskrit word *dharma* (*dhamma* in Pali), simply meaning the way of the universe, its law of being, while *pada* in both languages is a foot or a step. Thus the holy book represents a path guide to the universal way of love and truth that can lead us to *nirvana*, or personal liberation, as Juan Mascaró says in the note to his 1973 translation. The Dhammapada expresses both the law of the universe and how we can live in alignment with it while on earth.

Who Buddha was

Siddhartha Gautama Buddha lived 500 years before Jesus. "Buddha" is not his real name but a title of honor. He was the son of a king ruling over a small state in what is now Nepal, and if you have seen the movie *Little Buddha* with Keanu Reeves as The Enlightened One, you will have some idea of the luxury and indolence that Indian royalty enjoyed.

Nevertheless at age 29, after looking outside the walls of the palace and discovering just how miserable most people's lives were, Siddhartha fled into the jungle to spend years as a loin-clothed hermit. It was famously under the bough of a bodhi tree that "enlightenment" came to him. Unlike Jesus, the Buddha lived into old age, spending the next 45 years wandering northern India as a teacher.

Why Buddha succeeded

Among the hundreds of faiths of the time, Buddha's triumphed. Why? Buddha sought out people from all levels of society, having little respect for the caste system and the exclusive language and ceremony of the Brahmin priesthood. He knew that power corrupted and the religion that grew around him was dogma free, seeking to remove the barriers between individuals and enlightenment. Buddha was not a god, a divine incarnation, or even a prophet; through his own dedication, he had achieved perfect wisdom and purity of mind, laying down the example for anyone to follow him.

The spread of Buddhism was also guaranteed by the Master's identification of clear practices that promised to banish suffering for ever. This was obviously a revolutionary idea, and still is—the promise of a pain-free life continues to hold incredible allure. Buddhist scholar Thomas Cleary believes that the Buddha succeeded because his teachings stood outside of time and culture, grasping the essential nature of the human condition and our relationship to the universe.

What The Dhammapada says

The Dhammapada is symbolic of Buddhism's timelessness and accessibility. It has chapters but no obvious sequence. You can open it at any page and find an inspirational thought that may well have been spoken by Buddha himself, a sacred communication across the ages. It has been suggested that while the New Testament has the energy of a young man who seeks to transform the world, The Dhammapada carries the wisdom, serenity, and patience of an older person.

It covers perennial subjects such as pleasure, happiness, and evil through almost poetic sayings, and unlike some writings in Buddhism the style is unscholarly and to the point. As each era and culture has interpreted it afresh, the book does not date. The following are some of its subjects.

Happiness

It is our duty to free ourselves from hate, disease, and restlessness. This is not to be done by rejecting the world, but by cultivating love, health, and calmness within it. The ideal state is to "feed on joy," joy that can be self-generated, flowing from an ever-reliable source; one no longer has to rely on the events and conditions of the world for happiness. Self-contained, we see ambition and acquisition to be inferior routes to happiness.

Non-attachment
Sorrow arises from what is dear, as does fear. For someone free from liking, there is no sorrow, so how could there be fear?

How can we not have likes and dislikes? Perhaps it is impossible, but we should know that strong desires have a price. It makes sense that if we are attached to something, we have an attendant fear of its loss. By witnessing the transitory nature of the world and accepting whatever comes to us, we can reduce attachment and therefore fear and misery.

Self-mastery
Discipline is all-important. The following verses speak for themselves:

"By energy, vigilance, self-control, and self-mastery, the wise one may make an island that a flood cannot sweep away."
"He who can be alone and rest alone and is never weary of his great work, he can live in joy, when master of himself, by the edge of the forest of desires."

Enlightenment
The idea of leaving normal life behind and becoming a hermit can sometimes seem very attractive! But The Dhammapada says that taking solitary refuge is a sign of egocentrism or fear. We are better off dealing gracefully with the challenges of work and family life—through them we can become enlightened. Cleary says that the key teaching of The Dhammapada is "being in the world but not of the world."

Retribution and its avoidance
The following two statements are possibly the most profound in The Dhammapada, with implications for every aspect of human life and relationships:

"For hate is not conquered by hate: hate is conquered by love. This is a law eternal."
"Overcome anger by non-anger, overcome evil by good. Overcome the miser by giving, overcome the liar by truth."

Note that there is nothing in these statements about not taking action; they simply mean that whatever is done must be consciously chosen, not an "emotional response."

Accept criticism as a fact of life

"They disparage one who remains silent, they disparage one who talks a lot, and they even disparage one who talks in moderation. There is no-one in the world who is not disparaged."

You can never please everyone! The main thing is to concentrate on your own work, your integrity—to be independent of the good opinion of others.

The Path

There is a myth that Buddhism is pessimistic, which comes from the fifth saying in Chapter 20, "The Path." A conventional translation would be: "All is transient, all is sorrow. When one sees this, one is above misery. This is the clear path." Western culture has interpreted these statements as implying that life is suffering.

In fact, and as Cleary argues in his translation, Buddhism is inherently optimistic, believing that an individual, and humanity overall, can rise above its folly, fear, and aggression.

"When one sees by insight that all conditioned states are miserable, one then wearies of misery; this is the path to purity."

If we are independent of mind and do not let ourselves become robotic reflections of our environment, life will not equate with suffering. *Nirvana* is not obliteration of the world of the senses but being able to live within it in total independence. In Pali, *nirvana* means "extinction"—of the afflictions of greed, hate, conceit, delusion, doubt, and arbitrary opinion.

The famous "four statements" are central to Buddhism because they are the recipe for ending suffering:

❖ That misery or sorrow is a conditioned state.
❖ That it has a cause.
❖ That it has an end.
❖ That the way to end it is through practice of the eightfold path to Nirvana.

The eightfold path involves:

1 Accurate perception.
2 Accurate thinking.
3 Accurate speech.
4 Appropriate action.
5 Appropriate way of making a living ("right livelihood").
6 Precise effort.
7 Mindfulness.
8 Meditation.

Final comments

It is amazing to think that a person may pick up a 2,500-year-old book and be instantly refreshed by its insights. Of course, not only are Buddha's teachings still relevant, they are fashionable. Its lack of dogma and ritual make Buddhism the perfect religion for contemporary life. Though uprooted from tradition, we still want a level of spiritual discipline, and it comes with the least baggage of the major world religions, with an in-built resistance to zealotry; you don't often hear of Buddhist fundamentalists.

Somehow we expect spiritual truths to be complicated, only understood by a keen theological mind. The sayings from The Dhammapada show us just how unintellectual it all is. What may seem like empty platitudes are accurate instructions for the best life imaginable.

The Power of Habit

2011

"Small wins are exactly what they sound like, and are part of how keystone habits create widespread changes. A huge body of research has shown that small wins have enormous power, an influence disproportionate to the accomplishments of the victories themselves . . . Small wins fuel transformative changes by leveraging tiny advantages into patterns that convince people that bigger achievements are within reach."

"To figure out which cravings are driving particular habits, it's useful to experiment with different rewards. This might take a few days, or a week, or longer. During that period, you shouldn't feel any pressure to make a real change—think of yourself as a scientist in the data collection stage."

In a nutshell

The science of habitual behavior is now so advanced that there is little excuse not to exchange our bad habits for good ones.

In a similar vein
Stephen R. Covey, *The 7 Habits of Highly Effective People* (p110)

CHAPTER 22

Charles Duhigg

ward-winning journalist Charles Duhigg begins *The Power of Habit: Why We Do What We Do in Life and Business* with the story of a young woman whose life had fallen apart after her husband announced he had fallen in love with someone else and was leaving her. She smoked, she was overweight, she was in debt, and became a stalker of her ex-husband. In desperation she went on a trip to Cairo to see the pyramids, and while there resolved to come back and walk across the desert. To do so she thought she would need to stop smoking. Focusing on conquering this single habit taught her how to change all the other habits in her life that prevented her return to physical and psychological health. She was able to quit for good, became a runner, lost a lot of weight, and found a new partner. When habit researchers did scans of her brain, they showed that the parts relating to cravings and hunger still light up when she sees food, but it is overridden by new activity in the frontal region of the brain relating to self-discipline and inhibition.

Good habits, as moral codes and religions have taught, create a good life, but it is only in the last 30 years that neurology and psychology have turned habit formation and self-discipline into a science. Duhigg's book was one of the first to bring this emerging science to a popular audience, and makes fascinating reading. He divides it into three parts, looking at the power of habits in individuals, in organizations, and in societies. We focus on the first.

Creatures of habit

Though habits had long been of interest to psychologists, it was not until the 1990s that the scientific study of habits began to really advance. At the Massachusetts Institute of Technology, researchers deactivated the basal ganglia, a golf-ball-sized bit of the brain, in the brains of rats. The effect was that the rats had to start all over again to work out how to negotiate their way through a maze. Where before they relied on habits to find food, now their brains were

working overtime, each time, to find it. However, as habits of searching developed, brain activity decreased. In time, their internalization of routes was such that they hardly needed to think at all. This conversion process in which patterns became recalled with ease seemed to happen in the brain's storehouse of habits, the basal ganglia, which allowed the rest of the brain to virtually go to sleep.

Humans do not differ greatly from rats in the way we initiate and lay down habits in our minds. Our brains can take even very complex and sophisticated tasks, such as backing a car out of a driveway and moving into traffic—which involves most of our senses, complex judgments and motor coordination, that it has taken years for driverless car technology to come close to replicating—and reduce them to an unthinking routine that involves very little conscious brain power. The brain does this, Duhigg says, because it is "constantly looking for ways to save effort." It means our brains can be smaller yet more powerful, allowing us to focus on more abstract and higher order things such as inventing or designing.

The habit researchers found that habits never really disappear; they are part of the software of our brains. This is good in the sense that we don't have to relearn tasks anew each day, from brushing our teeth to being polite to driving to work, but bad if we are trying to get rid of a habit we don't like. We may find that an old habit can quickly resurface if the right cue or reward appears. Indeed, once habits swing into action, they are like a script that our brain wants to see through to its logical end. Having received the cue or the trigger, it wants to get the reward that comes at the end of the routine. If there is some trigger for our anger, it doesn't feel right if we don't follow through and have the emotional reaction or angry response that goes with it. If we see some erotic image that we associate with great pleasure, it seems to be going against our nature not to act upon it. Yet what is our "nature" is surprisingly malleable; it may just be some old habit or bundle of habits that can be replaced by new ones.

How habits work

There is a three-stage process in which a habit forms: first, some cue or trigger, which informs the brain that it can go into habitual autopilot, and which habit should swing into action; second, the habitual routine itself, which can be physical or emotional; third, some kind of reward, which reminds the brain that the habit is worth it. This three-stage process of cue-routine-reward becomes more automatic over time, and the very automaticity of habits is why, unless they are consciously fought, they tend to take over. But the beauty of knowing how habits work is that it is like learning how a gadget works—once you have the knowledge, you can tinker with it.

Cues can be so powerful, so deeply lodged in our minds as being associated with pleasure, that even if the reward changes such that it is damaging to us, we will feel powerless to stop the habit. The junkie keeps taking the drug, even though it no longer has much effect and is ruining his life. We get a thrill just ordering a double cheeseburger, even if we know it will ruin our diet and best intentions to be slim. A family may start out going to a fast food place once a week for convenience sake, but since the payoff to the taste buds is so great in terms of fat and sugar hits, they find ways to justify it twice a week, then three times, until it is affecting the family's health. One reason why fast food chains have uniform restaurant layouts and design is that the colors and architecture themselves become triggers. We sense the reward as we enter the place, even before eating. If cues and rewards are powerful, we can easily fall into a habit scarcely without realizing it.

At the same time, researchers have found that habits are also surprisingly "delicate," in the sense that the absence of a trigger can lead us to quickly change our behavior. For instance, the fast food joint we were spending so much time at closes down, so we start eating more at home (rather than finding an alternative fast food place). "By learning to observe the cues and rewards," Duhigg writes, "we can change the routines." We can control to a large extent the cues we are exposed to, to avoid a habit swinging into action.

All about the craving

Habits are so powerful, Duhigg notes, because they create neurological cravings.

We only have to see the cue (for example, a pack of Marlboros), for us to demand the reward for ourselves of the nicotine high. If we get the cue but don't follow through with the reward, we are left with a craving. It is for good reason that there are laws around the world that not only ban cigarette advertising, but hide cigarette packs behind a screen in a special part of supermarkets. If there's no cue or trigger, then no routine will swing into action that produces a craving.

You know how toothpastes leave a fresh, tingling sensation after you've brushed, and foam? Unless we get that sensation, or see the foaming, we won't feel we have a "signal" that we have completed the routine, and so won't feel rewarded. Yet the tingling doesn't do anything to stop tooth decay. Duhigg reveals the extent to which the increase in brushing was fuelled by psychological, not dental, observations, in his profile of advertising guru Claude Hopkins. At a time when few people brushed their teeth, Hopkins created the Pepsodent campaign that got half of Americans brushing their teeth. Hopkins researched dental textbooks and learned about the natural filmy substance that covers teeth. You could easily get rid of the film by eating an apple or brushing it away, and toothpaste didn't help in removing it. But the campaign Hopkins launched blamed this film for tooth discoloration and tooth decay, neither of which was true. The ads asked people to "feel the film" (the cue), and if it was there, then Pepsodent would remove it (the routine). A "Pepsodent smile" would make you look beautiful (the reward). Pepsodent would establish itself as the bestselling toothpaste in America for 30 years, and became an international brand. Hopkins put his success down to understanding human psychology, particularly the science of cues and rewards. His fortune was built on creating a craving.

Lessons from AA

The 12-step recovery program of Alcoholics Anonymous (AA) has been heavily criticized for being unscientific and even cultish, particularly the admonition to addicts to make "a decision to turn our will and our lives over to the care of God as we understand him." While psychiatry and addiction research has added mountains of new insights and data on addiction, the techniques of AA, Duhigg notes, seem "frozen in time." Yet in the last 15 years there has been a re-evaluation of the 12-step program from researchers at Harvard, Yale, and other universities, who have found that it actually follows the de-addiction pattern validated by research, in which the cue and the reward are not changed, only the routine (in this case, the drinking).

For instance, AA's step 4, to make "a searching and fearless inventory of ourselves" could include all the triggers that set off a reaching for the bottle. AA also gets people to look closely at the rewards that they seem to get from alcohol, including escape from life, emotional release, relaxation, companionship, and the stifling of anxieties and worries. It is not necessarily the feeling of being drunk that alcoholics crave (indeed some don't even like it), but the emotional release that alcohol brings. German neurologist Ulf Mueller notes that the parts of the brain linked to craving for physical pleasure are in a totally different area to those linked to the cravings for relief or emotional release. The reason that AA is focused on constant meetings, friendly sponsors, and camaraderie, is to provide a strong sense of connection, and the catharsis of a meeting provides as much of an emotional release as would a Friday night bender. The early meetings, "90 in 90 days," provide something for the alcoholic to do at night instead of being at home or going to a bar. It puts one routine in place of another.

Yet successfully recovered alcoholics say that it isn't enough to identify cues and rewards and put in place new routines, they need something else: God. In 2005, researchers found that the ones who became believers in a higher power seemed to be able to call on some extra source of strength in a period of temptation that would have turned others back to drink. In their objective way, the researchers zoomed in on what they felt was the positive effect that "God" was having: belief itself. If alcoholics believed that their lives were getting better, and that they were supported, then even a stressful event wouldn't shake that belief (and it is stressful events that are the most likely cause of relapses). The group and the community back up this belief; through the example of others, you can see living proof that it is possible to overcome and triumph against addiction. As new addicts join and in turn look to you as an example, the feeling of connection strengthens into responsibility. What groups and communities do is make change believable. They give us a chance to try out a new self, and in time these novel outlooks and routines become who we are.

The mechanics of change

Although science shows us that behavior and habit modification are eminently possible, ultimately they involve a consciously made *decision* to change. We must do the hard work of identifying the cues and triggers that seem to pull us unconsciously into our habits, being clear on the rewards they seem to offer, and then change our routines. A compulsive gambler knows she has a habit that threatens the prosperity of her family, and so has a responsibility to seek help. She cannot simply blame the casinos for bombarding her with free offers of accommodation and lines of credit. It is her responsibility to create a strategy that either makes her immune to such temptations, or does not receive them in the first place. Unless we clearly see, admit, and list the triggers and cues that start us off on our behaviors, we won't understand our cravings.

So how exactly do you change a habit? First, become aware of what you are feeling and thinking just before you engage in an addictive behavior. It could be boredom, or a wish to relax, or what feels like a physiological urge. Carry around a piece of paper, and mark down on it every time you feel an urge. A woman with a strong fingernail biting habit kept a diary and marked down 28 instances of biting in one week. She discovered that what set her biting off was a craving for physical stimulation, and it tended to happen when she was bored trying to do homework or watching TV. Therefore, it wasn't too hard to replace the biting of nails with some other kind of physical stimulation, such as rubbing her arm or tapping her knuckles on a surface.

Duhigg had a habit of going to the cafeteria each day, between 3 and 4 pm, to get a big chocolate-chip cookie. After analyzing the habit, he realized that what he was really after was a moment of distraction from work and the chance to socialize with his colleagues.

So he implemented a plan: every day at 3.30, he would walk to a friend's desk and talk for ten minutes. It took him a while for this to become a routine, and there were days he went for the cookie instead. But after a few weeks the plan became automatic, and it gave him a real sense of accomplishment. Duhigg quotes Nathan Azrin, who helped develop habit reversal training:

"It seems ridiculously simple, but once you're aware of how your habit works, once you recognize the cues and rewards, you're halfway to changing it. It seems like it should be more complex. The truth is, the brain can be reprogrammed. You just have to be deliberate about it."

Emotional habits

Duhigg discusses the café chain Starbucks, which realized that unless staff learned emotional self-control, they would bring their problems to work and take it out on customers and staff. Starbucks began training its staff in role-playing, imagining what they would do when, for instance, a customer started screaming about an order, or some other difficult moment. With the help of experts in self-discipline and habits, the chain trained people in what it cutely called the "LATTE" method: Listen to the customer; Acknowledge their complaint; Take action by solving the problem; Thank them; and Explain why the problem occurred. The point of such "inflection point" planning is that you practice what you will do at certain points again and again until your behavior becomes automatic. When the cue happens—an angry customer—the routine swings into action, and always has a reward, such as getting a pat on the back from management.

Duhigg refers to various studies that show that self-discipline matters more than IQ as an indicator of how successful someone will be. Brains can take you far, but if your responses to situations and people are not regulated, a year's work can easily be undone by a furious outburst, or some setback can make you give up just before things turn around. As every religion and ethical system teaches, emotional habits of restraint are key. Unless our reactions to people and events are habitual in a positive way, we can't be in control of our lives.

Final comments

"When we look at creatures from an outward point of view," William James wrote in *The Principles of Psychology* (1890), "one of the first things that strike us is that they are bundles of habits." We can have some great epiphany, but unless the neural pathways in our brains actually receive a rewiring, we can't really be said to have changed. The key, James noted, was to make the nervous system our ally instead of our enemy:

People grow and change, William James wrote, "to the way in which they have been exercised, just as a sheet of paper or a coat, once creased or folded, tends to fall forever afterward into the same identical folds."

If you get the habits right, the effects and outcomes of life take care of themselves. You want your habits to be so automatic, that they cannot *not* produce certain outcomes. One of Duhigg's profiles is Tony Dungy, an American football coach who took the Tampa Bay Buccaneers from loser status to one of the best teams in the NFL, simply by focusing on players' on-field habits of play and strategy. "Champions don't do extraordinary things," Dungy said. "They do ordinary things, but they do them without thinking, too fast for the other team to react. They follow the habits they've learned."

A lot of the motivational literature is about imagining great goals, and letting these aims fall into your subconscious mind—a sort of "set and forget" approach. But the science of habit formation confirms what philosophy, religion, and folk wisdom have always said: that we are a mass of habits, emotional and physical, and to realize our potential we have to be very deliberate about the routines that fill our days. We have great power in the sense that we can choose our habits, but also great responsibility because the habits we have chosen, much more even than the goals we have selected, in the end make us what we are.

Charles Duhigg

Duhigg was born in 1974 and grew up in New Mexico. His first degree was from Yale University, and he has an MBA from Harvard Business School. After a stint as a reporter for the Los Angeles Times, *in 2006 he began working for the* New York Times.

He won a 2013 Pulitzer Prize for a series of articles on Apple and Silicon Valley technology companies, and has won awards for other reporting. Duhigg's other book is Smarter Faster Better: The Secrets of Being Productive in Life and Business *(2016).*

Real Magic: Creating Miracles in Everyday Life

1992

"*As I look back at the entire tapestry of my life I can see from the perspective of the present moment that every aspect of my life was necessary and perfect. Each step eventually led to a higher place, even though these steps often felt like obstacles or painful experiences.*"

"*Know that if anyone has gone from sickness to health, fat to slim, addiction to choice, poor to rich, clumsy to agile, miserable to happy, or discontentment to fulfillment, then that capacity is part of the universal human condition . . . And, even if it has never been before—such as a cure for polio prior to 1954, or an airplane ride in 1745—the fact that one unique individual is capable of conceiving it in his or her mind is all that is required for humankind to be open to the possibility.*"

In a nutshell

When you are aligned with your higher self and your life purpose, miraculous things happen.

In a similar vein
The Bhagavad-Gita (p18)
Deepak Chopra, *The Seven Spiritual Laws of Success* (p90)
Louise Hay, *You Can Heal Your Life* (p190)
Pierre Teilhard de Chardin, *The Phenomenon of Man* (p290)

CHAPTER 23

Wayne Dyer

Wayne Dyer was a much-loved bestselling author and prolific speaker who, with his friend Deepak Chopra and the likes of Anthony Robbins, John Gray, and James Redfield (author of *The Celestine Prophecy*), has made life transformation into such a massive contemporary phenomenon. The success of *Your Erroneous Zones* (1976) saw Dyer leave respectable academia for the realm of talk shows and book signings. If that first book was his most fun to read (the play on the word erogenous is an indication), his most complete and arguably finest book is *Real Magic*. Packed full of insights, it is a self-actualization guide for real life that borrows freely from the best thinkers of East and West.

What is real magic?

Dyer took the phrase "real magic" from Harry Houdini, the famous escape artist. Late in his career, Houdini admitted that most of his feats were performed by illusion, but others he could not even explain to himself; these he called "real magic." For Dyer, real magic is the paradoxical truth that anyone can become a magician, a miracle maker in their everyday lives. This might seem far-fetched, but as Dyer says, it is simply a matter of changing the way you define your existence. He quotes Teilhard de Chardin: "We are not human beings having a spiritual experience, we are spiritual beings having a human experience."

The book takes the "impossibilities" in your life and, instead of suggesting mere goal setting or strong beliefs, shows you how to develop powerful "knowings" about who you are and what you can do. In this state of higher awareness, your purpose in life becomes very clear, relationships become more spiritual, work endeavors begin to "flow," and decisions are made with ease.

As Dyer sees it, there are no accidents in life. Each experience we have, no matter how painful, eventually leads us to something of higher value. When looking back, we can see that everything made sense and was part of an unfolding plan.

Enlightenment through purpose

The thread running though *Real Magic* is the need to become aware of our unique purpose in life. People learn or become "enlightened" about life and themselves in three main ways:

❖ *Enlightenment through suffering*. This might also be called the "why me?" path. Events occur, suffering takes place, and something is learned. But when suffering is our only teacher, we shut off the possibility of the miraculous.
❖ *Enlightenment through outcome*. In this path we have goals and ambitions that make sense of life. While superior to enlightenment through suffering, we must still be reactive and struggle, missing out on the higher awareness that creates magic.
❖ *Enlightenment through purpose*. Everything in the universe has a purpose, and by living according to our true purpose we begin to walk in step with it, magically creating what we want instead of battling against life.

A good indication that you are "on purpose" is if you lose track of time while doing your task, if it gives so much pleasure that you would want to do it even if you won $10 million tomorrow. Dyer remembers Montaigne's statement, "The great and glorious masterpiece of man is to live with purpose." Are you merely alive, or are you creating a masterpiece?

Creating a miracle mindset

Apart from purpose, we create a miracle mindset through:

❖ Withholding judgment ("you do not define people with your judgments, your judgments define you").
❖ Developing intuition.
❖ Knowing that intentions create your reality.
❖ Surrendering to the universe to provide for your needs.

Particularly important is the need to separate what we do from any rewards it may bring. This is hard when we live in a culture of want, yet Dyer observes the strange-but-true dictum that ambition can bite the nails of success. We cannot will miracles to happen, but must let them flow through us when we are fully concentrating on what we do, not what it might bring. By all means have a relaxed intention about the future, but do not let it interfere with your task in the present.

Purpose and relationships

Purpose also extends to our love life. Dyer says that all our relationships are part of a divine necessity; they were meant to be, so make the most of them. Spiritual partners go beyond what they may superficially have in common to see that their relationship has to do with the evolution of their souls. With this basic insight, we treat people as a gift, not a chattel. We try to be kind, rather than right. We allow people as much space and time as they need, which renews the relationship.

Lastly, since we know that each person is a wonderful mystery, we no longer have to understand them. We "honor the incomprehensible"!

Purpose and the prospering self

Dyer is particularly valuable on prosperity. Mostly we worry about whether we have money or do not have it, but his conception is that we must not try to "get" anything: "There is no way to prosperity, prosperity is the way." Prosperity is chiefly a state of mind, just as scarcity is. It is not about getting, but being. Prosperity consciousness is about the knowledge of how much we already have in abundance; as the biblical phrase has it, "To him that hath, more will be given."

In contrast, poverty consciousness is based on feelings of lack, which are manifested in your circumstances. Dyer echoes James Allen in saying that circumstances do not make us, they reveal us. This is obviously a sensitive area, as it could be interpreted that the poor deserve their situation. But Dyer makes a crucial distinction: While most of us have had the experience of being broke, "poor" is a set of beliefs that are strengthened each time we blame "circumstances" for our plight. Living out our purpose is a sure way to enter the stream of prosperity, as it involves constant giving. Another way is automatically to give away at least 10 percent of what we earn, even if that is not much.

Who am I meant to be?

Real Magic also covers personal identity. The chief point is that until we see that the personality we have now is not set in stone, that we can reinvent ourselves, we will not have a magic-filled life. The faint intuition or nagging inside about your possibilities knows more about you than you are willing to admit—treasure it and let it grow. Instead of focusing on what we lack, this growth should come from a knowledge that "we are it all already." Reinvention of our personality simply means exposing more of our true and greater self to the air.

Final comments

Real Magic also has excellent chapters on physical health, "becoming a spiritual being," and helping to usher in a "spiritual revolution." Dyer has the gift of talking about the non-material without sounding too serious or mystical. He draws on his psychotherapy experience, the great figures of eastern and western religions, and philosophy and quantum physics to prove his points, all the while avoiding intellectuality.

The very personal way in which Dyer speaks to the reader has made him a favorite to millions. People identify with him as a person who managed to combine the spiritual path with the patience-snapping demands of family life. Indeed, in his public talks he could be very amusing on this subject, telling once of his teenage daughter slouching against a door and saying, "Someone at school said you wrote a book on parenting. Tell me it's not true!"

Dyer's secret is meditation, and he is fond of quoting Pascal: "All man's miseries derive from not being able to sit quietly in a room alone." If sitting quietly in a room alone seems an impossible task for you, a good alternative would be to read this book.

Wayne Dyer

Born in 1940 in Detroit, Michigan, the youngest of three boys, Dyer spent many of his childhood years in foster homes. After high school he enlisted in the US Navy for four years' service, including a posting in Guam working as a cryptographer. After college in Detroit he worked as a teacher and acquired a Master's degree in school counseling, but envied the fewer teaching hours of the professors who had given his classes and so enrolled in a doctorate program in psychotherapy.

Six years of university teaching followed, including an associate professorship at St. John's University in New York; during this time he wrote three textbooks. Your Erroneous Zones *was written after the emotional discovery of his father's grave (related in* You'll See It When You Believe It*) in Biloxi, Mississippi. Dyer spent a year on the road promoting it before it became a bestseller.*

Dyer's other books include Pulling Your Own Strings, What Do You Really Want for Your Children?, You'll See It When You Believe It, Your Sacred Self, Manifesting Your Destiny, Wisdom of the Ages *(60 essays on the great spiritual figures of the last 2,500 years),* The Power of Intention, *and* Change Your Thoughts, Change Your Life: Living the Wisdom of the Tao.

Dyer was a keen runner. He had eight children and lived in Florida. He died of a heart attack in Hawaii in 2015.

Self-Reliance

1841

"Insist on yourself; never imitate. Your own gift you can present every moment with the cumulative force of a whole life's cultivation; but of the adopted talent of another you have only extemporaneous half possession. That which each can do best, none but his Maker can teach him . . . Where is the master who could have instructed Franklin, or Washington, or Bacon, or Newton? . . . Do that which is assigned to you, and you cannot hope too much or dare too much."

"We lie in the lap of immense intelligence, which makes us receivers of its truth and organs of its activity. When we discern justice, when we discern truth, we do nothing of ourselves, but allow a passage to its beams."

"Society is a joint-stock company, in which the members agree, for the better securing of his bread to each shareholder, to surrender the liberty and culture of the eater. The virtue in most request is conformity. Self-reliance is its aversion. It loves not realities and creators, but names and customs. Who would be a man, must be a nonconformist."

In a nutshell

Whatever the pressures, be your own person.

In a similar vein
The Bhagavad-Gita (p18)
Samuel Smiles, *Self-Help* (p284)
Henry David Thoreau, *Walden* (p296)

CHAPTER 24

Ralph Waldo Emerson

At only 30 pages, *Self-Reliance* is the shortest text covered in this book. It has the qualities of a concentrate, perhaps the very essence of personal development, and its ideas have had immeasurable influence. *Self-Reliance* was one of the key pieces of writing that helped carve the ethic of American individualism, and forms part of the intellectual bedrock of today's self-help writers.

As one of the great philosopher-sages of western culture, Emerson still matters; in fact, he has never been more relevant. The yearning to fulfill our potential has always been human nature; now, however, we are likely to see it as a right rather than a starry wish. Emerson called his philosophy idealism, but it was not romantic, unrealistic, or fuzzy. Rather, as Geldard says in *The Vision of Emerson*: "It has a touch of granite in it."

For Emerson, self-reliance was more than the image of a family carving out a life on the frontier. Though he admired the do-it-yourself attitude and reveled in nature, Emerson's frontier, the place of real freedom and opportunity, was a mental landscape free of mediocrity and conformity.

Unique and free

Like his friend and protégé Henry David Thoreau (see *Walden*), Emerson thought it silly to run around reforming and bettering the world, even giving to "good causes," before we had found our place in it. He famously observed:

"All men plume themselves on the improvement of society, and no man improves."

If we could not examine ourselves and identify our calling, we would be of little use. Lack of awareness would see us quickly molded into shape by a society that cared little for the beauty and freedom of the individual.

This is the path most of us take, happy to go along with society's program in exchange for a level of status and reasonable material circumstances. Though we profess to break away from limitations, the reality is comfort in conformity.

But why should we bother breaking out? Why risk the insecurity? Just as an ant cannot appreciate the level of living that a human can enjoy, so most of us do not know what we are missing if we never look beyond our little worlds. We tend to rely on things like sex, work success, eating, and shopping for that feeling of aliveness. Emerson saw though the veil of the external, knowing that it is the inner domains that reveal true riches, peace, and power. The only proper defense against numbing conformity is to find and walk the trail of uniqueness. In *Self-Reliance* there are many calls to that end:

> *"We but half express ourselves, and are ashamed of that divine idea which each of us represents."*

In expressing this divine idea that is ourselves, the apparently strong and necessary bonds to society and other people fall away; we no longer need their approval to function. We stand in the same position as Martin Luther, who said: "Here I stand—I can do no other"; this is me, this is what I'm about.

Our primary duty is not ultimately to our family, to our job, to our country, but only that which calls us to do or to be. Too often "duty" hides a lack of responsibility in taking up a unique path. We can push aside a calling for some years, choosing obvious sources of money or satisfaction or a more comfortable situation, but it will eventually make its claims.

For Emerson, genius was not owned by the great artists and scientists. The genuine things we do, those that don't refer to what others are likely to think, are fragments of genius that must be expanded to form all the days of our life. Only by finding and expressing this essence is a person's true nature revealed, whereas "Your conformity explains nothing."

Clarity and knowledge

Emerson was heavily influenced by the ancient eastern religious texts (Upanishads, Vedas, The Bhagavad-Gita). Their philosophy is a revelation of the oneness of all things; life is full of illusions and false ties that prevent us from being reunited with what is eternal and unchanging. Through awareness of our own thought processes we might hope to clear the fog of self-deception and illusion, what we now call the "scripting" of our lives by society. To be self-reliant is not to take anyone's word for anything. Emerson did not disagree with Thoreau's contention that Harvard, which they both attended, taught many disciplines, but the roots of none of them.

Emerson was aware that conventional education was not really up to this job of lifting the veil, as it mainly dealt in intellectual categorization. We would achieve real awareness in meditative thought that, instead of closing down knowledge into compartments, involved opening up to receive whole, changeless wisdom. This primary knowing Emerson called intuition, while all later teaching was merely tuition. He tried to make us think twice about depending on the strength of our will alone. Meditative thought, because it puts us in tune with universal forces and laws, leads us to ways of being and doing that are inherently right and "successful."

Inner treasure

The people of his time saw Emerson as a sage or a prophet, with fewer of the faults of human nature than anyone they knew. But Emerson had, as does anyone, the hopes, the highs, the setbacks of which life seems to consist. What made him stand out was a belief that we did not have to have a seesawing emotional life reacting to good or bad events. These are the final lines of *Self-Reliance*:

"A political victory, a rise of rents, the recovery of your sick or the return of your absent friend, or some other favorable event raises your spirits, and you think good days are preparing for you. Do not believe it. Nothing can bring you peace but yourself. Nothing can bring you peace but the triumph of principles."

This speaks to the very heart of the human condition and the ideas about fortune by which we live. Yet Emerson believed that all happiness was ultimately self-generated. It was not human nature to be permanently hostage to events—we are quite capable of detachment or transcendence.

Final comments

The reader may find no better writer than Emerson to help make the leap into self-reliant freedom. It is difficult to read *Self-Reliance* simply as a historical work, because you are easily pulled into Emerson's orbit of pure responsibility and self-awareness, a world in which there are no excuses, only opportunities.

His message is that the wish to succeed is not about our steely will against the universe. Rather, by becoming more fully aware of the patterns and flow of nature, time, and space, by working with the grain of the universe, we are part of an infinitely greater power. The principles he talked of in the quote above are not restrictive, but our creative, conscious response to the world; our lives should reflect this perfect universe, rather than being shaped by the crooked turns and boxes of culture. The self-reliant individual should be able to live in the world and improve it, not be merely another product of it.

Ralph Waldo Emerson

Born in 1803 in Boston, Emerson was the second oldest of eight children. Enrolled at Harvard at the age of 14, he graduated four years later halfway down in his class. After some time as a schoolteacher, he attended Divinity College at Harvard, became a Unitarian pastor, and married, only to see his wife Ellen die of tuberculosis. After resigning his post because of doctrinal disputes, Emerson traveled to Europe and met Carlyle, Coleridge, and Wordsworth.

Returning to America in 1835, he settled in Concord and married again, to Lydia Jackson, with whom he had five children. In 1836 he published Nature, which set down transcendentalist principles; other transcendentalists included Thoreau, Margaret Fuller, Amos Bronson Alcott, Elizabeth Peabody, and Jones Very. In the following two years Emerson delivered controversial addresses at Harvard, the first asserting American intellectual independence from Europe, the second attracting the wrath of the religious establishment in its plea for independence of belief above all creeds and churches.

In 1841 and 1844 two series of essays were published, including "Self-Reliance," "Spiritual Laws," "Compensation and Experience" and, in the decade 1850–60, "Representative Men," "English Traits," and "The Conduct of Life." Emerson stopped writing and lecturing ten years before his death in 1882.

Women Who Run with the Wolves

1992

"Wildlife and the Wild Woman are both endangered species. Over time, we have seen the feminine instinctive nature looted, driven back, and overbuilt. For long periods it has been mismanaged like the wildlife and the wildlands."

"A healthy woman is much like a wolf: robust, chock-full, strong life force, life-giving, territorially aware, inventive, loyal, roving. Yet, separation from the wildish nature causes a woman's personality to become meager, thin, ghostly, spectral . . . When women's lives are in stasis, or filled with ennui, it is always time for the wildish woman to emerge; it is time for the creating function of the psyche to flood the delta."

"The modern woman is a blur of activity. She is pressured to be all things to all people. The old knowing is long overdue."

In a nutshell

Reconnecting with your wild nature is not a mad indulgence but vital to mental and physical health.

In a similar vein
Robert Bly, *Iron John* (p28)
Joseph Campbell with Bill Moyers, *The Power of Myth* (p72)
James Hillman, *The Soul's Code* (p194)

CHAPTER 25

Clarissa Pinkola Estés

Modern psychology does not really cater to the deeper side of woman; it leaves no real explanation for her longings, it does not shine light on her mysteries, it does not allow her time. Estés has spent her life in the belief that the old stories from many cultural traditions can reconnect women with their soul, their wilder nature. She is what is known as a *cantadora*, a keeper of the old stories.

The title of the book came from the author's study of wolves, who she realized had much in common with women in their spiritedness, their intuitive and instinctive nature, and their travails. Like wolves, women have been demonized for any sign of wildness and their homelands concreted over; but just as many wild wolf populations have been re-established, it is about time that women regained access to their wild spaces.

Women Who Run with the Wolves is, overall, a spectacular work that has left many in its thrall. It has revolutionized many women's lives in the way that *Iron John* has for men. With myths and tales for every conceivable aspect of life, to say it is rich is an understatement. We can only really gloss over its contents, but the following couple of stories, abstracted from the book, may give you some idea.

The seal woman

Once, in a very harsh place, a hunter was out in his kayak. It was past dark and he had not found anything. He came upon the great spotted rock in the sea, and in the half-light the rock appeared to be full of graceful movement. As he drew closer, he saw a group of stunningly beautiful women, and in his loneliness he felt pangs of love and longing. He saw a sealskin on the edge of the rock and stole it. As the women donned their skins and swam back into their watery home, one of them realized she was without her skin.

The man called out to her to "Be my wife, I am lonely" but she said, "I

157

can't, I am of the Temeqvanek, I live beneath." But he said this to her:
"Be my wife, and in seven summers I'll give you back your skin, and
you can do as you wish." Reluctantly, the seal woman agreed.
They had a much-loved child, Ooruk, whom she taught all the stories
about the creatures of the sea that she knew. But after a time her flesh
started to dry out, she turned pale and her sight began to darken. The
day came when she asked for her skin back.
"No," said the husband—did she want to leave the family motherless
and wifeless?
In the night Ooruk heard a giant seal calling in the wind, and he fol-
lowed the call to the water. In the rocks he found a sealskin and, on
smelling it, realized it was his mother's. Taking it to her, she was
delighted, and took him with her under the water where she introduced
the boy to the great seal and all the others.
She regained her color and her health, because she had returned
home. She became known as the seal no one could kill, Tanquigcaq,
holy one. After a while she had to return the child to land, but when
he grew up he was often seen communing with a particular seal near
the water.

The seal, Estés says, is an old and beautiful symbol of the wild soul.
Seals are generally comfortable with humans, but like young or inexpe-
rienced women they are sometimes not aware of potential harm or the
intentions of others. All of us at some point will experience a "loss of
our sealskin," a robbing of innocence or spirit, a weakening of identity.
At the time it always seems horrible or at least difficult, but later you
will hear people say that it was the best thing that happened to them,
because it clarified who they are and what life is to them. It puts us in
touch with deeper things.

The story evokes the duality between the "above-water" world of
family and work, and the oceanic world of private thoughts, emotions,
and desires. The soul-home cannot be left unvisited for too long or, like
the seal woman, our personalities dry up and the body is leached of
energy. Many women lose their "soulskin" by giving too much or by
being too perfectionistic or ambitious, by constant dissatisfaction, or by
lacking the will to do anything about it.

Everyone wants a bit of the modern woman, but there has to be a
point where she says "no" and reclaims her soulskin. This might
involve anything from a weekend away in the woods, to a night with

friends, to setting side an hour a day when no one can ask for anything. Others might not understand it, but in the long term it benefits them as much as you, and you'll come back refreshed and psychically refueled.

The skeleton woman

Once there was a lonely arctic fisherman who, one day, thought he had hooked a big fish that would stop him having to hunt for a while. He got excited when there was a big pull on the nets, but was shocked when he saw what he'd pulled up: a woman's skeleton.

The woman had been thrown over the cliffs by her father, and she had sunk to the bottom. Appalled at his "catch," the fisherman tried to throw it back, but the skeleton came to some sort of life and pursued him back to his ice-home.

He took pity on her and cleaned her up and let her rest, before falling asleep himself. During the night she saw a tear coming from his eye, and she drank and drank the tears, so thirsty was she. And in the night she took his heart and used it to make her come alive again, as flesh and blood. A person again, she crawled into his sack with him.

Thereafter, the couple were always well fed, thanks to the sea creatures the woman knew when she was at the bottom of the sea.

Estés understands the story to be about relationships. When you are single, you look for someone who is loving enough or rich enough so that, like the fisherman, you "won't have to hunt for a while." You are just after more life in your life, something enjoyable and fun.

However, once you get a good look at what you've pulled up (maybe after the first flittery phase), like the fisherman you try to "throw him or her back." You realize that you've got more than you bargained for, that this is getting serious. The other person stops meaning good times to you, they become the skeleton woman—the horror of settling down, mortality, long-term commitment, ups and downs, age, ending of the current life. Yet if you are lucky, the "skeleton" will not accept your rejection but chase you to your home (your limits and insecurities). In time you realize that this being has a lot to offer, attractive even if scary; for some reason you want do something for this person.

In return the being gives you abundance, but of things and from sources that you didn't know existed.

The skeleton woman story is about what Estés calls the "life/death/life" cycle. In modern cultures we are terrified of any sort of death, whereas in older ones everyone was aware that new life came as the companion to death. When we shy away from serious relationships, it is never the other person we can't face up to, it is the unwillingness to enter into the time-honored cycle. We will not grow in this relationship, but seek another one and perhaps then another, so that we only experience a continual high of "life." This shrinks the psyche. Every relationship has many endings and beginnings within it, and what to our horror may seem like the final end is much more likely to be a necessary change so that the relationship can renew itself.

A woman, and indeed a man, must become aware of and willingly embrace the life/death/life cycle if they are ever to be in touch with their wild nature. Estés says of the skeleton woman:

"She surfaces, like it or not, for without her there can be no real knowledge of life, and without that knowing, there can be no fealty, no real love or devotion."

Final comments

Most people don't read this book as they normally read. You will find yourself taking in a chapter at a time then going away to ruminate on it. This is how it should be. It seems too big to tackle at first (over 500 pages), but treat it as a family of voices that you listen to one by one. Let it sink in slowly and you will begin to understand why it has inspired so many people, not only women.

A final word. You may be thinking: "If I embrace the wild nature in me, I will turn my world and my family upside down!" Not so, Estés says: Doing this brings more integrity to your personal life and your existence, because you will not be trying to walk around in a disguise, you won't be afraid of being a creator, a lover, someone who chases after what is right, an intuition truster, a woman truly aware of her power and attuned to nature. All these things are your birthright and nothing to fear.

Clarissa Pinkola Estés

Born in 1945, Estés was fostered by immigrant Hungarians near the Great Lakes in Michigan. She grew up amid nature and hearing stories from a long non-literate tradition. Her roots are Mexican-Spanish.

She has a doctorate in ethno-clinical psychology, or the study of tribes and groups, and is a Jungian psychoanalyst. She is also a renowned poet. Estés worked for many years as a post-trauma specialist and is presently managing editor of The Moderate Voice, a politics and culture website.

The writing of Women Who Run with the Wolves *was begun in 1971 and the stories collected from across North America. Other books include* The Gift of Story; The Faithful Gardener, *which is based on her childhood experiences; and* The Creative Fire: Myths and Stories on the Cycles of Creativity.

Man's Search for Meaning

1959

"*At times, lightning decisions had to be made, decisions which spelled life or death. The prisoner would have preferred to let fate make the choice for him. This escape from commitment was most apparent when a prisoner had to make the decision for or against an escape attempt. In those minutes in which he had to make up his mind—and it was always a question of minutes—he suffered the tortures of Hell.*"

"*We were grateful for the smallest of mercies. We were glad when there was time to delouse before going to bed, although this in itself was no pleasure, as it meant standing naked in an unheated hut where icicles hung from the ceiling.*"

"*If someone had seen our faces on the journey from Auschwitz to a Bavarian camp as we beheld the mountains of Salzburg with their summits glowing in the sunset, through the little barred windows of the prison carriage, he would never have believed that those were the faces of men who had given up all hope of life and liberty. Despite that factor—or maybe because of it—we were carried away by nature's beauty, which we had missed for so long.*"

In a nutshell

The meaning of life is the meaning that you decide to give it.

In a similar vein
Boethius, *The Consolation of Philosophy* (p34)

CHAPTER 26

Viktor Frankl

Viktor Frankl's wife, father, mother, and brother died in the concentration camps of Nazi Germany. Only his sister survived. Enduring extreme hunger, cold, and brutality, first in Auschwitz and then Dachau, Frankl himself was under constant threat of going to the gas ovens. He lost every physical belonging on his first day in the camps, and was forced to surrender a scientific manuscript that he considered his life's work.

This is, if there ever was one, a story that could excuse someone believing that life is meaningless and suicide a reasonable option. Yet having been lowered into the pits of humanity, Frankl emerged an optimist. His reasoning was that even in the most terrible circumstances, people still have the freedom to choose how they see their circumstances and create meaning out of them. As Gordon Allport notes in his preface to the third edition, this is what the ancient Stoics called the "last freedom." The evil of torture is not so much the physical torment, but the active attempt to extinguish freedom.

Redefining human achievement

A favorite quote of Frankl's was from Nietzsche, "He who has a why to live can bear with almost any how." The most poignant bits of this classic are Frankl's recollections of the thoughts that gave him the will to live. Mental images of his wife provided the only light in the dark days of the concentration camp, and there is a beautiful scene when he is thinking of her with such intensity that when a bird hops on to a mound in front of him, it appears to be her living embodiment. He also imagined himself after liberation in lecture halls, telling people about what must never happen again. This proved to be prophetic. Finally, there was the desire to jot down notes remembered from his lost manuscript.

The men who had given up, in contrast, could be recognized because they smoked their last cigarettes, which could otherwise have

163

been traded for a scrap of food. These men had decided that life held nothing more for them. Yet this thinking struck Frankl as a terrible mistake. We are not here to judge life according to what we expected from it and what it has delivered. Rather, he realized, we must find the courage to ask what life expects of us, day by day. Our task is not merely to survive, but to find the guiding truth specific to us and our situation, which can sometimes only be revealed in the worst suffering. Indeed, Frankl says that "rather than being a symptom of neurosis, suffering may well be a human achievement."

The book's impact

Man's Search for Meaning has sold over nine million copies and been translated into 24 languages. It was voted one of America's ten most influential books by the Library of Congress. Yet Frankl, who originally wanted the book to be published with only his prisoner number on the cover, stated that he did not see the work as a great achievement. Its success was "an expression of the misery of our time," revealing the ravenous hunger for meaningful existence.

Apart from its bestseller status, *Man's Search for Meaning* has been a big influence on the major self-help writers. The emphasis on responsibility that we find in Covey's *The 7 Habits of Highly Effective People*, for example, is directly inspired by Frankl, and the work is referenced in a number of books covered in this volume.

The current edition has three parts: the autobiographical "Experiences in a concentration camp"; a theoretical essay "Logotherapy in a nutshell" (1962); and a piece titled "The case for a tragic optimism" (1984). With this structure, the unputdownable personal story leads the reader on to its intellectual implications.

The will to meaning and logotherapy

What is amazing about Frankl's experiences is that they caused him to live out the ideas about which, as a doctor before the outbreak of the Second World War, he had been theorizing. The theory and the practice became the Third School of Viennese psychotherapy, logotherapy (from the Greek *logos*, "meaning"), following Freud's psychoanalysis and Adler's individual psychology. Whereas psychoanalysis requires introspection and self-centeredness to reveal the basis of someone's neurosis, logotherapy tries to take the person out of themselves and see their life in a broader perspective. Where psychoanalysis focuses on the "will to pleasure" and Adlerian psychology on the "will to power," logotherapy sees the prime motivating force in human beings as a "will to meaning."

Frankl remembers an American diplomat coming to his office in Vienna who had spent five years in psychoanalysis. Discontented with his job and uncomfortable about implementing US foreign policy, this man's analyst had laid the blame on the relationship with his father: The United States government represented the father image and was therefore the superficial object of his angst, but the real issue was his feelings toward his biological father. Frankl, however, simply diagnosed a lack of purpose in the man's work and suggested a career change. The diplomat took his advice and never looked back.

The point of the anecdote is that in logotherapy, existential distress is not neurosis or mental disease, but a sign that we are becoming more human in the desire for meaning. In contrast to Freud or Adler, Frankl chose not to see life simply as the satisfaction of drives or instincts, or even as becoming "well adjusted" to society. Instead, he (and humanistic psychology in general, for example Abraham Maslow and Carl Rogers) believed that the outstanding feature of human beings is their free will.

Sources of meaning

Logotherapy says that mental health arises when we learn how to close the gap between what we are and what we could become. But what if we are yet to identify what we could become? Frankl noted that the modern person has almost too much freedom to deal with. We no longer live through instinct, but tradition is no guide either. This is the existential vacuum, in which the frustrated will to meaning is compensated for in the urge for money, sex, entertainment, even violence. We are not open to the various sources of meaning, which according to Frankl are:

1 Creating a work or doing a deed.
2 Experiencing something or encountering someone (love).
3 The attitude we take to unavoidable suffering.

The first is a classic source, defined as "life purpose" in the self-help literature. Our culture expects happiness, yet Frankl says that this is not something that we should seek directly. He defines happiness as a by-product of forgetting ourselves in a task that draws on all our imagination and talents.

The second is important as it makes experience (inner and outer) a legitimate alternative to achievement in a society built around achieving. The third gives suffering a meaning, but what meaning? Frankl admits that we may never know, or at least not until later in life. Just because we do not comprehend meaning, it does not mean that there is none.

To the people who say that life is meaningless because it is transitory, Frankl's response is "only the unfulfilment of potential is meaningless, not life itself." Our culture worships the young, yet it is age that is to be admired, since the older person has loved, suffered, and fulfilled so much. Fulfillment of your own potential, however humble, will make a permanent imprint on the history of the world, and the decision to make that imprint defines responsibility. Freedom is only one half of the equation. The other half is responsibility to act on it.

Final comments

If there is a thread running through personal development writing, it is a belief in the changeability of the individual. Determinism, in contrast, says that we can never arise above our childhood or our genetic make-up. Freud believed that if a group of people were all to be deprived of food, their individual differences would lessen, to be replaced by a single mass urge. But Frankl's concentration camp experience often revealed to him the opposite. The hunger, torture, and filth did serve to desensitize the prisoners, but despite being herded as animals, many somehow avoided a mob mentality. We can never predict the behavior of an individual and can make few generalizations about what it means to be human:

"Our generation is realistic, for we have come to know man as he really is. After all, man is that being who invented the gas chambers of Auschwitz; however, he is also that being who entered those gas chambers upright, with the Lord's Prayer or the Shema Yisrael on his lips."

What makes humans different as a species is that we can live for ideals and values. How else, as Frankl noted, would you be able to hold your head up as you entered the gas chamber? Aware that most of us would never even come close to such a horrible fate, he used it as a reference point, a symbol of personal responsibility that could guide the decisions we make in our everyday lives. No matter what the circumstances, his book says, we can be free.

Viktor Frankl

Frankl was born in 1905 in Vienna. Before the Second World War he graduated with two doctorates in medicine and philosophy from the University of Vienna. During the war he spent three years at the Theresienstadt, Auschwitz, and Dachau concentration camps. Man's Search for Meaning *was written on Frankl's return to Vienna after liberation, and was dictated over nine days.*

The ensuing years were spent as chief of the neurology department of the Policlinic Hospital, Vienna, but in the 1960s he moved to the United States. He held visiting professorships at Harvard and other US universities and did over 50 American lecture tours. Throughout his life he was a keen mountain climber.

Frankl wrote more than 30 books, including Psychotherapy and Existentialism, The Unconscious God *and* The Unheard Cry for Meaning, *and in the year of his death published an autobiography,* Viktor Frankl: Recollections. *There have been at least 145 books and more than 1,400 journal articles written about Frankl and logotherapy, and Frankl himself received 28 honorary degrees.*

He died in 1997, in the same week as Mother Teresa and Princess Diana.

Autobiography

1790

"*And I was not discourag'd by the seeming Magnitude of the Undertaking, as I have always thought that one Man of tolerable Abilities may work great Changes, & accomplish great Affairs among Mankind, if he first forms a good Plan, and, cutting off all Amusements or other Employments that would divert his Attention, makes the Execution of that same Plan his sole Study and Business.*"

"*When another asserted something that I thought an Error, I deny'd myself the Pleasure of contradicting him abruptly, and of immediately showing some Absurdity in his Proposition; and in answering I began by observing that in certain Cases or Circumstances his Opinion would be right, but that in the present case there appear'd or seem'd to me some Difference etc. I soon found the Advantage of this Change in my Manners. The Conversations I engag'd in went on more pleasantly.*"

In a nutshell

Constant self-improvement and a love of learning form your ticket to unusual success.

In a similar vein

Stephen Covey, *The 7 Habits of Highly Effective People* (p110)
Samuel Smiles, *Self-Help* (p284)

CHAPTER 27

Benjamin Franklin

Benjamin Franklin is best known as a historical figure, for his role in the American Revolution and experiments with electricity. But as Franklin scholar Ormond Seavey notes in his introduction to the *Autobiography*, his great influence on the affairs of the eighteenth-century western world in business, politics, and science was built on his skill as a writer. In the history books he looms large as a co-drafter of the Declaration of Independence and the American Constitution, but the *Autobiography* has been lauded by biographer Richard Amacher as "The first great book written in America."

It helped to create the modern literary form of the autobiography and has been a bestseller for two centuries, despite the fact that it was never finished or properly edited. Franklin's attitude to written work is summed up in one of his own aphorisms:

"If you would not be forgotten, as soon as you are dead and rotten, either write things worth reading, or do things worth the writing."

The book

The *Autobiography* was not a chronicle of Franklin's brilliance; the idea was to show how a person's life and character could become a noble one through constant self-assessment. Franklin, as a scientist, wrote it almost as if it were a report on the failures and successes of experiments in living.

At no point did he claim any special mastery over how to live life, but he was committed to finding a formula that could assure a person of some success. This motivation makes the *Autobiography* one of the original self-help classics.

Franklin never tried to show superiority; he spoke directly to the reader and laced the book with subtle humor, giving it the intimate feel of a fireside chat. The first part detailed experiences with family, friends, bosses, and work colleagues, in addition to travels and attempts to start new businesses, all of which will strike chords with today's reader.

Creating the best possible self

Franklin believed that virtue had worth for its own sake, whether or not it was to the glory of God. His background was Puritan and culturally he remained one, self-examining and self-improving. In his famous *The Protestant Ethic and the Spirit of Capitalism*, Weber names Franklin as a key exponent of this ethic. Franklin was a printer by trade and believed that character was the result of correcting the "errata" that prevent us attaining perfection. Life is not something we must suffer through, but is ripe for endless tinkering.

This is why Franklin is seminal in self-help literature—he disregarded any religious conception that we are naturally bad or good people, but saw humans rather as blank slates designed for success. Seavey notes, "It was always natural for Franklin to be trying on a fresh identity, as if he were putting on new clothes." He was truly modern in seeing that the individual was not a fixed proposition at all, but self-creating.

Franklin's law of constant self-improvement

Franklin wrote the *Autobiography* as an old man, considered a great man. He had arrived in Philadelphia from Boston with a couple of shillings and three bread rolls, two of which, characteristically, he gave to a woman in need. Instinctively knowing that mastery of words would be his ticket out of mediocrity, he would persuade a friend working at a booksellers to "lend" him books overnight, devouring them between finishing his day's work and starting another. Franklin would have agreed with the phrase "leaders are readers": Read at least a dozen non-fiction books a year and your life will be immeasurably enriched and improved.

Nevertheless, as a young man Franklin never dreamed of becoming an independence leader or ambassador to France. The reader of his life should not dwell on his actual accomplishments; they are less important than the efforts to achieve self-mastery that he described. Franklin's message is timeless: Greatness is not for the few, but is the duty of all of us. We protest that we are not that special, that we don't have the alent or the drive, but Franklin knew that an ethic of constant self-improvement is the yeast that makes an individual rise.

Franklin and the self-help ethic

The famous example of Franklin's self-help ethic is what has become known as *The Art of Virtue*, in which he listed the 12 qualities he aimed to possess.

By a system of graphs and daily self-appraisal, he claimed to have (mostly) achieved the desired virtues, having some difficulty with Order, or what we might now call time management; but realizing he was too proud at having lived up to his own standards, he created a thirteenth, Humility!

1. *Temperance*. Eat not to Dullness. Drink not to Elevation.
2. *Silence*. Speak not but what may benefit others or yourself. Avoid trifling conversation.
3. *Order*. Let all your Things have their Places. Let each Part of your Business have its Time.
4. *Resolution*. Resolve to perform what you ought. Perform without fail what you resolve.
5. *Frugality*. Make no Expense but to do good to others or yourself; that is, Waste nothing.
6. *Industry*. Lose no Time. Be always employed in something useful. Cut off all unnecessary actions.
7. *Sincerity*. Use no hurtful Deceit. Think innocently and justly; and if you speak, speak accordingly.
8. *Justice*. Wrong none, by doing Injuries or omitting the Benefits that are your Duty.
9. *Moderation*. Avoid Extremes. Forbear resenting injuries so much as you think they deserve.
10. *Cleanliness*. Tolerate no Uncleanness in Body, Clothes or Habitation.
11. *Tranquillity*. Be not disturbed at Trifles, or at Accidents common or unavoidable.
12. *Chastity*. Rarely use Venery but for Health or Offspring; never to Dullness, Weakness, or the Injury of your own or another's Peace or Reputation.
13. *Humility*. Imitate Jesus and Socrates.

Franklin also advocated use of a "morning question" — "What good shall I do this day?" — and an "evening question" — "What good have I done today?"

The *Autobiography* has had a major influence on self-help writing. Anthony Robbins's blockbuster *Awaken the Giant Within* recommends these questions as part of a daily success ritual. Franklin's slightly bizarre idea of writing one's own epitaph early on in life, in order to gain control of what you do in it, is now an established self-improvement technique. Stephen Covey (*The 7 Habits of Highly Effective People*) makes no secret of his debt to Franklin, whose life he describes as "the story of one person's heroic effort to make principles the basis of existence." This attention to character, rather than personality techniques, is the foundation of Covey's seven habits.

The secret of influence

Finally, Franklin's built-in skill at winning friends and influencing people did not escape the attention of Dale Carnegie. As a young man, Franklin believed himself to be highly skilled in argument, but came to the conclusion that this "skill" actually stood in the way of getting things done. He developed the habit of only ever expressing himself in terms of "modest Diffidence," never saying words like "undoubtedly" or trying to correct people. Instead, he used measured phrases such as "It appears to me . . ." or "If I am not mistaken . . ." The result was that, even though he was not a great speaker, people focused on his ideas and he was quick to gain credibility.

Final comments

Franklin's *Autobiography* is an up-by-the-bootstraps story representing the freedom to create and prosper that is the essence of American morality. Yet given the author's great sense of humor, his chameleon qualities, and his skill at self-promotion, it would be naïve to take *The Art of Virtue* or the *Autobiography* as one's gospel. Reverence is not a very Franklinesque trait.

His prescriptions have not gone without criticism. Thoreau believed that they made for a dreary race against time to amount wealth, never stopping to enjoy nature or the moment. Franklin scholar Russel B. Nye termed his subject "the first apostle of frugality and the patron saint of savings accounts." This comment was probably more directed at Franklin's collections of aphorisms on money and thrift, *The Way to Wealth*. The man's life, however, did not fit the image of penny-pinching Puritanism, for it is obvious that he lived with panache. Franklin appreciated that the self-help ethic is not about earnest striving, but more about excitement at the prospect of a richer life.

Benjamin Franklin

Franklin was born in Boston in 1706, the son of a chandler and the youngest of 17 children. His formal education lasted up until the age of 10. From age 12 to 17 he was an apprentice printer to his brother—who produced one of America's first newspapers—before settling in Philadelphia. Eventually he set up his own printing shop, and by his late 20s was publishing the highly successful Poor Richard's Almanacks, *a mix of practical information with aphorisms, many of which are still in use. By age 42 he was wealthy enough to retire but pursued civic projects and experiments with electricity, inventing the lightning rod.*

Franklin's party leadership in the Pennsylvania Assembly led to involvement in negotiations between Britain and colonial America, and he served on a committee that drafted the Declaration of Independence. Made American ambassador to France at age 69, during a decade in that post he negotiated France's assistance for the US and a peace accord with Britain. He was selected as a delegate to the Constitutional Convention of 1787.

When he died in 1790, Franklin was arguably the most famous American in the world. The Autobiography *was then published, but covered his life only up to 1758. It had been written in fits between 1771 and 1790 while he was living in France.*

Franklin has been called America's first entrepreneur. Apart from his other successes, he charted the Gulf Stream, designed a domestic heater, created a public library, originated a city fire department, and served on a French committee looking into hypnotism.

Creative Visualization

1978

"Creative visualization is magic in the truest and highest meaning of the word. It involves understanding and aligning yourself with the natural principles that govern the workings of our universe, and learning to use these principles in the most conscious and creative way."

"If you had never seen a gorgeous flower or a spectacular sunset before, and someone described one to you, you might consider it to be a miraculous thing (which it truly is!). Once you saw a few yourself, and began to learn something about the natural laws involved, you would begin to understand how they are formed and it would seem natural to you and not particularly mysterious. The same is true of the process of creative visualization. What at first might seem amazing or impossible to the very limited type of education our rational minds have received, becomes perfectly understandable once we learn and practice with the underlying concepts involved."

In a nutshell

Life tends to live up to the thoughts and images you have about it, good or bad. Why not imagine your future the way you want it?

In a similar vein
Wayne Dyer, *Real Magic* (p144)
Louise Hay, *You Can Heal Your Life* (p190)
Joseph Murphy, *The Power of Your Subconscious Mind* (p248)

CHAPTER 28

Shakti Gawain

There is nothing weird or New Age about creative visualization. We live out so much of our lives in our imaginations, making pictures or movies of what we'd like to happen or what we fear will happen. We visualize all the time, but in an unconscious way. With creative visualization, you consciously decide and take responsibility for what you want to manifest as reality in your life.

Practicing creative visualization is about appreciating the join between imagination and reality, between the unseen laws that govern the world and its physical reality. Could it be, then, that the failure to bring about what you have wanted in life may simply be a lack of knowledge or appreciation of the way the universe operates? This book will be particularly useful if you are a "go with the flow" person yet realize that you need to have more control over your future. This is the paradox that Shakti Gawain appreciated when she sat down to write the book, so you are not alone.

The technique

Think about things in your life that you want: a new job or to start a business, a beautiful relationship, a feeling of peace or serenity, improved mental skills, sporting prowess.

With creative visualization, the key to success is to quieten your mind so that your brainwaves are at "alpha" level. You will often find this state just before sleep, first thing in the morning, while meditating, or perhaps sitting next to a river or in a forest. While your first instinct may be to dream up nice "things" that you want, the real purpose is to peel away the layers of your normal reactive self and let thoughts flow that express the higher you. From this position you are only likely to think about what is really best for you and what would make you truly happy.

If, for instance, you have been having trouble with someone at work, instead of your usual feelings of spite and dislike, picture yourself communicating in a relaxed and open way with that person. Whatever has been said before between you, let it go and mentally bless the person anyway. The next time you come into contact, the normal barriers may seem to have evaporated and you may be surprised how quickly things change for the better.

Gawain notes that the purpose of creative visualization is not to "control" people with your mind—it doesn't work if used for negative or manipulative ends—but to "dissolve our internal barriers to natural harmony."

The science of creative visualization

How can creative visualization work?

❖ The physical universe is energy. All matter, when you break it down to smaller and smaller bits, is made up of particles of energy that when put together in a specific way create the illusion of "solidity."

❖ Different types of matter have different levels of particle vibration. A rock, a flower, or a person is energy moving at different vibrations. Energy of a certain quality or vibration tends to attract that of a similar vibration. A thought is a form of light, mobile energy that tends to find physical expression.

❖ When we creatively visualize or make affirmations of positive outcomes and states, we are radiating thought energy into the universe. The universe responds in the form of matter or events. Creative visualization is literally "sowing the seeds" of the life we want.

Some further points include the following:

❖ *Affirmations.* You don't have to actually "see" images to be a creative visualizer. Some people aren't very good at this and find it more effective merely to think about what they desire, or turn it into an affirmation (e.g., "I deserve the best and the best is coming to me now.") Affirmations, Gawain says, "make firm what you are imaging." They must be in the present tense and should include verbs. Power also tends to be added if you invoke God, infinite intelligence, or the universe.

❖ *Accepting your good.* You may feel that you are unworthy of getting all that you'd like in life. Before you visualize, make sure that you are willing to accept what comes to you. Love yourself first.

- ❖ *Belief*. You don't need to believe in any spiritual or metaphysical ideas for creative visualization to work; all the power you need to do it successfully is already in you.
- ❖ *Health and prosperity*. You can heal yourself and others through visualizing perfect health, and begin to gain an awareness of the true abundance of the universe through picturing all that is constantly being created.

Final comments

Creative Visualization is a rather slim volume and you may be disappointed when first leafing through it, but its principles and many exercises have changed a lot of lives. Consider that it has sold over three million copies and been translated into 25 languages, and the term "creative visualization" has entered the public vocabulary and become its own subject area.

While saying to yourself an affirmation such as "The divine light is within me and is creating miracles in my life" may seem peculiar at first, you may find that this, or another affirmation, brings a sense of peace and confidence. Once an image or an affirmation becomes part of you, miraculous things can indeed happen. The book has many affirmations to guide you, so it's worth buying if only for these.

Gawain says that, as you get deeper into it, creative visualization becomes less of a technique and more a state of consciousness in which you realize just how much you are the continuous creator of your world. You can eliminate the need to worry, plan, or manipulate, because it dawns on you that these things in fact have a lot less power to change than does the relaxed visualization of outcomes that reflect your higher purpose.

Shakti Gawain

Gawain studied psychology and dance at Reed College and the University of California, and after graduating traveled for two years in Europe and Asia studying eastern philosophies, meditation, and yoga. After returning to America she involved herself in the human potential movement, reading intensively and working with various teachers.

Other books include Living in the Light: A Guide to Personal and Planetary Transformation *(1986),* Return to the Garden *(1989),* Gawain's personal story, The Path of Transformation *(1993),* Creating True Prosperity *(1997), and* The Creative Visualization Workbook *(1995).*

Emotional Intelligence: Why It Can Matter More than IQ

1995

"Emotional life is a domain that, as surely as math or reading, can be handled with greater or lesser skill, and requires its unique set of competencies. And how adept a person is at those is crucial to understanding why one person thrives in life while another, of equal intellect, dead-ends: emotional aptitude is a meta-ability, determining how well we can use whatever other skills we have, including raw intellect."

"I have had to wait till now before the scientific harvest was full enough to write this book. Now science is finally able to speak with authority to these urgent and perplexing questions of the psyche at its most irrational, to map with some precision the human heart."

In a nutshell

The truly successful person will always have achieved emotional self-mastery.

In a similar vein
David D. Burns, *Feeling Good* (p66)
Ellen J. Langer, *Mindfulness* (p220)
Martin Seligman, *Learned Optimism* (p278)

CHAPTER 29

Daniel Goleman

The book is almost 300 closely set pages long, with endless case studies and footnoting, but the thrust of *Emotional Intelligence* can be summed up in three points:

❖ Through the application of intelligence to emotion, we can improve our lives immeasurably.
❖ Emotions are habits, and like any habit can undermine our best intentions.
❖ By unlearning some emotions and developing others, we gain control of our lives.

If this were all there was it would not be a very interesting book, but *Emotional Intelligence* is one of most successful self-help tomes of the last decade and has reached well beyond what would normally be considered a traditional self-help audience. Researchers had been expanding our idea of what intelligence is for some time, but it took Goleman's book to catapult the idea of emotional intelligence (EQ) into the mainstream.

How much the average person hates the IQ test must have something to do with the success of the work. Whether or not that test is a good measure of anything, its effect has been to restrict choices and damage self-esteem for millions. Saying that IQ is not a particularly good predictor of achievement, that it is only one of many "intelligences," and that emotional skills are statistically more important in life success, *Emotional Intelligence* was bound to be well received.

Following is a breakdown of the book and some of its key points.

Civilizing the brain

In looking at the way the brain is wired, the first part of the book removes some of the mystery from our feelings, particularly the compulsive ones. The physiology of our brains is a hangover from ancient times when physical survival was everything. This brain structure was designed for "acting before thinking," useful when in the path of a flying spear or in an encounter with an angry mammoth. We are still walking around in the twenty-first century with the brains of cave dwellers, and Goleman tells us about "emotional hijackings" (floodings of the brain with intense, seemingly uncontrollable emotion) that can trigger spur-of-the-moment murder, even of a longstanding spouse.

Using emotional intelligence

Parts Two and Three go into the elements of emotional intelligence and its application in real life. Goleman notes that the problem is not the emotions *per se*, but their appropriate use in given situations. He quotes Aristotle:

"Anyone can become angry—that is easy. But to be angry with the right person, to the right degree, at the right time, for the right purpose, and in the right way—this is not easy."

Aristotle's challenge becomes all the more important in a technologically advanced world, because the meaning of "civilization" ceases to be technological, defaulting to the nature of man and the quest for self-control.

Part Three applies the lessons of emotional intelligence to intimate relationships, work, and health. The relationships chapter alone is worth more than many entire books on the subject, intricately describing the neuroscience behind the Martian and Venusian worlds of the sexes.

Emotion and morality

In making the link between emotional life and ethics, Goleman notes that if a person cannot control their impulsiveness, damage will be done to their deepest sense of self. Control of impulse "is the base of will and character," he says. Compassion, that other benchmark of character, is enabled by the ability to appreciate what others are feeling and thinking. These two elements are fundamental to emotional intelligence, and therefore are basic attributes of the moral person.

Emotional intelligence makes a winner

Other major qualities of emotional intelligence are persistence and the ability to motivate oneself. These are not emotions *per se* but require self-control and the ability to put negative emotions and experiences into context.

Goleman validates the "power of positive thinking" as a scientifically proven approach to achieving success, and says that an optimistic outlook is a key clinical predictor of actual performance, borrowing from research done by Martin Seligman (see *Learned Optimism*).

The obsession with IQ was a product of the twentieth century's model of mechanistic achievement. EQ, with its focus on empathic people skills and relationships, is a basic success element in a more fluid and creative twenty-first-century economy.

The world of work

Goleman's book has had a significant impact on the workplace and business world. Though he only devotes one chapter to management, it is clear that the concept of emotional intelligence has struck a nerve with workers angry or hurt by the low emotional capacities of their bosses. Similarly, it has shone a light for many bosses and team leaders who wonder what they can do to improve maddeningly poor performance. As you suddenly see that half your organization is emotionally stupid, your standards will inevitably rise.

One fascinating chapter, "When smart is dumb," puts IQ in its place among several other types of intelligence. As anyone who has worked in an office environment will know, you may be producing the most exciting product around but it will still be a miserable place to work if it is also an arena for clashing egos. Business success is the result of passion for a vision or a product. Though big egos are often associated with such success, better companies are notable for their ability to create harmony and excitement by focusing on the product or the vision, not the organization. These ideas are further spelled out in the spin-off *Working with Emotional Intelligence*.

Teaching EQ

Emotional Intelligence has its roots in the concept of "emotional literacy" and in the final part of the book Goleman expounds on the need for EQ skills to become part of the school curriculum. With facts and figures he has no trouble convincing us of the high costs—monetary and societal wellbeing—of not teaching children how to deal with their emotions constructively and resolve conflict.

Final comments

Part of Goleman's motivation in writing *Emotional Intelligence* was the thought of millions of readers relying on self-help books that "lacked scientific basis," and indeed the book comes from an impeccable academic and research milieu. Goleman appears to know all the key people in the field, notably Harvard intelligence researcher Howard Gardner, New York University's Joseph LeDoux, and Yale's Peter Salovey, who first provided the concept of emotional intelligence.

Yet this is still a self-help book in the classic mold. Pointing to the extraordinarily malleable circuitry of the brain and our ability to shape the experience of our emotions, one of Goleman's great points is that "temperament is not destiny." We are not beholden to our habits of mind and emotion, even if they seem an unchangeable part of us.

The most alluring implication of *Emotional Intelligence* is that greater awareness and control of our emotions on a large scale would mean an evolution of the species. We believe that hate, rage, jealousy, and so on are "only human," but when we look at the finest human beings of the twentieth century—Gandhi, Martin Luther King, Mother Teresa—we find that such negative emotions were remarkably absent. These people were able to express anger according to Aristotle's dictum: They could use their emotions instead of letting their emotions use them. What could be a better definition of civility or humanity?

Daniel Goleman

Goleman grew up in Stockton, California. His doctorate in psychology from Harvard University was supervised by David McClelland, who wrote a groundbreaking paper arguing that traditional tests for occupational hiring or college entrance (academic record and IQ) were inaccurate predictors of how well a person actually would perform. Instead, candidates should be tested for competencies in a core of emotional and social skills — Goleman's emotional intelligence.

For 12 years Goleman wrote a column for the New York Times *in the behavioral and brain sciences. He has also been senior editor of* Psychology Today. *Other books include* The Meditative Mind, Vital Lies, Simple Truths, The Creative Spirit *(co-author),* Social Intelligence, *and* Focus: The Hidden Driver of Excellence. *He also edited* Healing Emotions: Conversations with the Dalai Lama on Mindfulness, Emotions, and Health. Emotional Intelligence *has been translated into 33 languages,* Working with Emotional Intelligence *into 26.*

Goleman is now co-chair of the Consortium for Research on Emotional Intelligence in Organizations.

Men Are from Mars, Women Are from Venus

1992

"*To feel better, women talk about past problems, future problems, potential problems, even problems that have no solutions. The more talk and exploration, the better they feel. This is the way women operate. To expect otherwise is to deny a woman her sense of self.*"

"*Just as a glass of water can be viewed as half full or half empty, when a woman is on her way up she feels the fullness of her life. On the way down she sees the emptiness. Whatever emptiness she overlooks on the way up comes more into focus when she is on her way down into her well.*"

"*In Chuck's mind, the more money he made at work, the less he needed to do at home to fulfill his wife. He thought his hefty paycheck at the end of the month scored him at least thirty points. When he opened his own clinic and doubled his income, he assumed he was now scoring sixty points a month. He had no idea that his paycheck earned him only one point each month with Pam—no matter how big it was.*"

In a nutshell

Before we can treat each other as individuals, we must take into account the behavior differences of the sexes.

CHAPTER 30

John Gray

Before *Men Are from Mars, Women Are from Venus*, John Gray wrote a book entitled *Men, Women, and Relationships*. He began that book with a story.

His father had offered a lift to a hitchhiker, who promptly robbed him before locking him in the trunk of the car. Police responded to two reports of an abandoned car, but bad directions stopped them from finding it. They made it to the car after the third call, but by then it was too late. Gray Snr. had died of heat asphyxiation in the trunk of his own car.

When coming back home for the funeral, Gray asked that he be locked in the trunk to see what it must have felt like. In the darkness he ran his fingers over the dents where his father's fists had hammered, and put his hand through the space where the tail-light had been knocked out for air. His brother suggested that he extend his arm further, to see if maybe he couldn't touch the hood button. He reached—and pressed it open.

Gray took the manner of his father's death as a sign for what his work was about: liberating people by telling them about the emotional release buttons within their grasp.

Gray under the microscope

A good story, but do John Gray's books in fact liberate? A feminist critique of his writing is easy to make. Websites have sprung up with titles like "A Rebuttal from Uranus" (Susan Hamson) arguing that *Men Are from Mars* institutionalizes sexism.

Sex-role theory, of which Gray is a prime exponent, says that men and women are by nature very different, and that gender forms the core of a person's identity. Gray is particularly insidious, these critics say, because he never presents his views as a theory, simply saying "this is the way things are" (biological fact). His millions of readers, caught in a marketing blizzard, are blinded to the alternatives and the fact that gender roles are actually culturally conditioned. Gray's ultimate aim—conscious or not—is to make women feel better about their subordinate place in a hegemonic masculine culture.

Men Are from Mars in brief
Before taking sides, we must first describe the book. What are Gray's main points?

❖ The golden key to better relationships is the acceptance of differences. In our parents' day everyone accepted that men and women were different, but the culture changed to the other extreme of there being no differences.

❖ A woman aims to improve a man, but a man only wants acceptance. Her unsolicited advice is never welcomed, being interpreted as negative criticism. Rather than presenting a problem to a man, which is often taken to mean that he is the problem, a man should be approached as if he may embody the solution. Men are focused on their competence and if they cannot solve problems they feel as if they are wasting their time. Women, on the other hand, actually like to discuss problems even without a solution in sight, because it gives them the all-important chance to express their feelings.

❖ Women are like waves, rising to peaks, falling into troughs, then back up again. Men must know that the trough time is when women need men most. If he is supportive and does not try to get the woman out of the trough immediately, she feels validated. In order to be motivated a man must feel needed—but a woman must feel cherished.

❖ Men alternate between the need for intimacy and the need for distance. Men's going away into their "cave" is not a conscious decision but is instinctive. Women who don't know about the need for the cave and seek constant intimacy will see relationship turmoil. Like a rubber band, a man needs to stretch—but will usually spring back.

❖ Arguments quickly descend into hurt feelings about the way a point is being made, rather than its content. It is the uncaring sound of the point being made that is upsetting. Men do not see how much their comments hurt and provoke, because they focus on "the point."

Most arguments start because a woman expresses a worry over something and the man tells her that it is not worth worrying about. This invalidates her and she gets upset with him. He then gets mad because she seems to be getting angry at him for nothing. He will not say sorry for something he believes he has not done, so the initial argument goes into cruise control for hours or days.

❖ Men will argue because they do not feel trusted, admired, or encouraged and are not spoken to with a tone of trust and acceptance. Women will argue because they are not listened to or put high on a man's list of priorities.

The broader message

Gray suggests that at our time in history, we are right to expect maximum fulfillment in our romantic life. However, our bodies and brains, evolving over millennia, required the refinement of sex differences for greater survival success. (As Daniel Goleman argues in *Emotional Intelligence*, we are modern people walking around with brains built for the plains and the forests of distant ancestors.) To wear the bright expectation of perfect relationships, unarmed with any knowledge of the basic differences between male and female thought patterns, is naïve and unwittingly invites a saboteur aboard the loveship. Gray doesn't focus on the nature or nurture debate. He just says that this is how men and women tend to act, and if we understand it there will be fewer relationship problems.

In Gray's defense

As we noted to begin with, the criticism that often greets this book is that it increases the division between the sexes. We are, after all, in the twenty-first century—can't we see each other simply as people and not by sex? Or skin color or nationality or anything else? And why doesn't Gray ever write about gay relationships? He does admit that he generalizes, yet he writes as if what he is saying is fact.

These are all valid points, but they fail to see Gray's basic intention. He wrote for an audience of people who do not read genetics or sociology textbooks—they want better relationships now. *Men Are from Mars* does not advance cutting-edge theories, but neither does it say that men and women are roped to the poles of their sex; we have tendencies to action that, if recognized, need no longer be our master. By highlighting sex differences, Gray may be guilty in some courts of entrenching patriarchy, but nowhere in his writing does he go so far as to say that gender *determines* the person. The public would not have touched the book if he had. If the goal of focusing on sex differences is, paradoxically, to move beyond them, then Gray is a liberator.

Final comments

There are thousands of books on relationships. What made *Men Are from Mars* stand out?

Gray has said that he deliberately wrote *Men Are from Mars* in such a way that people "would not have to think." It seems made for lunchtime television and "cheesy" probably sums up the book in many people's eyes. Readers interested in this whole area of intersex communication who want something a little more brainy might like to read the books of linguistics expert Deborah Tannen (for example Y*ou Just Don't Understand, That's Not What I Meant*). A page of Tannen may be more interesting than ten of Gray, but the key to Gray's success is that his statements and analogies stick in the mind and many points involve quite subtle distinctions.

Gray's influence in the relationship realm is a lot like Dr. Benjamin Spock's in child rearing. Both authors' books became the standard text to have around the house on these subjects. Spock's ideas were blamed for producing a generation of spineless pacifists, but millions also swore by him. What verdict will eventually be passed on *Men Are from Mars*? Who knows, but it is clear that the book has been right for its times, and perhaps we needed to be reminded of our differences before we could move beyond them. As Emerson noted, the finest people are able to marry the two sexes in the one person. We should not get caught up in differences (gender or otherwise) if they will sidetrack our consideration and wonder at people *per se*.

The healthy attitude to take to Gray would be to accept some of what he says and disregard other parts. Both unquestioning embrace and outright rejection would indicate a closed mind. It is very easy to dismiss this book—but read it when you are miserable following a fight with your partner and it may come alive for you. As a simple guide to the ups and downs of living with a member of the opposite sex, it does have touches of brilliance.

John Gray

Born in Houston, Texas, in 1951, after high school Gray attended St. Thomas University and the University of Texas. He spent nine years as a Hindu monk, working in the Transcendental Meditation (TM) organization in Switzerland, as personal assistant to its leader, the Maharishi Mahesh Yogi, and obtained a Master's degree in eastern philosophy. Back in the US, Gray became a doctoral student and received his PhD in Psychology and Human Sexuality from Columbia Pacific University in San Rafael, California. He is a certified family therapist.

Men Are from Mars *was the bestselling book of the 1990s in the US and has sold 15 million copies according to its publisher. Other books include* Mars and Venus in Love, Mars and Venus in the Bedroom, How to Get What You Want, and Want What You Have: A Practical and Spiritual Guide to Personal Success, *and* Beyond Mars and Venus: Relationship Skills for Today's Complex World *(2017), which updates his thinking with recent research.*

Gray lives with his wife Bonnie and three daughters in Northern California. He was once married to personal growth adviser Barbara De Angelis.

You Can Heal
Your Life

1984

"If you want to understand your parents more, get them to talk about their own childhoods; and if you listen with compassion, you will learn where their fears and rigid patterns come from."

"They will often tell me they can't love themselves because they are so fat, or as one girl put it, 'too round at the edges.' I explain that they are fat because they don't love themselves. When we begin to love and approve of ourselves, it's amazing how weight just disappears from our bodies."

"Be grateful for what you do have, and you will find that it increases. I like to bless with love all that is in my life right now—my home, the heat, water, light, telephone, furniture, plumbing, appliances, clothing, transportation, jobs—the money I do have, friends, my ability to see and feel and taste and touch and walk and to enjoy this incredible planet."

In a nutshell

You will only begin to change your life when you learn how to love yourself properly.

In a similar vein
James Allen, *As a Man Thinketh* (p10)
Florence Scovell Shinn, *The Game of Life and How to Play It* (p272)

CHAPTER 31

Louise Hay

With its almost child-like motif of a rainbow-colored heart on the cover, *You Can Heal Your Life* offers a message of non-judgmental love and support that has endeared it to people everywhere. It has sold millions of copies, and Hay is now a matriarch of the self-help, New Age, and holistic healing movements. She attributes the book's success simply to her ability to "help people change without laying guilt on them" and the book has the calmness of a person who has gone through the worst and survived. The title only really makes sense when we read the final chapter, a plain-speaking record of Hay's personal history.

Hay's story

Hay's mother tried early on to foster her out. Raped by a neighbor at five years old, she continued to be sexually abused until the age of 15, when she left home and school to become a waitress in a diner. She gave birth to a girl a year later, but the child was adopted and she never saw her again. Hay left for Chicago, spending a few years in menial work, before basing herself in New York, becoming a fashion model. There she met an "educated, English gentleman" and married him, leading an elegant and stable lifestyle until, 14 years on, he met someone else and divorced her. A chance attendance at a Church of Religious Science meeting changed Hay's life. She became a certified church counselor and subsequently a transcendental meditator, after attending the Maharishi's International University in Iowa.

After becoming a minister and developing her own counseling service, Hay wrote a book called *Heal Your Body*, which detailed metaphysical causes of bodily illness. At this point she was told that she had cancer, but was healed through a combination of radically changed diet and mental techniques. After spending most of her life on the East Coast, she moved back to LA and was reunited with her mother before the latter's death. Now in her 90s, Hay is one of the world's best-known motivational speakers and writers, who often toured with the likes of Deepak Chopra, Wayne Dyer, and James Redfield.

The book

You Can Heal Your Life is the message of a person who has crawled out of victimhood, and this aspect of it has had enormous appeal, particularly to women with similar histories. The essence of Hay's teaching is love of the self and evaporation of guilt, a process she believes makes us mentally free and physically healthy, as the study of psycho-immunology attests.

All the familiar self-help messages are given attention, including breaking free of limiting thoughts, replacing fear with faith, forgiveness, and understanding that thoughts really do create experiences. Some of the main points are:

❖ Disease (or "dis-ease," as Hay calls it) is the product of states of mind. She believes that the inability to forgive is the root cause of all illness.

❖ Healing requires us to release the pattern of thought that has led to our present condition. The "problem" is rarely the real issue. The superficial things that we don't like about ourselves mask a deeper belief that we are "not good enough." Genuinely loving the self (but not in a narcissistic way) is the basis for all self-healing. Chapter 15 lists just about every illness and its likely corresponding mental "blockage." Skeptics may find the list remarkably accurate if they open their minds a little.

❖ Affirmations are about remembering our true self and utilizing its power. Therefore, trust in the power of affirmations to manifest what you want. They must always be positive and in the present tense; for example, "I am totally healthy" or "Marvelous work opportunities are coming to me." The book contains many affirmations to choose from.

❖ "Whatever we concentrate on increases, so don't concentrate on your bills." You will only create more of them. Gratefulness for what you do have makes it more abundant. Become aware of the limitless supply of the universe—observe nature! Your income is only a channel of prosperity, not its source.

❖ "Your security is not your job, or your bank account, or your investments, or your spouse, or parents. Your security is your ability to connect with the cosmic power that creates all things." If you have the ability to still your mind and invoke feelings of peace by realizing you are not alone, you can never really feel insecure again.

❖ One of the first things Hay says to people who come to see her is "Stop criticizing yourself!" We may have spent a lifetime doing this, but the beginning of real self-love—one of the main ingredients in healing your life—happens when we decide to give ourselves a break.

Final comments

You Can Heal Your Life will not be for everyone. It is quite New Age, fitting into the "journey to wholeness" mold of writing that is now so common, though Hay was a pioneer. For those who have read a number of self-development books, it may seem a little simplistic and contain nothing new; it is certainly no intellectual undertaking to read. On the other hand, it has a directness and enthusiasm that help it stay in the mind, and it intuitively makes sense.

In the true spirit of self-help, the book is not content to fix problems but to strip all authority from them. This outlook, which on first consideration seems naïve, is in fact philosophically rigorous: Dwell on your problems and they become insurmountable; consider your possibilities and they provide hope and motivation. Millions have had similarly difficult lives to Hay, but not everyone has the will to leave their problems behind or even the knowledge that they can; deprivation forms the illusion that "this is all there is." Hay's insistence to herself that pain and setbacks would not define her led her out of multiple psychological black holes. Her book has the credibility of the successful escapee.

Louise Hay

Hay has spent a lot of time working with people with AIDS through the Hayride Support Group. In 1988 she wrote The AIDS Book: Creating a Positive Approach. Her first book was Heal Your Body and later works include Gratitude: A Way of Life, and Mirror Work: 21 Days to Heal Your Life. *She was the founder of Hay House, a successful publisher of personal development books.*

Hay now lives in San Diego, California

.

The Soul's Code: In Search of Character and Calling

1996

"At the outset we need to make clear that today's main paradigm for understanding a human life, the interplay of genetics and environment, omits something essential—the particularity you feel to be you. By accepting the idea that I am the effect of a subtle buffetting between hereditary and societal forces, I reduce myself to a result."

"As democratic equality can find no other logical ground but the uniqueness of each individual's calling, so freedom is founded upon the full independence of calling. When the writers of the Declaration of Independence stated that all are born equal, they saw that the proposition necessarily entailed a companion: All are born free. It is the fact of calling that makes us equal, and the act of calling that demands we be free."

In a nutshell

Not only celebrities and nuns have "callings." All of us have in our heart the image of the person we can be and the life we can live.

In a similar vein
David Brooks, *The Road to Character* (p50)
Joseph Campbell with Bill Moyers, *The Power of Myth* (p72)
Clarissa Pinkola Estés, *Women Who Run with the Wolves* (p156)
Thomas Moore, *Care of the Soul* (p242)

CHAPTER 32

James Hillman

I s there a code to our souls, a DNA of destiny? The question compelled Hillman to trawl through the lives of actress Judy Garland, scientist Charles Darwin, industrialist Henry Ford, musicians Kurt Cobain and Tina Turner, and many others, searching for the "something" that drove them on and made them live as they did. His premise is that, just as the giant and majestic oak is embedded in the acorn, so does a person carry inside them an active kernel of truth, or an image, waiting to be lived. The idea is not a new one: The Greeks had the word *daimon* to describe the invisible guiding force in our lives, the Romans the *genius*.

We are a story, not a result

The idea of a soul image has a long history in most cultures, but contemporary psychology and psychiatry ignore it completely. Image, character, fate, genius, calling, *daimon*, soul, destiny—these are all big words, Hillman admits, and we have become afraid to use them, but this does not lessen their reality. Psychology can only seem to break down the puzzle of the individual into traits of personality, types, and complexes. The author mentions a psychological biography of Jackson Pollock, which stated that the rhythmic lines and arcs of his paintings were the result of being left out of his brothers' competitions of "creative urination" on the dust of their Wyoming farm!

Such interpretations kill the spirit, denying that inner visions, rather than circumstances, are what drive people. The way we see our lives, says Hillman, dulls them. We love romance and fiction, but don't apply enough romantic ideals or stories to ourselves. We cease to be a creation and become more a result, in which life is reduced to the interplay between genetics and environment.

Another way in which we restrict our existence is in how we see time, or cause and effect. That is, "This happened, which caused me to . . ." or "I am the product of . . ." The book looks rather at what is timeless about us, whether we are just born, middle-aged, or old.

Who are our parents?

Hillman is brilliant at exposition of what he calls the "parental fallacy," the belief that the way we are is because of how our parents were. Childhood, *The Soul's Code* argues, is best understood in terms of the image with which we are born coming into contact with the environment in which we find ourselves. The child's tantrums and strange obsessions should be seen in this context, rather than trying to "correct" them in therapy.

Yehudi Menuhin was given a toy violin for his fourth birthday, which he promptly dashed to the ground. Even at this age, it was an insult to the great violinist-in-waiting. We treat children as if they are a blank slate, without their own authenticity, and the child is therefore denied the possibility that they may have an agenda for their life, guided by their genius.

In terms of our *daimon*, a parental union results from our necessity: The *daimon* selected the egg and the sperm as well as their carriers, called "parents." This certainly turns the tables, but Hillman suggests that it explains the impossible marriages, quick conceptions, and sudden desertions that form the stories of so many of our parents.

He goes further to point out the poverty of seeing our mothers and fathers as, literally, mum and dad, when nature could be our mother, books our father—whatever connects us to the world and teaches us. Quoting Alfred North Whitehead, who said that "religion is world loyalty," Hillman says that we must believe in the world's ability to provide for us and lovingly reveal to us its mysteries.

"I must have you"

The Soul's Code shows how the *daimon* will assert itself in love, giving rise to obsessions and torments of romantic agony that defy the logic of evolutionary biology. Identical twins separated at birth are often later found to be wearing the same aftershave or smoking the same brand of cigarette, but in the most important choice of choosing a mate there can be great differences.

When Michelangelo sculpted portraits of gods or of his contemporaries, he tried to see what he called the *immagine del cuor*, the heart's image; the sculpture aimed to reveal the inner soul of the subject. Hillman says that the same heart's image lies within each person. When we fall in love, we feel super-important because we are able to reveal who we truly are, giving a glimpse of our soul's genius. The meeting between lovers is a meeting of images, an exchange of imaginations. You are in love because your imagination is on fire. By freeing imagination, even identical twins are freed of their sameness.

The bad seed

The Soul's Code is engrossing when it comes to love's opposite, the "bad seed." Hillman devotes most of a chapter to the phenomenon of Adolf Hitler. Hitler's habits, reported by reliable informants, give evidence of possession by a "bad" *daimon*. The principal difference to other lives discussed in the book is the combination of acorn and personality: Not only was Hitler's acorn a bad seed, but it was wrapped in a personality that offered no doubts or resistance to it. From a single seed, we can see how the fascinating power in this man charmed millions into a collective demonic state. We can apply the same idea to modern psychopaths like Jeffrey Dahmer to understand how they can enchant their victims.

This is not to suggest in any way that the terrible actions arising from a bad seed are justified. However, appreciating the criminal mind in terms of the *daimon*/acorn gives us a better understanding of it than our conventional idea of evil (that is, something to be eradicated or "loved away"). What makes the seed demonic is its single-track obsession, but its ultimate aim is glory. As a society, we should be willing to recognize this drive and find ways of channeling it to less destructive ends.

We live in a culture of innocence that despises darkness. American popular culture in particular, with its Disneylands and *Sesame Street*, cannot accept seeds that are not sugar coated. Nevertheless, innocence actually attracts evil, Hillman says, and "*Natural Born Killers* are the secret companions of *Forrest Gumps*."

The soul mystery

Having spent the book looking at the lives of the famous, Hillman raises the question of mediocrity—can there be a mediocre *daimon*? His answer is that there are no mediocre souls, a truth reflected in our sayings. We speak of someone having a beautiful soul, a wounded soul, a deep soul, or a child-like soul. We do not say that people have a "middle-class," "average," or "regular" soul, he notes.

Souls come from the non-material realm, yet they yearn for the experience of this very physical world. Hillman recalls the film *Wings of Desire*, in which an angel falls in love with life, the normal life of regular people and their predicaments. To the angels and the gods, there is nothing "everyday" or ordinary about our lives.

Final comments

Picasso said, "I don't develop; I am." Life is not about becoming something, but about making real the image already there. We are obsessed with personal growth, reaching toward some imaginary heaven, but instead of trying to transcend human existence, it makes more sense to "grow down" into the world and our place in it. Hillman is not surprised that the people we call "stars" often find life so difficult and painful. The self-image that the public gives them is an illusion and inevitably leads to tragic falls to earth.

The twists and turns of your life may not be as extreme as those of the celebrities, but they may have a greater positive effect. For character, Hillman says, we now look as much to "the soldier's letter back home on the eve of battle, as the plans laid out in the general's tent." One's calling becomes a calling to honesty rather than to success, to caring and loving rather than to achieving. In this definition, life itself is the great work.

James Hillman

Hillman was born in a hotel room in Atlantic City, New Jersey, in 1926. He served in the Hospital Corps of the US Navy from 1944–6 and as a news writer with the US Forces Network in Germany. After the war he attended the Sorbonne in Paris and Trinity College, Dublin, and established a private practice as an analyst. In 1959 he was awarded his PhD by the University of Zurich, and for the following decade worked at the Jung Institute in Zurich, developing the concept of psychic ecology (later archetypal psychology), which places the individual within a larger context of mythology, art, and ideas.

Hillman had lectured and held positions at Yale, Harvard, Syracuse, Chicago, Princeton, and Dallas universities. Books include Suicide and the Soul, Re-visioning Psychology, The Dream and the Underworld, Healing Fiction, We've Had a Hundred Years of Psychotherapy and the World's Getting Worse *(with M. Ventura), and* Lament of the Dead: Psychology after Jung's Red Book *(with Sonu Shamdasani). Hillman died in 2011.*

Feel the Fear and Do It Anyway

1987

"*I remember a time in my life when I was frightened by just about everything—fearful that I would fail in all my attempts to fulfill my dreams. So I just stayed at home, a victim of my insecurities. I'd like to report that it was an ancient Zen master who snapped me back into awareness. But it wasn't. it was actually an Eastern Airlines commercial that used the slogan 'Get into this world.' When I saw this commercial, I suddenly realized I had stopped participating in the world.*"

"*Are you a 'victim' or are you taking responsibility for your life? So many of us think we are taking responsibility for our lives when we simply are not. The 'victim' mentality is subtle and takes many forms.*"

In a nutshell

The presence of fear is an indicator that you are growing and accepting life's challenges.

In a similar vein
Norman Vincent Peale, *The Power of Positive Thinking* (p254)
Anthony Robbins, *Awaken the Giant Within* (p266)
Martin Seligman, *Learned Optimism* (p278)

CHAPTER 33

Susan Jeffers

Self-help ideas expand our idea of what is possible. They make us believe in our dreams and think big. "I'm going to do this!" we say, "I'm going to be that!" No longer will we sell ourselves short. Nevertheless, waking up to another day and the weight of "reality," those dreams suddenly seem more fiction than biography. In two minutes flat we are rationalizing the life we have now, and the fear that took a brief holiday is back.

How do we get to the point where pursuit of the dream is our daily norm? Between the experience of today and the vision is a Grand Canyon of doubt and fear that stops us dead, and it seems a great deal easier to turn around and go back to security and routine. But Susan Jeffers says that people see fear in totally the wrong way. Rather than being an indicator that you are reaching your limits, it is a green light to keep going; if you are not feeling any fear, you may not be growing. Don't deny the trepidation, but take the step anyway—ships were not designed to stay in harbor!

Following are some key points in Jeffers's philosophy of fearlessness.

Handling fear

There are different types of fear, but one is the killer: the simple but all-powerful belief that you won't be able to handle something. We won't be able to handle it if our partner leaves us, we won't be able to handle it if we don't have a certain income, and so on. The basic work to be done is to get to a point where you know you can handle anything that comes your way, bad and good. This sounds like an empty platitude, but Jeffers' point is that fear is not a psychological problem but an educational one. You must re-educate yourself to accept fear as a necessary part of growth, then move on.

Saying "yes" to your universe

Refreshingly, Jeffers does not say that you can totally control your world. Things happen for reasons of their own. The key to not getting bogged down in fear is to affirm what is. This not only applies to small things like losing a wallet, but to more significant ones like pain. Positive thinking may not make pain disappear, but if you include it as part of your universe—if you don't deny its right to be—it loses its terror. Jeffers mentions Viktor Frankl's concentration camp classic *Man's Search for Meaning*, which describes some of the most hideous conditions that humans have had to endure, yet within the barbed-wire fences the author could still find people who were saying "yes" to it all, choosing responsibility instead of giving up.

Throughout our lives we are told to take responsibility. We interpret this as meaning going to college, getting a job, getting a mortgage, marriage. Jeffers' understanding of it is closer to Emerson's ideal of self-reliance, that is, being responsible for how you interpret your life experiences. Hate your job? Then either take a conscious decision to stay and make something out of it (an emphatic "yes"), or go.

Why positive thinking works

Positive thinking is fine, but it does not reflect reality. It's too "Pollyanna." This is the common accusation, but Jeffers asks: If 90 percent of what we worry about never happens (as studies demonstrate), how is negativity more "realistic" than positivity? The fact is that what is realistic is up to us, depending on how we shape our thoughts.

A positive mindset will not save you from bad news, but your reactions to it can be different. Replace "It's terrible!" with "It's a learning experience." OK, but what about serious stuff, like getting cancer? Jeffers says that this attitude made all the difference in her own cancer experience. If the rule applies in such extreme situations, then there is no excuse for overreaction on a day-to-day basis. We love to denounce things and be drama queens, but Jeffers says to look at how it weakens us.

The key to positive thinking, the most elemental yet most overlooked aspect to it, is that you must practice it all the time. Even Susan Jeffers, a famous motivational figure, cannot afford to go a day without positive mental refueling. We won't go without breakfast, or a morning jog, or a child's hug, she says, so why do we think that a program of daily positive energizing is optional? Build a collection of inspirational books and tapes and read/play them daily, she advises. The effect will probably be greater than you think, both on yourself and the world you inhabit. Write out your favorite inspirational quotes and keep them next to your computer, in your car, by your bed. The positivity you create will start to seem closer to how things should be (to "reality") than the way you are used to being. The former life will begin to appear as if it was lived in a gray fog.

Program the subconscious

You can be sure that whatever exists in your subconscious mind will find a way to express itself in real life. It is therefore crucial to take control of your mental inputs at every level. One important way of generating change and overcoming fear, which requires little work or courage, is affirmations. Jeffers defines these as positive statements affirming that something is already happening. A statement like "I will not put myself down any more" won't work. It must be both positive and present. For example, "I am a confident person in every situation." You don't even have to believe in affirmations for them to work, as long as they become your mantra. The mind reacts to what it is fed, whether it is true or false. We can either listen to our "chatterbox" or to our higher self.

Other points

There are many other good messages in the book, including:

❖ There is always plenty of time. "The biggest pitfall as you make your way through life is impatience." Impatience is merely self-punishment, creating stress, dissatisfaction, and fear. One has to trust that whatever one is doing, it is all unfolding perfectly and in the right time.

❖ How to make "no-lose" decisions: Stop believing that there is usually only one "right" or "wrong" way to go. We have to get into a position where we are no longer hostage to a single outcome, knowing that the world has endless opportunities for achieving what we want.

❖ Never be fearful of mistakes. Remember that even the very best baseball hitters have a .400 average. The best miss six times out of ten! Lighten up and be happy that you've had the experience, even if it isn't successful this time. You're a success because you tried.

❖ On the fear of commitment in relationships: We have to realize that we are committing to the person and their advancement and well-being, not necessarily to an inflexible union for all time.

Final comments

At the beginning of the book, Jeffers sets out a number of "fear truths." The most profound is number five:

"Pushing through fear is less frightening than living with the underlying fear that comes from a feeling of helplessness."

In other words, those who never take any risks ironically live with a dread of something going wrong. They seek security above all else, but the effect is chronic insecurity. It is actually easier (and infinitely more life fulfilling) to try new things. The decision to incorporate more challenge into your life brings a feeling of security because you know that you can tackle anything.

This type of straightforward insight is typical of *Feel the Fear*. It has an empathy that makes you feel you're not alone, crucial given the sense of isolation that fear causes. And there is a lightness of touch to the writing that invigorates as you get into the book.

Embarrassed to buy a self-help book? Feel the fear and walk up to the counter anyway . . .

Susan Jeffers

Jeffers was a young mother of two when she decided to go to college, and she eventually gained a doctorate in psychology from Columbia University. On graduation she became the executive director of the Floating Hospital (a hospital on a boat) in New York City, where she remained for almost a decade.

Feel the Fear *evolved out of a course at the New School for Social Research in New York. The manuscript received many rejection letters, the worst stating that "Lady Di could be bicycling nude down the street giving this book away and nobody would read it" (as noted on Jeffers' website). The publishers claim 2 million copies sold.*

Other books include Feel the Fear . . . and Beyond, End the Struggle and Dance with Life, Dare to Connect, Opening Our Hearts to Men, *and* The Journey from Lost to Found. *Jeffers lived in Los Angeles, and was a regular guest on* Oprah.

She died in 2012.

The 80/20 Principle:
The Secret of Achieving
More with Less

1998

"The 80/20 principle has helped to shape the modern world. Yet it has remained one of the great secrets of our time—and even the select band of cognoscenti who know and use the 80/20 principle only exploit a tiny proportion of its power."

"Conventional wisdom is to not put all your eggs in one basket. 80/20 wisdom is to choose a basket carefully, load all your eggs into it, and then watch it like a hawk."

"The 80/20 principle, like the truth, can make you free. You can work less. At the same time, you can earn and enjoy more."

In a nutshell

By identifying what you're good at, then doing more of it, success will come easily.

In a similar vein
Mihaly Csikszentmihalyi, *Flow* (p116)

CHAPTER 34

Richard Koch

This fascinating book could revolutionize your life. Koch writes about the well-documented but counterintuitive principle that 80 percent of effects or results come from only 20 percent of efforts. Most sales will come from only 20 percent of the product line. 20 percent of a carpet gets the majority of its wear and tear. And applied to personal life, 80 percent of happiness comes from less than 20 percent of your time.

While the specific ratios will vary, the principle aims to show us the fundamentally unbalanced way the world works. This is the first book exclusively on the 80/20 principle, and the first to apply it to personal life. Originally pointed out by the Italian economist Pareto (and also known as Pareto's Law), the principle has been the mainstay of strategic management consultants and the secret of more successful companies. Its results may seem like magic for those not aware of it, because it defies conventional economic theory. Not surprisingly, it has also been termed the "Law of least effort."

Yet the principle is not a theory but simply an observation of reality. Unlike the spiritual or philosophical laws of many of the self-help classics, the 80/20 principle, Koch says, works whether you believe in it or not.

The 50:50 belief vs. the 80:20 rule

At an intellectual level, a ratio of 50:50 makes sense in relation to effort put in and results gained. If you put in a "good" effort, you will get a "good" result. If you "work hard," you can expect a certain level of reward. This is the mentality that has driven society for generations, and there is a certain merit in it in terms of maintaining societal coherence. A clear work–reward equation creates a stable society, within which mediocrity is accepted and conformity rewarded. Unfortunately, as Koch illustrates, this is no longer the world in which we live.

The new world says that merely "keeping up" will no longer be enough, that mere competence at something can no longer be rewarded with success. You must do something that comes easily to you and that you love, so that you have a tremendous advantage over others and can rise to the top of your field.

Only this type of effort, which may not really seem like "work" compared to what others do, will bring big rewards. In the 80/20 world, unlike the old one, those who apply its logic can expect exponentially greater returns compared to input. However, that input must be of a uniquely high standard and reflect the uniqueness of the giver.

According to the 80/20 principle, it makes perfect sense that Michael Jordan could earn more than half a dozen basketball teams put together, because of the supreme skills displayed and the corresponding entertainment provided. Stars are earning much more now relative to the past (look at the top actors), but this is almost beside the point. Koch refers to them merely to demonstrate the applicability of his principle to all of us, that "only by fulfilling oneself is anything of extraordinary value created."

Becoming a time revolutionary

Most of what we consider valuable comes from only a fraction of how we spend our time. In order greatly to increase our effectiveness, or our happiness, or what we earn, we must expand that fraction beyond 10 or 20 percent to a much greater share of our time. Koch says that our society's appreciation of time is poor. "We don't need time management," he says, "we need a time revolution."

Conventional time management is about increasing the efficiency of what we do and becoming better at prioritization. Koch believes that the failing of all types of time management is the assumption that we know what is and what isn't a good use of our time in the first place. Its second fault is the assumption that time is short, that we have many important things to do and are constantly under pressure.

To get phenomenally better in our use of time, however, the 80/20 principle requires us to go back to our "priorities" and see if they really reflect the best use of our life in general. Koch is blunt about it: "Most people try too hard at the wrong things." Since the principle reflects nature's imbalance in the way things actually operate, there is no use thinking about time rationally. To seek improvements of 15–25 percent in our use of time (as time management organizers promise) constitutes "tinkering around the edges." The unexpected and irrational reality is that there is an abundance of time once we start spending it on the 20 percent that matters. Instead of being always short of time, the author notes, the dangerous truth is that we are actually awash with it but "profligate in its abuse."

It's OK to be lazy if you are intelligent about it

Do you constantly strive while not really getting anywhere? Koch introduces us to the Von Manstein matrix. Von Manstein was a German general who concluded that the best officers, those who made the least mistakes and were the most far-sighted, were both intelligent and, by inclination, lazy. Koch applies the matrix to today's economy, stating that the key to becoming a star is to "simulate, manufacture, and deploy lazy intelligence." Instead of choosing the difficult, or a generic goal that we think will bring us respect, we should focus on what comes easily.

Amazingly, capitalism allows a person to become successful and rich just by being themselves: In fulfilling their highest expression, they automatically create a very small but highly valuable niche. This is in full accord with an information economy demanding ever-greater specialization, because no one does what we do, quite like we do. This applies even in markets where there appears to be endless supply and small demand, such as acting and sport. There are hundreds of professional tennis players, but only one is Andre Agassi, whose unique appearance and attitude win him many times the endorsements of players of similar rank. In all fields, the key to leadership is enthusiasm, inveterate curiosity, and continual learning. Yet these things are not work.

80/20 thinking is the combination of ambition with a relaxed and confident manner. It involves reflective thinking (allowing insights to come, rather than leaping into action), unconventional use of time, and a hedonistic philosophy. Koch believes that in our "work equals success" culture, hedonism has been smeared. Hedonism is not selfishness: The more we love doing something the better we will be at it, increasing the likelihood that it will benefit others.

Final comments

The 80/20 Principle is a recipe book for getting out of the rat race and living up to one's potential. It shows how trivia clogs up life and how protestations of "busyness" often hide the absence of purpose. These are familiar themes in self-help writing, but it is Koch's application of one of the universe's "power laws" that gives these insights special weight. Who could ignore a logic of action based on "working with the grain of the universe instead of against it"?

The book is particularly good for understanding the alchemy of success in today's economic world, managing to be both business book and exciting life guide. Koch refers to Joseph Ford's statement that while God may play dice with the universe, the dice are loaded. In showing us how the universe is "predictably unbalanced," the 80/20 principle allows us to rig the odds naturally in our favor. Expressing and finessing our unique talents, rather than pursuing "excellence" in something we do not love, is the key point. The great rewards never go to the merely excellent, but to the outstanding.

Richard Koch

Koch is both a successful entrepreneur and a bestselling author. His background is in management consulting (Bain & Co., Boston Consulting Group, co-founder of LEK Partnership) and he has advised many well-known corporations in Europe and the US. Business interests have included hotels, premium gin, restaurants, personal organizers, and most recently the online gambling platform Betfair.

The 80/20 Principle *has been a bestseller in the US, Asia, and Europe and translated into 18 languages. Other books include* The Power Laws: The Science of Success, The 80/20 Manager, Living the 80/20 Way, *and* Simplify: How the Best Businesses in the World Succeed.

Koch divides his time between homes in Spain, Portugal, and Cape Town.

The Life-Changing Magic of Tidying Up

2014

"I never tidy my room. Why? Because it is already tidy. The only tidying I do is once, or sometimes twice a year, and for a total of about one hour each time. The many days I spent tidying without seeing permanent results now seem hard to believe. In contrast, I feel happy and content. I have time to experience bliss in my quiet space, where even the air feels fresh and clean; time to sit and sip herbal tea while I reflect on my day. As I look around, my glance falls on a painting that I particularly love, purchased overseas, and a vase of fresh flowers in one corner. Although not large, the space I live in is graced only with those things that speak to my heart. My lifestyle brings me joy."

"By handling each sentimental item and deciding what to discard, you process your past. If you just stow these things away in a drawer or cardboard box, before you realise it, your past will become a weight that holds you back and keeps you from living in the here and now. To put your things in order means to put your past in order, too. It's like resetting your life and settling your accounts so that you can take the next step forward."

In a nutshell

**Our approach to things and spaces says a lot about us.
By changing your environment, you can change your life.**

In a similar vein
Shakti Gawain, *Creative Visualization* (p174)
Thomas Moore, *Care of the Soul* (p242)

CHAPTER 35

Marie Kondo

As a child, Marie Kondo's passion was reading women's lifestyle magazines, and investigating the latest storage solutions and cleaning tips. At school she enjoyed rearranging bookshelves, and at home drove her siblings and parents mad by stowing things away or discarding things. She only began to develop a philosophy of tidying after coming across, in junior high school, *The Art of Discarding* by Nagisa Tatsumi.

As Kondo became Japan's foremost "organizing consultant," people were surprised that she had made a career out of tidying, because everyone assumes that it is not something that needs to be taught. In Japan, courses in home economics teach students to cook or sew, but tidying goes unmentioned on the assumption that it is learned via experience, and so no training is needed. But there is an art and a logic to it that is far from obvious.

Indeed, Kondo's "KonMari" (her nickname) approach has created an impact because it is more a philosophy than a technique. In reading *The Life-Changing Magic of Tidying Up: The Japanese Art of Decluttering and Organizing*, what surprises is the psychological and spiritual aspects of the book—but this makes sense. After all, "When you put your house in order," she writes, "you put your affairs and your past in order, too."

Everything you know about tidying is wrong

Whenever Kondo read advice on tidying in women's magazines, it was always along the lines of, "Do a little each day to keep on top of it." If you throw away one unneeded item a day, that's 365 things in a year.

But Kondo was always buying things, so the thrown-out stuff would quickly be replaced with more. What she soon discovered is that tidying should be concentrated in a single burst. By doing your tidying in one go, it creates such a deep impression on the mind that you won't want to return to your old cluttered state. People are shocked when Kondo tells them that tidying is not something to do every day. It is not an endless chore, but must be seen as a special event. Of course, on a daily basis you will want to put things back in their place, but transformative tidying or reorganization is a one-off job.

We think of tidying as a physical effort, when in fact it is mainly *mental*, involving the decision of whether or not to keep something. Some of her clients think Kondo will teach them "what to put where," and provide some great storage ideas. But "storage solutions" are a superficial way of dealing with the underlying issue, which is your mental relationship with your possessions, and so-called "storage experts" are really people helping you to hoard. No, the real solution is thinking carefully about what's worth keeping, which makes us also more careful about what new things we bring into the house in the future.

A cluttered room serves a psychological purpose: to draw our minds away from the root issue, that of messy internal mental spaces. In contrast, Kondo observes, "When your room is clean and uncluttered, you have no choice but to examine your inner state. You can see any issues you have been avoiding and are forced to deal with them." For this reason, when you start tidying properly, it sets in chain a tidying up of your mind and a resetting of your life. Many of Kondo's clients get rid of four-fifths of what they own, and still do not miss anything that was discarded. Yes, some realize they've thrown out things they needed, but all are cheerful about it, because much more important than the lost belonging is the mental liberation that they experience.

Joy in your hands

Kondo tried out the many rules that had been offered to work out what to throw away, such as "Discard if you haven't used it in a year." She was assiduous, even neurotic, in her throwing out, but it never made her live space really tidy. Collapsing on to her bed one day in frustration, she realized that her focus was all wrong. She shouldn't be thinking about what to throw away, but what to *keep*. What things did she really love? What sparked joy? The key to this approach, she found, is not just to glance at what's in a cupboard and decide, but to pick up and handle each thing. How does it feel to hold this in my hands? Pick up any item of clothing, for example, and your body reacts. Which clothes make you feel happy, and which don't?

If we hold in our hands something that does not give us joy, but which we are finding hard to let go, Kondo observes, it can mean

214

only one of two things: either we can't give up the past, or we are afraid of embracing the future. If you are honest, you will see that many of your possessions involve a holding on to things, which stops you from receiving what you really need right now. Yes, doing so can be painful, because we have to face up to choices we made which are no longer how we see ourselves. A home full of stuff amounts to an inventory of previous choices. It is up to us to decide, item by item, what expresses who we are, *today*.

Faced with an object or piece of paper or photo that doesn't spark joy, the rational mind will put up reasons why you should keep it, such as that you might need it in the future, or it would be a waste to throw it away. With clothes that you have barely worn, but which don't fit or are "too good" to throw away, you can get around this by being thankful of the joy you got when purchasing them; you can be grateful for how the item taught you what doesn't suit you. When something no longer sparks joy, thank it for its service before sending it away. This gratitude ensures that its energy will come back to you in some other form, be it a brand-new thing that you love, or a new person or connection in your life. Remember: new, valuable, life-affirming things are more likely to come to you after you have relinquished your attachment to older stuff, which will thank you for liberating it from the darkness of your cupboard. Matter and energy demand to be used.

It is not enough to have a goal of, "I want to live without clutter," Kondo says. You must envision the kind of lifestyle you want. Visualize how you will feel as you look around your changed home, and how it inspires you every day with its order and beauty. Kondo had a woman client who lived in a seven-tatami-mat (10 by 13 foot) room which was so cluttered she had to move things off her bed to go to sleep at night, then when she left in the morning had to put the things back onto the bed. She dreamed of "a more feminine lifestyle" in which her room would be as elegant as a hotel suite, with a pink bedspread and antique lamp, and at the end of the day she would have a bath with aromatic oils and classical music, "falling asleep with unhurried spaciousness." Your vision will be different, but it's important to have one.

The next step is to ask *why* you want to live this way. By digging down past the obvious reasons, like "I want a restful environment so I can be energized for the next day at work," you will find that the reason you want change is simple: you want to be *happy*, and a beautiful living space is a means to that end.

Specifics

The reason why so many fail at tidying, Kondo notes, is ignorance of how much stuff they actually own. It only seems we have fewer books than we actually do, for instance, because they are spread in different rooms in the house. If we only tidy one room at a time, "we can never grasp the overall volume and therefore can never finish." It dawned on Kondo that it would make more sense to tidy by *category*.

Being ruthless about discarding clothes may lead you to worry that you won't have anything left to wear. But Kondo insists that you will be left with what you need. The biggest obstacle to throwing out clothes is the thought that "they are still perfectly usable." Some of Kondo's clients ask if they can keep clothes "only to wear at home." If she agreed, the wardrobes would be filled with this "loungewear" that is never worn. If you want or need loungewear, buy dedicated garments that are designed to make you feel relaxed. People feel that it's fine to wear sloppy old track gear in the home, but this does nothing for one's self-image. Have a set of work or leisure or sport clothes, and a set of clothes for relaxing at home, but don't wander around in ghastly old "comfortable" stuff that belongs in the bin.

Don't just chuck clothes into your wardrobe or stuff them into drawers; spend a minute folding them properly, thanking them as you do it for their protection of your body. The Japanese are known for their love and respect for folding, and for good reason. But surely folding is a waste of time? Actually, when people learn how to fold properly, they enjoy it, Kondo says. Every garment wants to be folded well, not treated like rubbish. Even in high school, Kondo was treating her possessions as if they were alive. It transformed her relationship to things. Respect and love your belongings by giving them a dedicated space in the home where they belong. Thank them for their daily service.

Kondo has plenty of book-loving clients. The first thing she tells them is to put all their books, no matter how many, on the floor. Wouldn't it be easier to select what they want to keep while the books are still in the shelves? Perhaps, she says, but the point is that you don't know whether a book sparks joy if it is sitting on the shelf. You have to pick it up, hold it and think about it (not read it). There has to be a little communication that goes on between you and the book. If there's none, let it go. Imagine, instead, what it would be like to have a book collection in which every book in it is loved. Wouldn't that be an amazing collection? Be as ruthless with the unread as with the read. If you haven't read it by now, almost certainly you never will, so it can go, along with half-read books. If, after throwing out a book you feel you made a mistake, then you can always buy another copy. More importantly, you will have learned something about what matters to you.

After noting the detailed systems that some people use for classifying and filing papers, Kondo somewhat shockingly states, "My basic principle for sorting papers is to thrown them all away." Minus things like love letters from your spouse and academic degree certificates, the vast majority of papers provide no joy and don't need to be kept after a certain amount of time has passed. "There are several spots within the house where papers tend to pile up like snowdrifts," Kondo writes. Put all the bits of paper that need to be dealt with soon, such as school forms or letters needing a reply, in one place in the house, and one place only. All other boring but important pieces of paper, such as leases or insurance policies or guarantees, can be stored in one clear plastic folder, out of sight.

Kondo provides further advice on whether or how to keep credit card statements, warranties, greeting cards, used chequebooks, mobile phone boxes, electrical cords, cosmetics samples, free novelty goods, *komono* (miscellaneous trinkets from buttons to rubber bands to key rings)—and gifts. When someone has put thought into giving you something, you can't just throw it away, can you? Well actually, the purpose of gift-giving is the conveying of a feeling, and your joy at receiving the gift was the main point. Whether or not it is of any use to you now, or suits your taste, is secondary, so you shouldn't feel guilty throwing it away. Equally, don't keep old presents from your children, or old letters from a school love. Their meaning was the emotion you felt *when you received them*. Hanging on to old stuff always means that we are missing great moments and opportunities that are happening now. Don't leave photos in boxes, waiting for your old age to look through them. Hold each and every photo in your hands and see if it means something. So many holiday photos are just of scenery, or multiple shots of something, and can be discarded. What photos you are left with should be put in a treasured album, not a box.

Final comments

Kondo confesses that she was never that confident in herself, but made up for it in fully understanding the power of the objects and spaces we surround ourselves with. When these spaces become beautiful, it provides tremendous self-confidence and optimism. Kondo admits that she is influenced by Japanese *feng shui*, which teaches that everything has its own energy, so objects and the spaces in which they exist deserve great respect. Within this philosophy, it is natural that you have around you only things that spark joy.

Hoarders and people with obsessive cleaning disorders are an indication of just how much our belongings and spaces reflect our state of mind. It is easy to feel superior to such people, or feel sorry for them, when in fact our own homes reflect our fears, delusions, attachments, and defenses. If your life is going well, your home tends to reflect it. Yet the paradox of her book, Kondo stresses, is that tidying is not something that should be done every day, or done obsessively. There are more important things in life than tidying. However, having a beautiful, orderly home provides a necessary foundation for the clarity and happiness we all seek.

Marie Kondo

Born in 1985, Kondo grew up the middle child in a Tokyo family. As a child she was obsessed with tidying the family home, and also put her hand up for any organizing chores at school. While at Tokyo Woman's Christian University, where she majored in sociology, she began her decluttering consultancy. She also spent several years as an attendant at a Shinto shrine.

The Life-Changing Magic of Tidying Up *was published in Japanese in 2010 and was a bestseller. Although a celebrity in Japan (where a dramatized film was made about her), when the book was published in English in 2014 (translated by Cathy Hirano) she was unknown.* New York Times *reporter Penelope Green wrote an article in which she tried out some of Kondo's methods, giving the book a boost. It has since sold over four million copies. Her other book is* Spark Joy: An Illustrated Masterclass on the Art of Organizing and Tidying Up *(2015). Kondo lives in Tokyo with her husband and daughter.*

Mindfulness: Choice and Control in Everyday Life

1989

"Unlike the exotic 'altered states of consciousness' that we read so much about, mindfulness and mindlessness are so common that few of us appreciate their importance or make use of their power to change our lives. This book is about the price we pay for mindlessness: the psychological and the physical costs. More important, it is about the benefits of mindfulness. Those benefits are greater control over our lives, wider choice, and making the seemingly impossible possible."

"When we are behaving mindlessly, that is to say, relying on categories drawn in the past, endpoints to development seem fixed. We are then like projectiles moving along a predetermined course. When we are mindful, we see all sorts of choices and generate new endpoints."

In a nutshell

Mental habits dull our lives. By regaining control of your thinking you can experience life anew.

In a similar vein
The Dalai Lama & Howard C. Cutler, *The Art of Happiness* (p122)
The Dhammapada (p128)
Daniel Goleman, *Emotional Intelligence* (p178)
Martin Seligman, *Learned Optimism* (p278)

CHAPTER 36

Ellen J. Langer

Have you ever said "excuse me" to a store mannequin or written a cheque in January with the previous year's date? For most of us the answer is probably "yes," but these small mistakes, Ellen Langer believes, are the tip of a mindlessness iceberg. A Harvard psychology professor, her research into rigidity of mind led to observations about mental fluidity, or mindfulness.

One of the great themes of self-help literature is the need to be free of unconsciously accepted habits and norms. Langer's classic shows how we can actually accomplish this. The book is in the best tradition of western scientific research, filled with the results of fascinating experiments that should appeal to those readers who enjoy *Emotional Intelligence* or *Learned Optimism*.

Who or what is a mindful person? Langer suggests that their qualities will include:

❖ Ability to create new categories.
❖ Openness to new information.
❖ Awareness of more than one perspective.
❖ Attention to process (doing) rather than outcome (results).
❖ Trust of intuition.

New categories

Langer says that we live and experience reality in a conceptual form. We don't see things afresh and anew every time we look at them; instead, we create categories and let things fall into them, which is a more convenient way of dealing with the world. Apart from the smaller things, such as defining a vase as a Japanese vase, a flower as an orchid, or a person as a boss, there are the wider categorizations under which we live, including religions, ideologies, and systems of government. Each gives us a level of psychological certainty and saves us from the effort of constantly challenging our own beliefs. We divide animals into "pets" and "livestock" so that we can feel OK loving one and eating the other, for example.

Mindlessness results when we don't know that the categories to which we subscribe are categories and have accepted them as our own without really thinking. Creating new categories, and reassessing old ones, is mindfulness. Or, as William James put it:

> *"Genius . . . means little more than the faculty of perceiving in an unhabitual way."*

New information

Langer talks about "premature cognitive commitments," which are like photographs in which meaning, rather than motion, is frozen. To evoke the dangers of false, frozen images, she reminds us of Miss Havisham in Dickens' *Great Expectations*, who still wore the wedding dress she had donned the day she was abandoned at the altar, but which now hung like faded curtains over her aged body.

At a more prosaic level, a child may know an elderly person who is grumpy and will hold on to a picture of "old people are grumps," taking it with him into adulthood. In not bothering to replace that picture with different images of later life, the person is locked into a false perception that is likely to be reflected in their own experience. They will turn into an old grump too.

This of course applies to other aspects of life: If we are mindful, we will be less willing to take "genes" as an excuse for our behavior or lack of action. Just because a parent never rose above middle management level, we don't assume that we couldn't become president of the company.

Perspective and context

Mindlessness occurs when people accept information in a context-free way. The ability to transcend context, Langer says, is the mark of mindfulness and creativity.

She notes that much pain is context dependent. Getting a bruise out on the football field will matter much less to us than if we sustain one at home. Imagination is the key to perceiving differently. The Birdman of Alcatraz, stuck in a cell for over 40 years, managed to make his life a rich one by his care of injured birds.

The personal development implication of these vignettes is clear: We can put up with anything as long as it is within a positive context. Without a defined personal vision, life might seem like a mass of constant worries and annoyances; with one, everything is put into perspective. As Nietzsche said, if you have a "why," you can put up with any "how."

Process orientation

Another key characteristic of mindfulness is a focus on process before outcome, or "doing rather than achieving." We look at a scientist's breakthrough and say "genius," as if what he or she discovered happened overnight. With the rare exception, like Einstein's great year of discovery, most scientific success is the result of years of work that can be broken down into steps. A college student looks at a professor's book in awe, thinking "I could never write something that good," assuming it must be higher intelligence, not years of study and work, that delivered up the weighty tome. These are all faulty comparisons.

The process orientation requires us to ask not "Can I do it?" but "How can I do it?" This "not only sharpens our judgment, it makes us feel better about ourselves," says Langer.

Intuition

Intuition is an important path to mindfulness, because its very use requires ignoring old habits and expectations to try something that may go against reason. Yet the best scientists are intuitive, many spending years methodically validating what appeared to them in a flash of intuitive truth.

The amazing thing about mindfulness and intuition is that they are both relatively effortless: "Both are reached by escaping the heavy, single-minded striving of most ordinary life." But intuition will give us valuable information about our survival and success; we cannot explain where it comes from, but we ignore it at our cost. The mindful person will go with what works, even if it doesn't make sense.

Final comments

In essence, mindfulness is about preserving our individuality. By choosing the mindset of limited resources, by opting to focus on outcomes rather than doing (process), and by making faulty comparisons with others, we become little more than robots. The true individual is characterized by openness to the new, is always reclassifying the meaning of knowledge and experience, and has the ability to see their daily actions in a bigger, consciously chosen perspective.

Langer recognizes the parallels with eastern religion in her work, for example the Buddhist understanding that meditation is about enjoying a mindful state that leads to "right action." Mindfulness, Langer hopes, has the same effect, and therefore has important implications for the health of society, not merely the individual. The beauty of mindfulness is that it is not work; in fact, because it leads to greater control of our own thinking, it is, to use Langer's word, "exhilarating," in a quiet way creating excitement about what is possible.

Its ideas may seem difficult, but *Mindfulness* was written for a popular audience and is not long. It may be more understated than most self-help books, but its insights tend to stay in the mind. Today, mindfulness practice is common and taught in many workplaces and institutions. Langer was one of the first to talk about it and highlight its benefits.

Ellen Langer

Langer obtained a BA in Psychology from New York University in 1970, and her PhD from Yale in 1974. From her position as Professor of Psychology at Harvard University, she has produced several scholarly works, numerous journal articles, and chapters in edited collections.

Mindfulness *was the product of over 50 experiments, mostly with elderly people. The experiments led Langer to believe that the protectiveness of nursing homes leads to reduced autonomy and responsibility, which hasten aging. The book has been translated into 13 languages and has gone through 10 printings.*

Langer's other popular works are Personal Politics *(with Carol Dweck, 1973),* The Psychology of Control *(1983),* The Power of Mindful Learning *(1997), and* Counterclockwise: Mindful Health and the Power of Possibility *(2009). She lives in Massachussetts.*

Tao Te Ching

5th–3rd century BC

"Flow around obstacles, don't confront them.
Don't struggle to succeed.
Wait for the right moment."

"Trying to understand
is like straining to see through muddy water.
Be still, and allow the mud to settle.
Remain still, until it is the time to act."

"Stop clinging to your personality,
and see all beings as yourself.
Such a person could be entrusted with the whole world."

"Whether faced with friend or enemy,
loss or gain,
fame or shame,
the Wise remain equanimous.
This is what makes them so extraordinary."

In a nutshell

**Make your life easier and more effective by attunement with the
natural "flow" of the universe.**

In a similar vein

Deepak Chopra, *The Seven Spiritual Laws of Success* (p90)

CHAPTER 37

Lao Tzu

The *Tao Te Ching* is one of the world's great philosophical and spiritual classics, revered by millions. The oldest scripture of Taoism and a meditational text, it is also a timeless philosophy of power based on harmony with nature. It has been adopted as a modern leadership manual and is well suited to contemporary life.

The title means "The Way of Power" or "The Classic (*Ching*) of the Way (*Tao*) and Virtue (*Te*)." The *tao* determines the *te*, or the manner in which a person might act who is attuned to the *tao*. Whatever can be defined is not *tao*—it is the timeless spirit that runs through all life, creating the essential oneness of the universe. The *tao* is not even "god," god being an entity that has sprung from the *tao*.

The *Tao Te Ching* paints a picture of a person in full attunement with the *tao*, and therefore with the universe. Martin Palmer, in his introduction to Timothy Freke's excellent translation, says that it represents "a world of order that we must work with, not a world where we must just fend for ourselves." In this world we no longer struggle, finding that it is attunement, rather than mindless striving, that delivers us what we need.

The idea of the *tao* is that as you get in harmony with it, your actions cease to seem like "action." Csikszentmihalyi has documented this feeling as "flow" and the physicist Bohm talks of it as being part of "the unfolding." In contrast, regular action involves an effort of will to accomplish something, usually involving manipulation or even exploitation. While *tao* action makes whole, its alternative fragments.

Tao leadership

Lao Tzu saw two types of leader: the conventional one, a warrior who uses force to achieve his ends, symbolized by the *yang* or masculine aspect; and the healer-leader, symbolized by the feminine *yin*. The latter is the concept of "servant leadership," in which the leader blends into the background so that their people can star.

Some in the business world say that the more power a boss has, the less they should use. This is borne out by the teamwork, synergy, and flat hierarchies of today's best-run companies, which aim to increase effectiveness by sharing power; these organizations have a better chance of creating ideas or products that genuinely improve life.

By 2020 the ideal leader may be very hard to spot, position or wealth no longer being good guides to impact or influence. In Lao Tzu's words:

> *"The wise stand out,*
> *because they see themselves as part of the Whole.*
> *They shine,*
> *because they don't want to impress.*
> *They achieve great things,*
> *because they don't look for recognition.*
> *Their wisdom is contained in what they are,*
> *not their opinions.*
> *They refuse to argue,*
> *so no-one argues with them."*

Listening, yielding, cooperating, being open, seeking the best possible outcomes—these *yin* aspects must balance the go-getting *yang* force that has given us civilization as we know it. The integration of the two will be a mark of the new leader, whose credibility rests not on what they say or even what they have so far achieved: "Their wisdom is contained in what they are."

Tao success

For a book essentially about leading a successful life, the *Tao Te Ching* offers what seems to be very strange advice. Consider: "Give up, and you will succeed."

How can we reconcile such a statement with so many other messages in self-help about the active steps one must take for success? Take Robbins' *Awaken the Giant Within*, the archetypal modern personal development book. Subtitled "How to take control of your mental, emotional, physical, and financial destiny!" it encapsulates the ethic of total self-creation, based on the belief that we know what we want, what will make us happy, and our limitless potential.

The *Tao Te Ching*, on the other hand, is about how to lead a very simple life, not seeking power, fame, or riches. There is a quiet ecstasy to living in the moment, not trying to force anything to happen or get others to do things our way. This is a book about the power of timing:

> *"Be still, and allow the mud to settle.*
> *Remain still, until it is the time to act."*

Which way is better? Using focus and never-give-up intensity to achieve something, or going with the flow and "allowing" something to manifest itself? Ultimately, it boils down to where one's faith lies: either in ourselves (reasonable enough), or in the intelligence governing the universe (*tao*). In Lao Tzu's mind, the *tao* that created everything is capable of giving us peace, joy, and personal power. The compulsion to strive surely arises out of a perception that we must gain mastery of the world, or a little section of it, in order to feel whole. It is therefore more probable that striving, while a natural way to express our identity through creating something, is not actually the best path to success. Instead, the goal for which we strive should be readily admitted to be only a symbol of the greater unity that the *Tao Te Ching* suggests. This unity is described as "the way of heaven."

Final comments

At first the *Tao Te Ching* seems a strange voice, but it will change and probably enlarge your current ideas of life and success. You may find yourself needing to incorporate your world view into its, rather than the other way around.

Don't read it from start to finish. There is no narrative, just meditations broken up into short chapters of a few lines, which don't seem to relate to each other. Its hypnotic power is summed up in one of its own stanzas:

> *"A traveler may stop for nice food and good music,*
> *but a description of Tao seems bland and tasteless.*
> *It looks like nothing special.*
> *It sounds like nothing special.*
> *But live by it, and you will never tire of it."*

Psycho-Cybernetics

1960

"*Man is by nature a goal-striving being. And because man is 'built that way' he is not happy unless he is functioning as he was made to function—as a goal-striver. Thus true success and true happiness not only go together but each enhances the other.*"

"*Insofar as function is concerned, the brain and nervous system constitute a marvelous and complex 'goal-striving mechanism,' a sort of built-in automatic guidance system which works for you as a 'success mechanism,' or against you as a 'failure mechanism,' depending on how 'YOU,' the operator, operate it and the goals you set for it.*"

In a nutshell

Our body/brain is a brilliant self-contained system for achieving goals. Use it.

In a similar vein
Anthony Robbins, *Awaken the Giant Within* (p266)

CHAPTER 38

Maxwell Maltz

Worldwide sales of *Psycho-Cybernetics* including the editions of five US publishers and the many foreign translations issued since 1960, run into millions of copies.

This huge readership alone would make the book worth investigating, but it becomes an enigma when you appreciate that Dr. Maltz never became famous in the way that Dale Carnegie or Norman Vincent Peale did. What was it that drew people to this unremarkable-looking paperback?

What is cybernetics?

The word comes from the Greek for "steersman," and in the modern sense usually refers to systems of control and communication in machines and animals; how, for instance, a computer or a mouse organizes itself to achieve a task. Maltz applied the science to humans to form psycho-cybernetics. However, while inspired by the development of sophisticated machines, his book denounced the idea that man can be reduced to a machine. Psycho-cybernetics bridges the gap between our mechanistic models of the brain's functioning (clichés like "Your brain is a wonderful computer") and the knowledge of ourselves as being a lot more than machines.

Maltz said that human beings have an "essence" or life force that cannot be reduced to a mere brain and physical body. Jung called it the "libido," Bergson the "*elan vital*." A person cannot be defined by their physical body or brain, just as electricity cannot be defined by the wire through which it travels. We are, rather, systems in constant flux.

Some readers will be uncomfortable with this distinction between the brain and the mind, but it does make sense in relation to Maltz's key statement: "Man is not a machine, but has and uses a machine." This distinction is crucial to understanding the larger subject of the book: setting and achieving goals.

Guided missile technology applied to humans

The founder of cybernetics was American mathematician Norbert Wiener, who spent the Second World War refining guided missile technology. Stressing the similarities between machines, animals, human brains, and societies, Wiener was way ahead of his time in predicting that there was nothing to prevent machines "thinking" in the way that humans do. He saw both computers and the human brain as systems that take in low-energy data and create new connections to be used in interactions with the external world. Feedback from the external environment is used to enhance subsequent communications with it.

This virtuous loop of control, communication, and feedback is the key feature of a "servo-mechanism" that needs to arrive at a preset goal. Once it knows where it is going, a guided missile hits its target via constant feedback and communication with itself.

Maltz thought: Why couldn't this technology be applied to human achievement? He realized that the key point about the loop is that it gains an automaticity when the target or goal is very clearly fixed. When you first learn to drive, you have to worry about every car and process every sign ahead of you on the road—the result is that you move slowly and are liable to get lost. In time, however, driving becomes easy because you know your destination when you sit behind the wheel, and body and mind automatically do what is necessary to reach it.

Cybernetics appeared such a breakthrough to Maltz because its implication was that achievement was a matter of choice. Most important to the dynamic of achieving was the "what" (the target), rather than the "how" (the path). The frontal lobes or conscious thinking part of the brain could devise the goal, or create the image of the person you wanted to be, and the subconscious mind would deliver its attainment. The "set and forget" mechanism of guided missiles would also work for our deepest desires.

The importance of the self-image

Maltz was a plastic surgeon. Distinguished as he was in his field, he was at a loss to explain why a minority of patients were no happier after their operations than before, even if disfiguring scars or other malformations had been removed. He found himself drawn into the new self-image psychology, which held that we generally conform in action and thought to a deep image of ourselves. Without a change to this inner image, patients would still feel themselves to be ugly, however excellent the cosmetic work.

He came to believe that self-image was the "golden key" to a better life. Without an understanding of it, we might forever be fiddling around the "circumference of the self," instead of at its center. Positive thinking, for instance, could be of no use if it simply related to particular external circumstances. Saying "I will get this job" will not do anything if the idea of being in the job is not consistent with how you see yourself deep down.

How it works

We acquire our self-image through our beliefs about ourselves, which grow out of past experience of success and failure and of how others see us. Maltz argued that both are unworthy of the privilege of determining our basic psychological template. The crucial and fascinating point about the self-image is that it is value neutral, that is, it doesn't care if it is empowering or destructive, but will form itself simply according to what psychological food it is fed. We can either create an image of the self that can accommodate prosperity, peace, and greatness, or we can stick with a defective one that can't even get us out of bed in the morning. The point is that a positive self-image that can see you fulfill your dreams does not happen by accident—it must be thought about and manufactured.

Nevertheless, how is the self-image actually changed? What of the person who has experienced little but failure? This was a disturbing question for Maltz, since the evidence was that the self-image was changed by experiencing, not by intellectual means. However, this was not the case in reality because—and this is one of the book's most significant points—experimental and clinical psychologists had established beyond doubt that the brain is not great at telling the difference between an actual experience and one imagined in full and vivid detail. (Such results had been understood years before by William James.) This meant that winning images of the self could replace negative ones, denying any authority to past events. The beauty of self-image was that while it was the supreme factor in determining success or failure, it was also extremely malleable.

Living out the image

The brain thinks in terms of images, therefore if you can consciously create the desired image of yourself the brain and nervous system will automatically provide continual feedback to ensure that it "lives up to" the preordained image. In a well-known clinical experiment, one group of basketball players was physically trained to throw more balls through the hoop, while another was taught merely to visualize throwing goals. Despite the absence of any physical practice, the second group far outscored the first.

The brain, nervous system, and muscles are obedient servants of pictures placed in your head. But the ability of your body and brain to manifest the desired self-image depends on its indelibility. It must be tattooed on the brain. With such a strong image of ourselves, it is difficult not to live out and manifest all that is associated with the self-image. Instead of just "having goals," we become them.

Final comments

Much of self-help writing is about goals, but how does goal setting work? Why does it work? Maltz was the first to explore its actual machinery, and in doing this he has been a key influence to a generation of success writers. The emphasis on positive self-image paved the way for hundreds of books on the power of affirmation and visualization techniques. *Psycho-Cybernetics* has sold in its millions because it provides a scientific rationale for dream fulfillment.

Notwithstanding its *Reader's Digest* style of writing, this is, in fact, a textbook. The science and computing references are now outdated, but the principles of cybernetics have only grown in influence. Complexity theory, artificial intelligence, and cognitive science all grew out of the cybernetic understanding of how the non-physical, the "ghost in the machine," guides matter. This makes *Psycho-Cybernetics* the perfect self-help book for a technological culture.

It is admirable because it was written at a time when behaviorism and time-and-motion studies, which tended to reduce people to the mechanical, were at their zenith. Maltz's genius was in saying that while we were "machines," and while the dynamics of goal setting and self-image might best be described in mechanistic terms, the fantastic variety of our desires and our ability to create new worlds were uniquely human. What could never be reduced to machine analogies were the fires of imagination, ambition, and will.

Maxwell Maltz

Born and educated in Europe, Maltz spent most of his adult life in New York where he established a reconstructive cosmetic surgery practice. His New Faces, New Futures *was a collection of case histories of patients whose lives had been transformed by facial surgery. Maltz's subsequent research into the few patients whose lives did not radically improve led him to the psychologist Prescott Lecky's work on "self-consistency." He was in his 60s by the time* Psycho-Cybernetics *was published.*

With its success, Maltz became a popular motivational speaker throughout the 1960s and the early 1970s. The wide audience for the book included Salvador Dali, who painted a "psycho-cybernetics" work as a gift to the author. Maltz died in 1971, aged 76.

Though rather overshadowed, other Maltz titles include The Magic Powers of the Self-Image, Live and Be Free through Psycho-Cybernetics, *three novels and an autobiography,* Dr. Pygmalion. Psycho-Cybernetics 2000, *edited by Bobbe Summer and Anna Maltz, is an updated version of the book.*

Motivation and Personality

1954

"*Being a human being—in the sense of being born to the human species—must be defined also in terms of becoming a human being. In this sense a baby is only potentially a human being, and must grow into humanness.*"

"*I certainly accepted and built upon the available data of experimental psychology and psychoanalysis. I accepted also the empirical and experimental spirit of the one, and the unmasking and depth-probing of the other, while yet rejecting the images of man which they generated. That is, this book represented a different philosophy of human nature, a new image of man.*"

In a nutshell

Full mental health is not the absence of neurosis but the fulfillment of our potential.

In a similar vein

Pierre Teilhard de Chardin, *The Phenomenon of Man* (p290)

CHAPTER 39

Abraham Maslow

I n the summer of 1962, Abraham Maslow was driving through heavy fog on the treacherous Big Sur coastal highway in California. Noticing an interesting sign, he decided to pull over. The place he had stumbled on turned out to be the world's first personal growth center, Esalen, where serendipitously staff were unpacking copies of his latest book, *Towards a Psychology of Being*.

With such a beginning, it was perhaps inevitable that Maslow would become the high priest of the 1960s human potential movement. Through the core idea of the "self-actualizing person," his *Motivation and Personality* had presented a new image of human nature that excited a whole generation. With Rollo May and Carl Rogers, Maslow founded the "third force" humanistic branch of psychology, and its extension, transpersonal psychology, which went beyond the regular needs and interests of people to their spiritual and cosmological context.

Yet Maslow was not an obvious revolutionary. As an academic psychologist his work was essentially a reaction against behaviorism, which broke people down to mechanistic parts, and Freudian psychoanalysis, which imagined us controlled by subterranean urges. Still working within the boundaries of the scientific method, *Motivation and Personality* instead sought to form a holistic view of people, one not dissimilar to how artists and poets have always imagined us. Rather than being simply the sum of our needs and impulses, Maslow saw us as whole people with limitless room for growth. It was this clear belief in human possibility and the organizations and cultures we could build that has made his work so influential.

The key concepts: Hierarchy of needs and self-actualization

Maslow's "hierarchy of needs" is a famous concept in psychology. He organized human needs into three broad levels: the physiological—air, food and water—the psychological—safety, love, self-esteem—and, finally, self-actualization. His insight was that the higher needs were as much a part of our nature as the lower, indeed were instinctive and bio-logical. Most civilizations had mistakenly put the higher and lower needs at odds with each other, seeing the animalistic basic drives as conflicting with the finer things to which we aspire like truth, love, and beauty. In contrast, Maslow saw needs as a continuum, in which the satisfaction of the lower needs came before a person's higher mental and moral development. Having met the basic bodily requirements, and reached a state where we feel we are loved, respected, and enjoy a sense of belonging, including philosophical or religious identity, we seek self-actualization.

Self-actualizing people have attained "the full use and exploitation of talents, capacities, potentialities and the like." These are the people who are successful as a person, aside from any obvious external success; by no means perfect, but seemingly without major flaws. Since Daniel Goleman wrote his bestseller on emotional intelligence people have "discovered" it as a key to success, yet for self-actualized people this type of intelligence is ingrained.

Maslow's research involved the study of seven contemporaries and nine historical figures: US Presidents Abraham Lincoln and Thomas Jefferson, scientist Albert Einstein, First Lady and philanthropist Eleanor Roosevelt, pioneer social worker Jane Addams, psychologist William James, doctor and humanitarian Albert Schweitzer, writer Aldous Huxley, and philosopher Baruch Spinoza. He identified 19 characteristics of the self-actualized person, including:

- ❖ Clear perception of reality (including a heightened ability to detect falseness and be a good judge of character).
- ❖ Acceptance (of themselves and things as they are).
- ❖ Spontaneity (a rich, unconventional inner life with a child-like ability to constantly see the world anew and appreciate beauty in the mundane).
- ❖ Problem-centeredness (focus on questions or challenges outside themselves—a sense of mission or purpose—resulting in an absence of pettiness, introspection, and ego games).
- ❖ Solitude seeking (enjoyed for its own sake, solitude also brings serenity and detachment from misfortune/crisis, and allows for independence of thought and decision).

- ❖ Autonomy (independence of the good opinion of other people, more interest in inner satisfaction than status or rewards).
- ❖ Peak or mystical experiences (experiences when time seems to stand still).
- ❖ Human kinship (a genuine love for, and desire to help, all people).
- ❖ Humility and respect (belief that we can learn from anyone, and that even the worst person has redeeming features).
- ❖ Ethics (clear, if not conventional, notions of right and wrong).
- ❖ Sense of humor (not amused by jokes that hurt or imply inferiority, but humor that highlights the foolishness of human beings in general).
- ❖ Creativity (not the Mozart type of genius that is inborn, but in all that is done, said, or acted).
- ❖ Resistance to enculturation (ability to see beyond the confines of culture and era).
- ❖ Imperfections (all the guilt, anxiety, self-blame, jealousy, and so on that regular people experience, but these do not stem from neurosis).
- ❖ Values (based on a positive view of the world; the universe is not seen as a jungle but an essentially abundant place, providing whatever we need to be able to make our contribution).

A further subtle difference sets these people apart. Most of us see life as striving to get this or that, whether it be material things or having a family or doing well career-wise. Psychologists call this "deficiency motivation." Self-actualizers, in contrast, do not strive as much as develop. They are only ambitious to the extent of being able to express themselves more fully and perfectly, delighting in what they are able to do.

Another general point is their profound freedom of mind. Despite the circumstances in which they may have been, and in contrast to the conforming pressures all around them, self-actualizers are walking examples of free will, the quintessential human quality. They fully grasp what Stephen Covey calls the gap between stimulus and response, the concept that no response should be automatic. In contrast, the merely "well-adjusted" (that is, neurosis-free) person may not really know who they are or have a defined purpose in life. As Theodore Rozsak saw it in *Person/Planet*:

"Maslow asked the key question in posing self-actualization as the proper objective of therapy: Why do we set our standard of sanity so

cautiously low? Can we imagine no better model than the dutiful con-sumer, the well-adjusted breadwinner? Why not the saint, the sage, the artist? Why not all that is highest and finest in our species?"

Maslow made the intriguing observation that, although his self-actualizers shared the above traits and therefore could be grouped as a type, they were more completely individualized than any control group ever described. This is the paradox of the self-actualizer: the more of these traits a person has, the more likely they are to be truly unique.

Final comments

Maslow's greatness was in re-imagining what a human being could be. Moving us away from the idea of mental health as merely the "absence of neurosis," he insisted that psychological health required the presence of self-actualizing traits. Such a fundamental recasting of psychology has had implications for all areas of human activity.

At the time he wrote *Motivation and Personality*, Maslow believed that only a tiny percentage of the population was self-actualized, but that these few could change the whole culture. Given the impact of the concept on the 1960s counter-culturalists, a generation that has changed the world in its image, you would have to say that Maslow was right.

Certainly, his hierarchy of needs has been seminal to understanding motivation in the workplace, and the self-actualization of the employee has become a serious concern in business. He foresaw the trend toward personal growth and excitement replacing money as the highest motivator in a person's working life.

The principle clearly sets higher standards for individuals and society, and the main criticism of Maslow has been that he was Utopian, creating an ideal human nature that does not exist. He died before he could address the problem that some say he ignored: evil. The desire for self-actualization may be a factor in the spread of democracy and the growth in recognition of human rights, but what light does it shine on horrors like the genocide in Rwanda and Kosovo?

If self-actualization is a facet of human nature, then its absence creates a vacuum that becomes filled by repression, poverty, and nationalism, making the world ripe for evil. Seen in this way, the fulfillment of the self should never be thought of as a luxury. The evolution of the species depends on it.

Abraham Maslow

Born in 1908 to Russian-Jewish immigrants in Brooklyn, New York, Maslow was the oldest of seven children. He was said to be shy, neurotic, and depressive, but with a passionate curiosity and incredible native intelligence (an IQ of 195) he excelled in school.

At college, Maslow's early influences were Harry Harlow, the distinguished primate researcher, and the behaviorist Edward Thorndike. While at Columbia University, Maslow's research into the sex lives of college women attracted controversy. During his 14-year professorship at Brooklyn College, his mentors included Alfred Adler, Karen Horney, Eric Fromm, and Margaret Mead. The anthropologist Ruth Benedict and founder of Gestalt therapy Max Wertheimer became friends and models for the idea of the self-actualizing person. In 1951 Maslow moved to Brandeis University, where he stayed until a year before his death, and where Motivation and Personality *was written.*

In 1962 Maslow held a visiting fellowship at a Californian high-tech company, which resulted in his adaptation of the self-actualization concept to the business setting, related in Eupsychian Management: A Journal *(1965).* Towards a Psychology of Being *was published in 1962 and the classic* The Farther Reaches of Human Nature *a year after Maslow's death in 1970.*

Care of the Soul:
A Guide for Cultivating Depth and Sacredness in Everyday Life

1992

"Care of the soul is a fundamentally different way of regarding daily life and the quest for happiness . . . Care of the soul is a continous process that concerns itself not so much with 'fixing' a central flaw as with attending to the small details of everyday life, as well as to major decisions and changes."

"Soul cannot thrive in a fast-paced life because being affected, taking things in and chewing on them, requires time."

In a nutshell

Fill your emptiness by living soulfully. Let your individuality out by accepting your idiosyncrasies and dark side.

In a similar vein

CHAPTER 40

Thomas Moore

Care of the Soul was a No. 1 *New York Times* bestseller and spent almost a year on that list. It is rare for a self-help title to have also received critical acclaim. This is a popular self-help book, but not like any you may have read. Steeped in a sense of the sacred and the profound, Moore's thesis is that modern lives lack mystery, and the success of the book would seem to indicate that most of us agree.

You should also find it a peaceful experience, almost like a letter from a forgiving friend; while knowing everything about you, they are unfazed in their belief in your godliness. This effect may derive from a combination of Moore's experience as a psychotherapist, his years as a monk, and his wide learning. Inspired by myth, history, and art, the book exudes the richness of human experience. Moore's chief influences are Freud (delvings into the psychic underworld), Jung (the belief that psychology and religion are indistinguishable), James Hillman (see *The Soul's Code*), and the Renaissance men Ficino and Paracelsus.

What is care of the soul?

Care of the soul is "an application of poetics to everyday life," bringing imagination back into those areas of our lives that are devoid of it, and re-imagining the things that we believe we already understand. Rewarding relationships, fulfilling work, personal power, and peace of mind are all gifts of the soul. They are so difficult to achieve because the idea of soul does not exist for most of us, instead making itself known through physical symptoms and complaints, anguish, emptiness, or a general unease.

Soulwork can be deceptively simple. Often you feel better just by accepting and going more deeply into what you apparently hate, for example a job, a marriage, a place. The book contains a quote by the poet Wallace Stevens: "Perhaps the truth depends on a walk around a lake." Instead of trying to remove any bad feeling or experience surgically from our mind, it is more human and honest to look squarely at the "bad thing" and see what it says to us. We will not receive the soul's messages if it is moved out of sight. An intent to heal, either on the part of the sufferer or the helper, may obscure insight into what is actually going on.

Conventional self-help and psychotherapy are problem solving. The literature on the soul, exemplified by Moore, is "problem-noticing and wondering." The soul has to do with turns of fate, which are often counter to expectations and against the desires of the ego and the will. This is a frightening idea, yet the only way it becomes less frightening is when we start to make space for its movements and respect its power. As Victor Hugo put it in *Les Misérables*:

"There is one spectacle grander than the sea, that is the sky; there is one spectacle grander than the sky, that is the interior of the soul."

Enjoying our depth and complexity

Moore asks us to re-examine the myth of Narcissus, the beautiful young man in love with an image of himself in a pond. His soulless and loveless self-absorption results in tragedy, but its intensity eventually pushes him into a new life of reflection and love for his deeper self and nature around him. "The narcissistic person simply does not know how profound and interesting his nature is," Moore suggests. Narcissus is like ivory: beautiful, but cold and hard. What he could become is a flower, with roots and part of a whole world of beauty. However, killing the Narcissus in us is not the way to go; instead of moving to the other extreme of false humility, it is best to keep our high ideals and dreams and find more effective ways to express them.

With the analysis of myths such as these, Moore counsels that we should avoid the simplistic single-mindedness of some self-help writing. There are many aspects to the self, and by accommodating its competing demands (for example solitariness vs. social life) life expands into something fuller. We can sometimes entertain our ego, at other times be the detached sage. Both are valid, and we don't always have to be making sure that life makes sense.

No one has a soul like ours

"The uniqueness of a person is made up of the insane and the twisted as much as it is of the rational and normal," Moore notes. This is attested to by the biographies of just about everyone you have ever admired—even Abraham Lincoln is getting the revisionist treatment. Why should you be any different? *Care of the Soul* warns us to be particularly careful that our efforts to "iron out the bumps" may only be a drive toward conformity and a sad loss of ourselves.

Most therapists now focus on specific problems that can be tackled in a short timeframe, that can restore you to "normality." Through drugs, cognitive therapy, and sciences like neuro-linguistic programming, there is no need for introspection. Care of the soul never ends, however, as the soul itself is outside of time. Only such things as mythology, nature, the fine arts, and dreams—which all defy time—can give us proper insight into our mystery.

The book has four parts and thirteen chapters, covering the gamut of the human condition. The following themes are from the first half.

Love

We should try not to see love in terms of "making relationships work." Rather, love is an "event of the soul" that may have surprisingly little to do with who you are with. Love is relief from the mundane, sanitized nature of modern life, a door into mystery, which is why we seize it with such force.

Jealousy

Moore had a young client who had whipped himself into a frenzy about his girlfriend's suspected affairs. Yet the man also believed that romantic attachment was not modern or acceptable. This purity of ideals had shunted out the possibility of real attachment, and the result was an ugly externalization of jealousy.

Nevertheless, jealousy is not all bad, serving the soul through the creation of limits and rootedness. Flying in the face of modern ideas about "co-dependency," Moore says that it is OK to find one's identity in relation to another.

Power

The soul's power is quite different to the ego's. With the ego we plan, direct, and work toward an end. The soul's power is more like a current of water: Though we may never understand its source, we still have to accommodate it and let it guide our existence. With the soul we have to abandon the "consumer logic" of cause and effect and the efficient use of time.

Violence

The soul loves power, but violence breaks out when the dark imagination is given no outlet. When a community or a whole culture lacks soulfulness, the soul is fetishized into objects, for example guns. As Oscar Wilde suggested, virtue cannot be genuine when it sets itself apart from evil.

Depression

Moore says that any culture that tries to protect itself against the tragic side of life will make depression the enemy, but that in any type of society "devoted to light" depression will be unusually strong in order to compensate for its unnatural covering up. Moore describes depression as a gift: It unwraps our neat little values and aims, giving us a chance to get to know the soul.

Final comments

Late in the book, Moore tells of the summer he spent working in a laboratory, having left the monastic life where he had been cloistered for 12 years. Enjoying his new-found freedom, he was shocked when a workmate said to him with conviction, "You will always do the work of a priest." The success of *Care of the Soul* is a perfect example of how self-help literature has taken the place of traditional carers-of-the-soul, to whose rituals and religious instruction we once would have turned automatically.

In place of the "salvation fantasy" that he believes characterizes contemporary self-help, Moore tries to return us to a self-knowledge quest that can encompass our shadows and complexities. His book is modeled on the less ambitious self-help manuals of the Middle Ages and Renaissance, which offered philosophical comfort for the trials of life. *Care of the Soul* may stand out from today's self-help writing, but in fact continues an old and venerable tradition.

Renaissance doctors, Moore tells us, believed that each individual soul originated as a star in the night sky. The modern idea, he notes, is that a person is "what he makes himself to be." We have to value the self-creating freedom that is enjoyed in our time, but Moore's book gives us something altogether different: the encouragement to wonder what is eternal in us.

Thomas Moore

As well as the 12 years he spent as a monk in a Catholic religious order, Moore obtained four degrees: a PhD in religious studies from Syracuse University, an MA in theology from the University of Windsor, an MA in musicology from the University of Michigan, and a BA in music and philosophy from DePaul University.

A writer and psychotherapist, he has been a leading exponent of the archetypal school of psychology, which seeks to reintroduce a mythic dimension to the discipline. Other books include The Planets Within, Rituals of the Imagination, Dark Eros, Soul Mates, *and* The Re-enchantment of Everyday Life. *He also edited* A Blue Fire, *an anthology of the writings of James Hillman. More recent works include* Dark Nights of the Soul *(2005), and* A Religion of One's Own *(2015).*

Moore lives in New Hampshire with his wife and two children.

The Power of Your Subconscious Mind

1963

"The result of the affirmative process of prayer depends on your conforming to the principles of life, regardless of appearances. Consider for a moment that there is a principle of mathematics and none of error; there is a principle of truth but none of dishonesty. There is a principle of intelligence but none of ignorance; there is a principle of harmony and none of discord. There is a principle of health but none of disease, and there is a principle of abundance but none of poverty."

"Whatever is impressed in your subconscious mind is expressed on the screen of space. This same truth was proclaimed by Moses, Isaiah, Jesus, Buddha, Zoroaster, Laotze, and all the illumined seers of the ages. Whatever you feel as true subjectively is expressed as conditions, experiences, and events. As in heaven [your own mind], so on earth [in your body and environment]. This is the great law of life."

"The law of your mind is the law of belief. This means to believe in the way your mind works, to believe in belief itself."

In a nutshell

By understanding how the subconscious mind works, you can learn how dreams become reality.

In a similar vein

Shakti Gawain, *Creative Visualization* (p174)
Florence Scovell Shinn, *The Game of Life and How to Play It* (p272)

CHAPTER 41

Joseph Murphy

D r. Joseph Murphy spent a good part of his life studying eastern religions and was a scholar of the *I-Ching*, the Chinese book of divination whose origins are lost in history. He was also, for 28 years, Minister at the Los Angeles branch of the Church of Divine Science, a New Thought church that promotes a practical spirituality, free of the usual religious creed and dogma.

It is a long way from the ancient East to LA, but Murphy felt that there were secrets he had found concerning the subconscious that were beyond time and culture, and that should find a wider audience.

How the subconscious works and what it can do

Murphy saw the subconscious mind as a darkroom within which we develop the images that are to be lived out in real life. While the conscious mind sees an event, takes a picture of it, and remembers it, the subconscious mind works backwards, "seeing" something before it happens (this is why intuition is infallible).

The subconscious responds to habit and habitual thinking. Being totally neutral in a moral sense, it is happy to adopt any habit as "normal"—good or bad. We blithely let negative thoughts drop into the subconscious every minute of our lives, then are surprised when they find expression in day-to-day experiences and relationships. While there are some things that will happen to us that we had no role in creating, in fact these are rare. Mostly the bad that happens is in us already, waiting for the light of day.

This is the harsh reality, but knowledge of the subconscious also delivers us a breakthrough: It means that we can remake ourselves anew simply by controlling the thoughts and images with which we feed it. This makes Murphy's book, with its instructions and affirmations that will have the greatest effect on the subconscious, a tool of liberation. Understanding your subconscious mind as a photographic mechanism removes the emotion and struggle from changing your life, because if it is simply a matter of replacing existing mental images with new ones, you begin to see the ease with which you may change.

Relaxed faith = Results

The subconscious is an entirely different kettle of fish to the conscious mind. It cannot be coerced, responding best to relaxed faith that it will do its transforming work with ease. Trying hard, which may work for a task given to the conscious mind, is a cause of failure with its subterranean other half. It suggests to your subconscious that there is a lot of opposition to what you want done.

Along with relaxed faith, the ease with which the subconscious accomplishes things increases with emotion. An idea or a thought alone may excite the rational, conscious mind, but the subconscious likes things to be "emotionalized." When a thought becomes a feeling, and imagination becomes desire, it will deliver what you want with speed and abundance.

Yet Murphy said that it is less important to know how your subconscious works than to develop the faith that it can. William James, the father of American psychology, believed that the greatest discovery of the nineteenth century was the power of the subconscious mind added to faith. The idea that you can change your life by changing the landscape of your mind may not have appeared in history books alongside the discovery of new continents or electricity or steam, but all the great minds have known it.

Believing it to be so

"The law of your mind is the law of belief itself," Murphy noted. What we believe makes us who we are. William James observed that whatever people expect to be true will be so, irrespective of whether the object of their belief exists. In the West we have made "the truth" our highest value; this motivation, while important, is weak next to the actual power of belief in shaping our lives. Whatever you give your subconscious—false or true, good or evil—it will register as fact. Be careful not to joke about misfortune, as the subconscious has no sense of humor.

A mentally disturbed person and a healthy person share the same power of belief; the sane differ from the insane only in that they retain objectivity about their beliefs. When a man in a hospital says he is Elvis Presley, he is not "making it up," he knows he is Elvis. We must use this same power for constructive ends, not wishing but knowing that we are a perfect spouse or a business genius. The trick is to choose to know something that seems almost mad but not quite—something that seemed impossible to us a year ago, yet at the same time would be an enactment of our heart's desire.

Health and prosperity

In the rituals of ancient times, with their weird mixtures and incantations, it was the power of suggestion and acceptance in the subconscious mind that healed. Even today, doctors report the power of placebos to produce miraculous recoveries if they are accompanied by doubt-free instructions that "this will do the trick." Miracles of healing, Murphy said, are simply the body obeying the subconscious mind's knowledge of "perfect health" when the questioning nature of the normal conscious mind is silenced.

The other aspect of mental healing is the premise that our individual minds are part of a larger human mind (as Emerson believed), which itself is linked to "infinite intelligence." This is why it is not crazy, Murphy claimed, to believe that you can heal people who are not even physically near to you, by visualizing all the health, energy, and love in the universe applied to that person, the life force pulsing through every cell of their body, cleaning and invigorating as it goes.

As there is a principle of health and harmony in the universe, so there is a principle of abundance. "The trouble with most people is that they have no invisible means of support," commented Murphy. Others, aware of the law of abundance, will not be thrown into a nervous breakdown if their bank account goes into the red or their business is lost. They will understand it as a message to get re-attuned and re-acquainted with the fact of a prosperous universe.

The "feeling of wealth," Murphy said, produces wealth in reality. The subconscious mind understands and follows the idea of compound interest. That is, little thought deposits made regularly over time compound to produce a large principal of mental abundance. He showed the reader exactly how to send the right signals to their subconscious to make sure that these abundant images manifest themselves in the real world.

Why prayers are usually in vain

Our universe is one of law and order, Murphy wrote, therefore there should be nothing "mystical" about getting answers to our prayers. It is a process no more mysterious than the erection of a building. One who knows the workings of the subconscious mind will learn how to pray "scientifically."

What does this mean? Prayers traditionally consist of earnest utterances to God followed by "hoping for the best." Logically, however, such prayers will carry little weight or power because they are framed in doubt. It is the great irony of conventional prayer (the pleading, wishing, hoping variety) that it involves no faith. Real faith is simple: the knowledge that something *is* happening, *is* being provided, present tense. When prayers become occasions to give thanks for the fact of assistance (even if it has yet to materialize), they cease to be a mystical ritual that we hope God will notice, and become a co-creating process with definite ends.

Final comments

The Power of Your Subconscious Mind is simply written and tries to be free of culture or religion. It is slightly repetitive, but this in itself mirrors the book's idea of subconscious programming. The first half is the best, as it explains how the subconscious works. The second half deals with its role and power to transform in areas like marriage, human relations, scientific discovery, sleep, fear, forgiveness, and "eternal youth." For full effect, the author's advice that it be read at least twice should be taken.

To some the book will be somewhat "way out," but many people say that their life was not the same after reading it. The subconscious is a powerful thing, and what you get from Murphy is the realization that if you refuse to try to understand the non-rational mind, your rational desires and plans will be forever sabotaged.

Joseph Murphy

Murphy was born in 1898 in Ireland. He joined a Jesuit seminary and was ordained, but left the priesthood and moved to the United States. He worked as a pharmacist before discovering Ernest Holmes' Religious Science. He always refused requests for profiles and biographies, saying that his life was to be found in his books. He wrote over 30, including The Amazing Laws of Cosmic Mind, Secrets of the I-Ching, The Miracle of Mind Dynamics, Your Infinite Power to be Rich *and* The Cosmic Power Within You. *There is a new edition of* The Power of Your Subconscious Mind, *revised by Ian McMahan.*

Murphy spent many years in India and was a Fellow of the Andhra Research University of India. He did a PhD in psychology at the University of Southern California before turning his hand to writing.

Murphy died in 1986.

The Power of Positive Thinking

1952

"*Faith is the one power against which fear cannot stand. Day by day, as you fill your mind with faith, there will ultimately be no room left for fear. This is the one great fact that no one should forget. Master faith and you will automatically master fear.*"

"*There was a time when I acquiesced in the silly idea that there is no relationship between faith and prosperity; that when one talked about religion he should never relate it to achievement, that it dealt only with ethics and morals and social values. But now I realize that such a viewpoint limits the power of God and the development of the individual. Religion teaches that there is a tremendous power in the universe and that this power can dwell in personality. It is a power that can blast out all defeat and lift a person above all difficult situations.*"

In a nutshell

You can achieve anything if you have faith.

In a similar vein

Florence Scovell Shinn, *The Game of Life and How to Play It* (p272)

CHAPTER 42

Norman Vincent Peale

I f it were not for Peale's wife's persistence, this book—which is one of the all-time bestselling self-help titles and made him a founder of the human potential movement—might never have been published. He was in his 50s when he wrote it and had received nothing but a stack of rejection slips. Dejected, he threw the manuscript into the wastebasket and forbade his wife to remove it. She took him literally, next day presenting the manuscript, inside the wastebasket, to what became the successful publisher.

The book has sold around 20 million copies in 42 languages. Along with *How to Win Friends and Influence People* it was one of the original twentieth-century self-help classics.

The perception

If likened to a television character, Peale's book might be Ned Flanders from *The Simpsons*, the Christian dad always ready with a cheery word for his neighbor Homer Simpson. Through Homer we see the world as it "really" is, through Ned Flanders the world as the do-gooders perceive it. The book has become linked with a Pollyanna-ish attitude to the world that sees no evil and hears no evil, and believes that a happy smile can melt all obstacles. "Every day, in every way, I am getting better and better" is Emile Coué's famous positive thinking mantra, which to most ears is superficial and even idiotic.

In *The 7 Habits of Highly Effective People*, Stephen Covey criticizes positive thinking by saying that before we can justifiably take on a positive frame of mind, we first have to accept that things are not OK, and then take responsibility. Otherwise we are fudging reality.

The reality

However, when we open up Peale's book, we read:

"The book is written with deep concern for the pain, difficulty and struggle of human existence."

He went on to say:

"It teaches positive thinking, not as a means to fame, riches or power, but as the practical application of faith to overcome defeat and accomplish worthwhile creative values in life."

These are not the ideas of someone with an unrealistic take on life. Peale saw plenty of human misery in his daily life as a minister in New York City, but he was not content to provide a weekly sermon; he wanted measurable change in the life of the people he met. Over many years, he created a "simple yet scientific system of practical techniques for successful living that works," tested and refined among thousands of people within and outside his ministry. And like Carnegie with *How to Win Friends and Influence People*, Peale ran the ideas as an adult course long before they were distilled into book form.

The source of positive thinking

For Peale there was no greater source of personal power or guidance than the Bible. Biblical quotes are the mainstay of the book (supplemented by the likes of Emerson, William James, and Marcus Aurelius) and perhaps because it is based on this timeless wisdom, Peale's classic has amazing power. When statements such as the following are highlighted for us, it is difficult to argue with Peale's conviction:

"If God is for us, who can be against us?" (Romans 8:31)
"If thou can believe, all things are possible to him that believeth." (Mark 9:23)
"According to your faith, be it unto you." (Matthew 9:29)

Peale's theme was that we don't have to depend on ourselves; there are incredible sources of power open to us if we only believe in their existence. We make life hard, but an appreciation of the universe's ability to make good and to provide would lead us to see life as flowing and abundant. Life seems difficult because we only believe in ourselves. He expressed the great secret of self-help that, in order to gain personal

power and peace, we have to be willing to go beyond the merely per- ▸
sonal to something greater than ourselves.

The book proceeds by cases and stories, some of them incredibly
touching. Filled with the struggle of humanity, its aim is to show that
defeat is not permanent. Some of the chapters, with examples of their
content, are described below.

"How to have constant energy"

Peale revealed the secret source of energy of every great person he had
known: attunement with the infinite. The knowledge that what one is
doing is supported outside oneself and is serving a divine end provides
a constantly renewable source of energy. Working only by oneself and
for oneself leads to burnout.

"Try prayer power"

Prayer is different to what you may have thought. It is a space to say
whatever is on your mind, in whatever language you choose. Instead of
asking for things, give thanks in advance for what you desire, leave it
in God's hands, and visualize the good outcome. The Peale formula is
"Prayerize, Picturize, Actualize." Be surprised at its effectiveness.

"Expect the best and get it"

Fearful creatures that we are, we tend to expect the worst. But an
expectation of the best has a way of organizing forces in your favor.
You are less likely to keep anything in reserve. The subconscious,
which regulates many of our actions, merely reflects your beliefs. Alter
the belief about an outcome and your actions will seem to be shaped in
order to achieve it. Peale's phrase is: "Doubt closes the power flow.
Faith opens it."

"New thoughts can remake you"

Use only positive and hopeful language for a 24-hour period. Then go
back to being "realistic" the next day. Repeat this over a week and you
find that what you considered realistic a week ago now seems pessimistic. In golfing terms, discover that "the rough is only mental."

Your new understanding of what is realistic moves up to a higher, permanently positive level.

Final comments

To really appreciate *The Power of Positive Thinking* you have to understand its background. Peale came from plain Mid-Western stock, and he believed he was writing, in his words, "for the plain people of this world." Most readers will find it quaint or amusing because the language conjures up simple church-going folk in the 1950s. It might be old-fashioned, but only a cynic would find it redundant—the book's principles are easily moved from its original time and place and applied to your life, as you would expect of a classic. It is refreshing because there are no gimmicky techniques; expect to find only a bag of well-worn tools for chiseling away cynicism and hopelessness.

Although the book contains things like a "prayer for salesmen," it is something more than a hotchpotch of Christian and capitalist morals. Consistent with most of the self-help classics, it says that the highest morality is fulfillment of potential; to "give up" is to deny yourself all the spiritual and material rewards that are rightfully yours.

If you are feeling down, there is an unassailable logic to Peale's book that can forcefully restore life again and again, clearing all doubt from the mind.

Norman Vincent Peale

Peale was born in Bowersville, Ohio, in 1898. Following college (Ohio Wesleyan University) and work on newspapers (Detroit Journal), he studied theology at Boston University. After ordination he quickly became a popular preacher who could swell congregation numbers tenfold. During his time at University Methodist Church in Syracuse, New York, he met and married Ruth Stafford, his life-long partner and collaborator.

At 34, Peale moved to Marble Collegiate Church in New York City, where he stayed through the Depression and the Second World War until the early 1980s. His sermons became so well known that they attracted tourists. In the 1930s he also began a radio broadcast, "The Art of Living," that was to be heard weekly for 54 years, and established a clinic of Christian psychotherapy with psychiatrist Smiley Blanton. In 1945 he established the inspirational magazine Guideposts, *which is still popular. Politically he was conservative: He traveled to Vietnam at President Nixon's request and was given the Presidential Medal of Freedom by Ronald Reagan.*

Peale was a prolific speaker; he was still addressing around 100 groups a year in his 90s. He died on Christmas Eve, 1993, aged 95, but the Peale Center in New York State carries on his work. Peale's life has been chronicled in Carol V. R. George's God's Salesman: Normal Vincent Peale and the Power of Positive Thinking.

The Road Less Traveled

1978

"Most do not fully see this truth that life is difficult. Instead they moan more or less incessantly, noisily or subtly, about the enormity of their problems, their burdens, and their difficulties in life as if life were generally easy, as if life should be easy."

"As Benjamin Franklin said, 'Those things that hurt, instruct.' It is for this reason that wise people learn not to dread but actually to welcome problems and actually to welcome the pain of problems."

"What are these tools, these techniques of suffering, these means of experiencing the pain of problems constructively that I call discipline? There are four: delaying of gratification, acceptance of responsibility, dedication to truth, and balancing . . . they are simple tools, and almost all children are adept in their use by the age of ten. Yet presidents and kings will often forget to use them, to their downfall."

In a nutshell

Once you admit that "life is difficult," the fact is no longer of great consequence. Once you accept responsibility, you can make better choices.

In a similar vein
Alain de Botton, *How Proust Can Change Your Life* (p38)
Thomas Moore, *Care of the Soul* (p242)
Marianne Williamson, *A Return to Love* (p302)

CHAPTER 43

M. Scott Peck

his is the self-help book read by people who don't read self-help
books. It contains none of the alluring promises of boundless joy
and happiness that are the feature of personal development writing, yet has still been a massive bestseller. Famously beginning with the
words "Life is difficult," it covers such gloomy topics as the myth of
romantic love, evil, mental illness, and the author's psychological and
spiritual crises.

Perhaps because of its lack of rosiness, it is easy to give this book
our confidence—it works on the premise that once we know the worst,
we are free to see what is beyond it. *The Road Less Traveled* is inspirational but in an old-fashioned way, putting self-discipline at the top of
the list of values for a good life. If you believe that there are no easy
ways to enlightenment or even full mental health, that factors like commitment and responsibility are the seeds of fulfillment, then you belong
in Dr. Peck's territory.

Peck was a conventionally trained psychotherapist, but has been
influential in the movement to have psychology recognize the stages of
spiritual growth. He saw the great feature of our times as being the rec-
onciliation of the scientific and the spiritual worldviews. *The Road Less
Traveled* was his attempt to bridge the gap further, and it has clearly
been successful. The book is welcomed by anyone who has found
themselves torn between the science of psychology and the spiritual
search.

Discipline
Self-control is the essence of Peck's brand of self-help. He says:

*"Without discipline we can solve nothing. With only some discipline
we can solve only some problems. With total discipline we can solve
all problems."*

A person who has the ability to delay gratification has the key to psychological maturity, whereas impulsiveness is a mental habit that, in denying opportunities to experience pain, creates neuroses. Most large problems we have are the result of not facing up to earlier, smaller problems, of failing to be "dedicated to the truth." The great mistake that most people make is believing that problems will go away of their own accord.

This lack of responsibility will damage us in other ways. Our culture puts freedom on a pedestal, yet as Eric Fromm showed in *Escape from Freedom*, people have a natural willingness to embrace political authoritarianism and give up their personal power. When it comes down to it, we shy away from real freedom and choice just as much as we avoid obviously negative things. Discipline is not only about "growing up" in terms of accepting reality, but in the appreciation of the tremendous range of choices before us.

The road and its rewards

One of the great insights of the book is how few people actually choose the spiritual path. Just as there are many well-qualified sergeants who baulk at becoming an officer, Peck observes, people in psychotherapy often have little taste for the power that comes with genuine mental health. Life on autopilot is preferable to any major challenge.

The Road Less Traveled is rich with the stories of real people. Some of the vignettes demonstrate the transformation of a life, but in other cases people merely refuse to change, or in the end can't be bothered. Does this ring true? It is in these less extreme cases that we are more likely to see our own quiet turning away from a bolder, richer life. Rather than the horror of a mental illness, Peck says, most of us have to deal with the straightforward anguish of missed opportunities.

Yet why is this so, when the rewards are so great? The road less traveled might be the spiritual path, but it is also much rockier and dimly lit next to the regular highway of life, on which other people seem happy enough. However, Peck says that to ask this question of "Why bother?" we must know nothing about joy. The rewards of spiritual life are enormous: Peace of mind and freedom from real worry that most people never imagine is possible. Burdens are always ready to be lifted, since they are no longer solely ours.

Nevertheless, deepened spirituality also brings responsibility; this is inevitable as we move from spiritual childhood to adulthood. Peck remembers St Augustine, who said: "If you are loving and diligent, you may do whatever you want." Just as our previous spiritual timidity and laziness resulted (as we can now see) in a very limited existence, so discipline opens the door to limitlessness in our experience of life. Only the more enlightened can be amused by the fact that others think they must lead a boring and restrained life; the walls that look stark from without may simply be shielding us from the glow of rapture within.

Love is a decision

What is the fuel on the road less traveled? Love, of course, and Peck is at his best discussing this thing that cannot be adequately defined. We tend to think of love as effortless, the freefall of "falling in love." While it may be mysterious, love is also effortful; love is a decision: "The desire to love is not itself love. Love is as love does."

The ecstatic state of being in love is in part a regression to infancy, a time when we felt our mother and ourselves to be one; we are back in communion with the world and anything seems possible. Yet just as the baby comes to realize that he or she is an individual, so the lover eventually returns to his or her self. At this point, Peck says, the work of "real" love begins. Anyone can fall in love, but not everyone can decide to love. We may never control love's onset, but we may—with discipline —remain in charge of our response. And once these "muscles" of love have been used they tend to stay, increasing our power to channel love in the most life-giving and appropriate way.

Final comments

The discerning reader will note the contrast between Peck's belief that psychological change is necessarily slow, and the cognitive psychology view that our limitations can be removed without much trouble if we know how (see Martin Seligman, David D. Burns, Anthony Robbins). This is a basic divide in the self-help literature: the hard work ethic, components of which include building character and discovering soul; and the belief in mental technology, that our problems are not deep-seated and can be addressed by practical psycho-technological methods. If the former way is characterized by discipline and self-knowledge, the latter says that if we only have the right tools, we can create whoever we want to be.

Those readers who exclusively cheer for the latter should balance themselves by reading Peck. He discusses, for instance, an experience that is not referred to in modern psychology at all: "grace." A surprise burst of peace, gratitude, and freedom, Peck feels this to be the highest point of human experience, fruit of a life of discipline and purpose.

In his insistence on morality, discipline, and admiration of long-suffering, Peck's writing can seem old-fashioned. Yet he is no conformist in his denouncement of the failure of psychotherapy to recognize people as spiritual beings, and the book has surprised many readers by its embrace of the Jungian, New Age concepts of the collective unconscious and synchronicity. Somehow, the blend of Christianity, the New Age, and academic psychology does work.

Peck's classic will seem a little earnest to some, to others it will be full of life-changing insights. It is one of the giants of the self-help canon, having sold over seven million copies, and its title has entered the public idiom. In spite of what Peck says about resistance to spirituality, the less traveled road is clearly getting more traffic.

M. Scott Peck

Born in 1936, Scott Peck had a privileged upbringing in New York and went to exclusive prep schools and Harvard. He gained his MD at Case Western Reserve University in 1963, after which he began a nine-year service in the Army Medical Corps. Over the following decade he established his own psychiatric practice.

Though The Road Less Traveled was written in the mid-1970s, when Peck was 39, it did not make it on to the New York Times bestseller list until 1983. Thereafter it stayed on the list for so long that it entered the Guinness Book of Records. The sequel is Further Along the Road Less Traveled (1993).

Peck's other books include People of the Lie (1983) on healing human evil and The Different Drum (1987) on community life. A World Waiting to Be Born (1993) looks at the idea of civility at the personal and societal level, while Denial of the Soul (1998) concerns euthanasia and terminal illness.

As a chain-smoking martini drinker, the author does not fit the usual profile of the self-help guru and wrote of his sometimes turbulent private life. He died in 2005.

Awaken the Giant Within

1991

"Any time you sincerely want to make a change, the first thing you must do is raise your standards. When people ask me what really changed my life eight years ago, I tell them that absolutely the most important thing was changing what I demanded of myself. I wrote down all the things I would no longer accept in my life, all the things I would no longer tolerate, and all the things that I aspired to becoming."

"We don't have to allow the programming of our past to control our present and future. With this book, you can reinvent yourself by systematically organizing your beliefs and values in a way that pulls you in the direction of your life's design."

"Though we'd like to deny it, the fact remains that what drives our behavior is instinctive reaction to pain or pleasure, not intellectual calculation. Intellectually, we may believe that eating chocolate is bad for us, but we'll still reach for it. Why? Because we're not driven so much by what we intellectually know, but rather what we've linked pain and pleasure to in our nervous systems."

In a nutshell

It is time to seize the day and live the life you've imagined. This is your starter kit.

In a similar vein
Susan Jeffers, *Feel the Fear and Do It Anyway* (p200)

CHAPTER 44

Anthony Robbins

Anthony Robbins is the embodiment of the personal transformation guru. In the United States at least he is a household name
and it would be difficult not to have seen one of his television
infomercials there. He has personally coached presidents, royalty, top
sports stars, and corporate leaders, and has reached huge new audiences through a combination of legendary personal energy and marketing prowess. Other self-help titans like Deepak Chopra and Wayne
Dyer are low key in comparison. Lots of people are willing to pay over
$2,000 to attend a Robbins weekend seminar, which features walks
across hot coals and the hysteria normally seen at pop concerts or
evangelical meetings.

Awaken the Giant Within begins with Robbins in a jet helicopter on
his way to a sellout seminar. Below he spots the building where, a
decade before, he was working as a janitor, and remembers the Robbins of that period: overweight, broke, and lonely. Now svelte, happily
married, and a millionaire with a mansion by the sea, this is the
moment Robbins realizes that he is living his dream.

Such details are part of the enjoyment of *Awaken the Giant Within*
and Robbins knows that the best advertisement for his products is his
life itself. But let's go back to the beginning . . .

Robbins and NLP

Robbins's first book, written while still in his mid-20s, was *Unlimited
Power*. Itself a bestseller, this laid the groundwork for its successor,
revealing the source of many of Robbins' methods: neuro-linguistic
programming (NLP).

NLP was pioneered by John Grinder and Richard Bandler and arose
out of the study of how language, verbal and non-verbal, can affect the
nervous system. Its premise is that we can control our nervous system
so that our responses and actions, though seeming to be "natural," are

in fact programmed. Another key premise is that if we "model" the actions and behavior of successful people we can achieve at least the same results as they have.

Robbins's genius has been to refine and market NLP to a general audience. His catchphrase "Change happens in an instant," for example comes directly from NLP, as do his points about linking our motivations to pain or pleasure.

Some points from *Awaken the Giant Within*

The book gets the reader's imagination going by the questions it asks, the possibilities it creates in your mind. Robbins is the master of unlimitedness, yet is careful to provide the practical steps and details for goal achievement. The book is 500 pages long. The following list covers some of the themes, all are of which are backed up by copious references, stories, and facts.

Pain and pleasure

These are the key shaping forces in life. We can either let them control us or understand them to suit ourselves. Be careful what you link pleasure to: Some people equate pleasure with heroin, others with helping people. Do you want to be like Jimi Hendrix, minus the talent, or Mother Teresa? By linking massive pain or massive pleasure with an activity or thought, we change who we are.

The power of belief

Two men are chained to a wall in a prison. One commits suicide, the other goes on to tell people about the power of the human spirit. Rather than the events of our lives shaping us, it is our beliefs about what those events mean that do so. Global beliefs (how we see the world and people in general), if changed, can alter virtually everything about the rest of our lives. All great leaders create a sense of certainty, never believing that their problems are permanent. The CIA has techniques to change a person's core beliefs in a very short period. You can apply the same techniques to your own limiting beliefs.

The power of questions

All human progress occurs through questioning current limitations. We don't need to have an answer prepared; ask a quality question and you will get a quality answer.

The power of words

Use the power of words and enlarged vocabulary to transform thinking and action. Appreciate also that "leaders are readers"—reading allows us to make crucial distinctions based on others' experience.

Clarity is power

Determine exactly what you want to achieve and write it down, creating a future so amazing that you are compelled to realize it. You must "focus on where you want to go, not on what you fear." Create a ten-year plan then work backwards; most people overestimate what they can do in a year and underestimate what they can do in a decade.

Raise your standards, change your rules

Make decisions rather than wishes about what you are and take action. Figure out the hidden personal rules by which you currently live and create new ones that will drive you to live out your destiny.

A closer look . . .

Awaken the Giant Within is the popular bible of psycho-technology. Converts will feel that if everyone read and applied Robbins, the world would be a vastly more empowered, fulfilled, and happy place.

For some readers, however, Robbins' world may seem too black and white. It shows you how to get out of any sort of negative state, hygienically removing the bad mood, depression, and so on. Other self-help writers like Thomas Moore and Robert Bly see great value in depression and even grief. It teaches us about ourselves, they say, and is part of a soulful existence.

Awaken the Giant Within is subtitled "How to Take Immediate Control of Your Mental, Emotional, Physical, and Financial Destiny!" Can we really control our destiny? Are the goals that Robbins inspires

ANTHONY ROBBINS

people to dream up really unique to them? His own life might appear
to be living fantasy, but does this mean that all our desires should be
fulfilled too? The tools he provides to achieve anything we want are
indeed impressive, but there is no caveat about the reasons for wanting
them.

People can be turned off by the superman aura around the book and
its conviction that the fantasy we might have about ourselves can be
realized. To a critic, everything is about "achieving your goals." Eric
Fromm wrote about the "marketized individual," the person who ends
up as a mere reflection of the capitalist economy, pursuing self-
improvement only to the extent that it may bring higher status.

In Robbins' defense

To address these criticisms, it is true that some people may use
Robbins' mental technology to achieve banal materialistic ends, but
what he actually says challenges the very hold of materialism in our
lives. The core of his philosophy is defying the culture that surrounds
us by refusing to be just another mole, burrowing away at our job so
that we can keep in step. In his world, everyone should be amazing.
And the book does have us question our idea of success: Is it, Robbins
asks, a product of our deepest creativity and highest vision? His philoso
phy holds that pursuing a dream is the only way of keeping ourselves
truly alive, and money is always secondary to that.

What Robbins does is get people to "step over the edge," to change
their beliefs about themselves, identify their core values, move on from
jobs or relationships that do nothing for them, and reveal that their
limitations are largely illusory.

Final comments

The Robbins message has mass appeal because we all believe that there
is much more to us than others recognize. The world is fond of putting
our ideas in the "unreasonable, unrealistic" category. We are taught
that we can't do what our heart desires and after a while we accept it
as fact. But Robbins' truly successful person refuses to be reasonable.

Awaken the Giant Within has been called "plastic surgery for the
mind," meaning if you're not happy with your identity, change it.
Though that idea will sound far-fetched or even distasteful to one per-

270

son, the reassurance that it is possible can be a lifeline for another. Re-invention, let's not forget, is the very basis of American culture, and *Awaken the Giant Within* could not have surfaced in any other place. Look on it as a sort of Statue of Liberty in words.

Anthony Robbins

Born in 1960, Robbins grew up in a low-rent suburb of Los Angeles, but was thrown out of home by his mother at age 17 for being "too intense." He obtained a reputation as a super-salesman, selling tickets to other motivational speakers' events. Claiming to have read over 700 personal growth books, he came across NLP in 1983 and went on the road to promote his brand of it, promising to heal people of phobias in 15 minutes. He was a millionaire by age 24, lost his money, then regained it. These incidents and others are related in The Life Story of Anthony Robbins, *by former Robbins associate Michael Bolduc.*

Robbins is now America's best-known "peak performance consultant" and has worked with IBM, AT&T, American Express, and the US Army, as well as professional sports teams and Olympic athletes. He has been a private coach to Bill Clinton (who apparently relied on Robbins for support during the Monica Lewinsky crisis), Andre Agassi, Mikhail Gorbachev, and he even had some sessions with Princess Diana.

The Anthony Robbins companies run seminars and events around the world, including a "Mastery University." His Foundation runs programs to help youth, the elderly, the homeless, and people in prison. Robbins lives in California with his wife and children. In 2016, Tony Robbins: I Am Not Your Guru, *a feature documentary film directed by Joe Berlinger, was released.*

The Game of Life and How to Play It

1925

"Most people consider life a battle, but it is not a battle, it is a game."

"The superconscious mind is the God mind within each man, and is the realm of perfect ideas. In it, is the 'perfect pattern' spoken of by Plato, The Divine Design for each person."

"A person knowing the power of the word, becomes very careful in his conversation. He has only to watch the reaction of his words to know that they do not 'return void'. Through his spoken word, man is continually making laws for himself."

"God's plan for each man transcends the limitation of the reasoning mind, and is always the square of life, containing health, wealth, love and perfect self-expression. Many a man is building for himself in imagination a bungalow when he should be building a palace."

In a nutshell

If life is thought of as a game, we are motivated to learn and apply the rules for our own happiness.

In a similar vein

Deepak Chopra, *The Seven Spiritual Laws of Success* (p90)
Shakti Gawain, *Creative Visualization* (p174)
Joseph Murphy, *The Power of Your Subconscious Mind* (p248)

CHAPTER 45

Florence Scovell Shinn

Until now, you may have conceived of life as a battle—your might and will against the rest, or alternatively the pain of constant struggle.

However, if you were to see life as a *game*, you would worry less about the outcomes and focus on the rules and laws that can lead you to success. This is the path of less resistance and more time for world-wonder. By taking it, you choose to be a person of faith instead of fear.

For Florence Scovell Shinn, the rules were to be found in the Old and New Testaments. Much of what is presented in her 100-page classic, however, such as the Laws of Nonresistance, *Karma*, and Forgiveness, are to be found in eastern holy books, and indeed the stated goal of her work is universal: An individual can achieve the "square of life," the four points of Health, Wealth, Love, and Perfect Self-Expression, if only they can attune themselves with the unchanging principles that govern life. This total wellbeing was, she believed, our "divine right."

Some of the principles from the book are described below.

The divine design

Do you ever get an inspirational flash across your mind, a picture of what you could achieve or the person you could be? You have received a snapshot of your "divine design" from the universe, showing you that this image is actually within yourself. Plato called it the "perfect pattern," the place you are to fill that no one else can.

Don't be like most people and pursue things that really have nothing to do with the real you, and would only make you dissatisfied if you were to achieve them. Ask for a sign or a message to tell you what your divine design is and it will be revealed. Don't be scared that it won't be what you want—it will most probably fulfill your deepest longing.

Divine right and selection

We should only ever ask for something if it is to be "by divine right." A woman was infatuated with a man who from an outsider's perspective did not treat her very well. Scovell Shinn made her repeat to herself something to the effect of: "If he is divinely selected for me, he will be mine. If he is not, I will not want him anyway." Sure enough, she fell for someone else who matched all her ideals and promptly forgot the first man.

Another woman had a strong wish to live in a house owned by an acquaintance. This man died and she moved into the house, only to have her own husband die and the house become a white elephant for her. This was the karmic effect of a want that had not first been put before God, or infinite intelligence. It is good that we desire, but it is better that we seek what is ours "by divine right," for when it is received we will know beyond any doubt that it is ours.

Non-resistance

Playing the game of life successfully involves following what works, instead of battling what you don't like. The book contains this insight, which intuitively we can all recognize:

"So long as a man resists a situation, he will have it with him. If he runs away from it, it will run after him."

The simple change from a view of life in terms of struggle and fight for victory to a simple faith in good outcomes will transform your life.

You will get everything you want, and probably very quickly, if you don't doubt it and you can "wish without worrying," that is, you know that your wishes are being fulfilled. Fear is "sin," it goes against nature, whereas faith is real, solid, and is what infinite intelligence or God requires from us in return for delivering our wishes. Faith is what links you to the universe: It expands your cosmic footprint, while fear can only shrink you.

Continually send out messages of goodwill and blessing to those close to you, to your work colleagues, even to your nation. This not only gives you a feeling of great peace, but you will find yourself "protected" from harm and wrath.

Faith over fear

"Cast thy burden upon the Lord." Many times the Bible says that the battle is not humankind's but God's. What we must learn to do is "stand still" and let God, or the superconscious mind within, go to work. This bears a startling resemblance to the sayings of the *Tao Te Ching*, which suggests to us that if we are in tune with the *tao* (or God, or universal intelligence), we need not worry or fear. In stillness we can see what must be done, if anything.

In Scovell Shinn's world, "man violates law if he carries a burden." It is actually wrong to fret and be cast down, as this is living by a false reality and can attract disaster and disease. Once we have cast the burden off, however, we are suddenly able to see clearly again. We feel reminded that we must live by faith, not fear.

Real love

A woman came to Scovell Shinn in desperation that the man she loved had left her for other women, and said he had no intention of marrying her. She did not like it when Scovell Shinn said to her, "You are not loving this man, you are hating him. Perfect yourself on this man, give him unselfish love, and bless him wherever he is." The woman went away and nothing changed, but one day she started thinking of him with more love. He was a captain and she always called him "the Cap." She began to say, "God bless the Cap wherever he is." Some time later a letter arrived on Scovell Shinn's desk: At the moment when the woman's suffering had ceased, the man returned. The two were then very happily married.

What the woman had learned was selfless love, a trait that all of us must acquire if we are to succeed in the game of life.

The power of words

Anyone who does not know the power of words, the author said, "is behind the times." Each of us has an ongoing conversation with ourselves, never realizing how it affects, for better or worse, the way we live out our life. Whatever words we say to ourselves fall into the blank slate of our subconscious mind as "fact," therefore we must take supreme care about the internal and external words we utter.

The people who came to see Scovell Shinn asked her to "speak the word." She gave them an affirmation for their particular situation that they were to repeat until their "good" manifested itself. She quoted Proverbs 18.21: "Death and Life are in the power of the tongue."

"God is my supply"
Many of Scovell Shinn's clients came to her in desperation—one needed $3,000 by the first of the month to repay a debt, another had to find an apartment soon or would be on the streets. She would remind them that "God is my supply," to stop worrying and fretting.

She made them affirm: "Spirit is never too late. I give thanks that I have received the money on the invisible plain and that it manifests on time." One woman had only a day to go until a payment was due, and a cousin happened to visit her who asked, as he was leaving, "By the way, how are your finances?" Her payment was made the next day.

Nevertheless, it is not enough merely to say the right words and have faith: We need to demonstrate to our subconscious mind that we seriously expect to receive. "Man must prepare for the thing he has asked for, when there isn't the slightest sign of it in sight." Open the bank account, buy the furniture, prepare for rain when there is no cloud in sight—"acting as if" opens the way for the moment of gain. The knowledge that "a feeling of opulence must precede its manifestation" will reinforce to you that God is your supply.

Final comments
Although written in the New York of the 1920s and full of religious references, this shortish book now has cult status. The anecdotes may be of people now long gone but the wisdom is timeless, and the book can have a soothing effect that brings us back to the right principles. To borrow one of the author's phrases, the book "salutes the divinity" in us and has the knack of restoring a sense of direction and confidence. If you are willing to keep an open mind as you read it, its insights and affirmations can have great effects.

Florence Scovell Shinn

Born in 1871, Scovell Shinn was by profession an artist and book illus-trator, and also taught metaphysics in New York for many years. She was married to the artist Everett Shinn, but they divorced in 1912.

Her down-to-earth style and humor endeared her to many people who might not otherwise have listened to spiritual advice. She wrote a number of books, but The Game of Life *was her classic work. She died in 1940.*

Learned Optimism

1991

"The traditional view of achievement, like the traditional view of depression, needs overhauling. Our workplaces and our schools operate on the conventional assumption that success results from a combination of talent and desire. When failure occurs, it is because either talent or desire is missing. But failure can also occur when talent and desire are present in abundance but optimism is missing."

"The commonness of being knocked flat by troubles, however, does not mean it is acceptable or that life has to be this way. If you use a different explanatory style, you'll be better equipped to cope with troubled times and keep them from propelling you towards depression."

"What we want is not blind optimism but flexible optimism—optimism with its eyes open. We must be able to use pessimism's keen sense of reality when we need it, but without having to dwell in its dark shadows."

In a nutshell

Cultivation of an optimistic mindset significantly increases your chances of health, wealth, and happiness.

In a similar vein
David D. Burns, *Feeling Good* (p66)
Mihaly Csikszentmihalyi, *Flow* (p116)
Daniel Goleman, *Emotional Intelligence* (p178)

CHAPTER 46

Martin Seligman

Martin Seligman is a cognitive psychologist who spent many years clinically testing the idea of "learned helplessness." His experiments giving mild electric shocks to dogs proved that dogs would give up trying to escape if they believed that, whatever they did, the shocks would keep coming. Another researcher tested the principle on people, using noise instead of shocks, and found that learned helplessness can be engineered in human minds just as easily. Yet the experiments contained an anomaly: As with the dog experiments, one in every three human subjects would not "give up," they kept trying to press buttons on a panel in an attempt to shut off the noise. What made these subjects different from the others?

Seligman applied the question to real life: What makes someone pick themselves up after rejection by a lover, or another keep going when their life's work comes to nothing? He found that the ability of some people to bounce back from apparent defeat is not, as we sentimentally like to say, a "triumph of the human will." Rather than having an inborn trait of greatness, such people have developed a way of explaining events that does not see defeat as permanent or affecting their basic values. Nor is this trait something that "we either have or we don't"— optimism involves a set of skills that can be learned.

Positive explanatory style

Pessimistic people tend to think that misfortune is their fault. The cause of their specific misfortune or general misery is, they believe, permanent—stupidity, lack of talent, ugliness—therefore they do not bother to change it. Few of us are wholly pessimistic, but most of us will have given pessimism free reign in reaction to particular past events. In psychology textbooks, such reactions are considered "normal." But Seligman says that it does not have to be this way, that a different way of explaining setbacks to yourself ("explanatory style") will protect you from letting crises cast you into depression. If you have even an average level of pessimism, Seligman says, it will drag down your success in every arena of life: work, relationships, health.

The author undertook groundbreaking work for life insurance company MetLife. Life insurance is considered one of the most difficult of all sales jobs, a real spirit crusher. The company was spending millions of dollars a year training its agents, only to see most of them move on. Instead of the usual criteria by which MetLife hired (career background and so on), Seligman suggested that applicants be hired if they tested well for optimism and explanatory style. The result: Agents hired on this basis did 20 percent better than the regular recruits in the first year, and 57 percent better in the second. They clearly had better ways to deal with the nine out of ten rejections that would make the others give up.

Optimism and success

Conventional thinking is that success creates optimism, but the evidence laid out by Seligman shows the reverse to be true. On a repeat basis optimism tends to deliver success, as the experience of the life insurance agents demonstrated. At the exact same point that a pessimist will wilt, an optimist perseveres and breaks through an invisible barrier.

Not getting through this barrier is often misinterpreted as laziness or lack of talent. Seligman found that people who give up easily never dispute their own interpretation of failure or disparagement. Those who regularly "vault the wall" listen to their internal dialog and argue against their own limiting thoughts, quickly finding positive reasons for rejection.

The value of pessimism

Yet *Learned Optimism* admits that there is one area in which pessimists excel: their ability to see a situation more accurately. Some professions (financial control and accounting or safety engineering, for example) and all firms could do with a few bring-us-down-to-earth pessimists. In *Business @ the Speed of Thought* (1999) Bill Gates discusses this very trait, lauding the Microsoft employees who can tell him what is going wrong and do so quickly.

Nevertheless, let's not forget that Gates is also a dreamer *par excellence*, who at a very young age imagined a world in which every home and office would be using his Windows software. Seligman is clear on the point that success in work and life results when we can both perceive present reality accurately and visualize a compelling future. Many people are good at one and not the other. Someone who wishes to learn optimism must keep the former skill, while becoming a better dreamer. The combination is unbeatable.

Most depression results from thinking badly

It is slightly ironic that *Learned Optimism* draws much of its data from studies of depression. Before cognitive therapy, depression was always thought of being either "anger turned in upon itself" (Freud) or a chemical malfunction in the brain. However, pioneering cognitive researchers Albert Ellis and Aaron T. Beck (see *Feeling Good*) set out to prove that negative thoughts are not a symptom of depression, they cause it. Most of us know this at a common-sense level, but psychotherapy allows us to believe that we are dealing with something beyond our control.

Seligman is a leading authority on sex differences in depression. He says that women are twice as likely to suffer from it because, although men and women experience mild depression at the same rate, how women think about problems tends to amplify them. Rumination on a problem, always connecting it back to some "unchangeable" aspect of ourselves, is a recipe for the blues. Millions of dollars have been spent by America's National Institute of Mental Health to test this idea that depression (i.e., the standard variety, not bipolar or manic) results from habits of thought. Seligman tells us the results in two words: "It does." Moreover, developing the mental muscles of optimism significantly reduces the likelihood that we will become depressed.

Habitual optimism

This brings us to a bigger question: Why is there so much depression around? Seligman argues that our recent preoccupation with individualism creates its own form of mental shackles. If we are invited to believe in our own endless possibilities, any form of failure becomes devastating. Combine this with the crumbling of previously solid psychological supports—the nation, God, the extended family—and we have an epidemic of depression.

However, while drugs like Prozac can be effective in eliminating it, there is a gap between successfully treated depression and habitual optimism. With the positive explanatory style that Seligman recommends problems are seen as temporary, specific, and external, rather than inevitable expressions of our failure as a person. Cognitive therapy changes the basic way a person sees the world and that altered perception tends to be permanent.

Final comments

Learned Optimism is a product of the sea change that occurred in psychology in the mid-1960s. Until then, a person's behavior was considered to be either "pushed" by internal urges (Freudianism) or "pulled" by the rewards or punishments that society provided (behaviorism).

Cognitive therapy, in contrast, showed that people could actually change the way they think, in spite of unconscious leanings or societal conditioning. As Seligman notes toward the end of the book, the upheavals of the modern era, such as mass migration, made rapid personal change necessary; now it is desirable. Yet we are a culture of self-improvers because we know self-improvement is possible—not just experience but psychological science proves it.

Learned Optimism is an important work within the self-help field because it provides a scientific foundation for many claims. It became a bestseller because it attracted readers who normally would consider personal development ideas as, to use the author's phrase, "metaphysical boosterism." The book is therefore not simply about optimism (though it may well turn you into an optimist) but about the validity of personal change itself and the dynamic nature of the human condition. Seligman's later work, *Authentic Happiness*, incorporates many of the findings and ideas of *Learned Optimism* but takes the idea of "positive psychology" further. It is highly recommended.

Martin Seligman

Born in 1942, Seligman was raised in Albany, New York. As an under-graduate he majored in modern philosophy at Princeton, then psychology. Licensed as a psychologist in Pennsylvania in 1973, for 14 years he directed the clinical training program of the University of Pennsylvania psychology department.

Apart from Learned Optimism, *other works are* What You Can Change . . . and What You Can't *(1994),* The Optimistic Child *(with Reivich, Jaycox, & Gillham, 1995), and* Flourish: A Visionary New Understanding of Happiness and Well-Being *(2011). More scholarly works include* Helplessness *(1975) and* Abnormal Psychology *(1982).*

He is a former President of the American Psychological Association, from which he has received two awards for Distinguished Scientific Contribution. He is currently Kogod Professor of Psychology at the University of Pennsylvania and is at the forefront of the "positive psychology" movement.

Self-Help

1859

"Thus the brave and aspiring life of one man lights a flame in the minds of others of like faculties and impulse; and where there is equally vigorous effort, like distinction and success will almost surely follow. Thus the chain of example is carried down through time in an endless succession of links—admiration exciting imitation, and perpetuating the true aristocracy of genius."

"There are many counterfeits of character, but the genuine article is difficult to be mistaken. Some, knowing its money value, would assume its disguise for the purpose of imposing among the unwary. Colonel Charteris said to a man distinguished for his honesty, 'I would give a thousand pounds for your good name.' 'Why?' 'Because I could make ten thousand by it,' was the knave's reply."

"No laws, however stringent, can make the idle industrious, the thriftless provident, or the drunken sober. Such reforms can only be effected by means of individual action, economy and self-denial; by better habits, rather than by greater rights."

In a nutshell

History is full of people who achieved amazing things by sheer will and persistence.

In a similar vein
Stephen Covey, *The 7 Habits of Highly Effective People* (p110)
Benjamin Franklin, *Autobiography* (p168)

284

CHAPTER 47

Samuel Smiles

*S*elf-Help was published the same year as Darwin's *Origin of the Species* and John Stuart Mill's *On Liberty*. While Darwin drew a picture of how closer adaptation to environment refines life and Mill sketched a society based on liberty, Smiles gave the world a work that still inspires in its scenes of individuals who have fashioned a life from pure will. *Self-Help* may not have the scholarly or philosophical depth of the other two, but it was seminal to the self-help genre and its ethos of personal responsibility.

In many Victorian homes the book had a status second only to the Bible and though it is now considered a classic display of Victorian values (industry, thrift, progress, and so on), the old-fashioned turns of phrase and unquestioning morality represent the cover by which we should not judge the book. It is a work within a broader literary tradition that includes Benjamin Franklin's *Autobiography* and the novels of Horatio Alger, one in which human beings advance despite the odds. The self-help ethic comes alive through biography. Smiles knew this and he packed his book with remarkable people, many now forgotten. He mentions:

❖ Sir William Herschel (1738–1822), who while working as an oboist in a traveling orchestra became curious about astronomy. He built his own reflecting telescope, discovered Uranus and other celestial bodies, and became astronomer to the King of England.
❖ Bernard Palissy (c.1510–89), a poor potter who threw his own furniture and fence palings into a furnace in order to create his famous enamelware, such tenacity eventually being rewarded by the position as potter to the French throne.
❖ Granville Sharp (1735–1813), a clerk who in his spare time began the anti-slavery movement in England, eventually getting the law changed to ensure that any slave setting foot in the country would be freed.

SAMUEL SMILES

Yet these lives are paraded before us not merely so that we can marvel, but to give some idea of the vast range of possible models for our own life. Smiles sorted these lives according to how they illuminate the great qualities like tenacity, industry, and endurance; they form the chapters of the book.

Hard work and genius

Smiles believed that, since it was about human nature, *Self-Help* would remain valid. However, to accept that you would have to believe that perseverance and unremitting work are still primary elements of success—are they?

The myth of the artist is a person of wild genius who produces masterpieces in creative bursts, while the common denominator in Smiles' "lives of the artists" is their singular industry and never-say-die application to the task, almost equal to their artistic talent. In showing that many of the methods they pioneered were the result of years of trial and error, he explodes the belief that the most famous artists have the most "talent." In fact talent is not thinly spread; what is rare is the willingness to put in the back-breaking labor to fulfill an artistic vision. Michelangelo would not have painted the Sistine Chapel ceiling if he had not been willing to lie on his back on boards for months on end. It took Titian seven years to produce his *Last Supper* for Charles V, yet the viewer might assume that it was created in a "burst of genius."

Smiles noted the motto of both painter Sir Joshua Reynolds and sculptor David Wilkie: "Work! Work! Work!" Johann Sebastian Bach reflected: "I was industrious; whoever is equally sedulous, will be equally successful." History has a tendency to turn unwavering commitment and hard graft into grand words like genius, when its subjects knew otherwise. Smiles wrote:

> *"It is not eminent talent that is required to ensure success in any pursuit, so much as purpose—not merely the power to achieve, but the will to labour energetically and perseveringly. Hence energy of will may be defined to be the very central power of character in a man—in a word, it is the Man himself."*

He told us about George-Louis Buffon (1707–88), author of the famous 44-volume *Histoire Naturelle*, which took stock of all that was known about natural history in his era and foreshadowed the theory of evolution. The massive self-discipline needed to complete such a project led Buffon to conclude that "genius is patience." Smiles went on to quote De Maistre: "To know how to wait is the great secret of success." He also noted Isaac Newton's understanding of what produced genius: constant thought about the solution of a problem.

Patience, ordering of the mind, and absorption in the task at hand are the key elements that Smiles cited in all our great advances, and neither government funding nor education can supply them. They are created talents.

Character

These days the phrase "character building" is usually uttered with a laugh to someone contemplating a cold shower or doing a 10-day trek across the Himalayas. As Smiles warned even back in the 1850s, education, wealth, or noble family does not come close to replacing character. Today we live in the so-called knowledge society in which the highest value is taken to be creative deployment of data and information, but Smiles asserted that "Character is power, more than knowledge is power."

Self-Help may be a simple book for a simpler time, but its dogged reiteration of the need to cultivate personal qualities that bring freedom of mind reveals a timeless truth: Character is something formed in spite of the great forces of instinct and cultural conditioning. Smiles included a statement by Sir Humphry Davy: "What I am I have made myself: I say this without vanity, and in pure simplicity of heart." Davy's admission spoke of courage, not as part of exciting tales of derring-do but of small daily decisions that reaffirm independence. This is the primary ingredient of Stephen Covey's "highly effective people."

But where will character get me? How will it make my living? In the nineteenth century, business was not seen as it tends to be now, as the arena for the brightest, most creative minds, yet Smiles was able to see that it would become so. He wasted no time in stripping business to its core element: integrity of word and deed. Since trust is the glue that holds free societies together, it follows that lasting success will be attracted to those who can be trusted. As Max Weber famously argued, this attribute had been so rare that early Protestant merchants, in their utter dependability, scooped up fortunes.

Nothing dulls the mind and destroys character as much as drugs and alcohol, and Smiles did not miss a chance to praise that most esteemed quality, temperance. How we laugh in the old movies when the preacher rails against the "road to ruin." It is the fevered fear of alcohol that amuses, because we are "sensible" about it. But who will admit its less dramatic consequences that add up over a lifetime: the things you don't get done the next day because of the night before, the drinking "to be social" that does little more than cover an acceptance of mediocrity. Smiles thought of Sir Walter Scott, who said, "Of all vices, drinking is the most incompatible with greatness."

Final comments

In Samuel Smiles' lifetime the British Empire covered roughly a quarter of the planet. Like any empire it spawned its fair share of misery among those forced into keeping the whole show going. Its good qualities—social reform, some enlightened political principles, sheer energy, and inventiveness—were held together by a larger belief in "progress."

One effect of Mill's *On Liberty* was to make us see such values in relative terms. By being a missive against political oppression, it also unwittingly beat a path for socialism, which raised the ideal of community to such a level that individuals were protected from having to push their own boundaries. Yet Smiles reminded us that Mill actually said, "The worth of the state, in the long run, is the worth of the individuals composing it."

If the progress ideal makes a comeback in the twenty-first century, it is less likely to be the property of governments than the faith of individuals. While Mill's principle of political liberty is the basic condition for personal progress, it is the ethos of *Self-Help* that can actually make us do something with our freedom. Interestingly, Smiles was in his earlier life a rabid political reformer, but gave this up when he realized that the more pressing type of reform was personal.

Self-Help is monumentally sexist, there being a total lack of women in the biographies. Its small defense is that it was developed from talks given to working men, who at that time would probably not have stomached female role models. With some more stories of women in the book it would perhaps be less obscure today, but any reader who can laugh off or forgive Smiles' oversight will be well rewarded. This *Titanic* of the self-help literature deserves to rise again.

Samuel Smiles

The eldest of 11 children, Smiles was born in 1812 in Haddington, Scotland, the son of a paper maker. At 14 he left school and worked for three years before enrolling at Edinburgh University to study medicine. After some time as a doctor, his interests soon shifted to politics, leading to his becoming editor in 1838 of the radical Leeds Times, *where he stayed until 1842. Influenced by the utilitarians Jeremy Bentham and James Mill (John Stuart's father), his causes included freer trade, extension of suffrage, and better conditions for factory workers.*

Smiles became disillusioned with political reform and increasingly advocated personal development, and in the same year that he began a career as a railway administrator gave the course of lectures that would later be molded into Self-Help. *Translated into many languages, it was one of a handful of English titles circulating in Japan after the Meiji restoration, becoming a bible for western-inspired businessmen. The millionaire industrialist Lord Leverhume and the American writer and founder of* Success *magazine Orison Swett Marden were among many who said that they owed their achievements to* Self-Help.

Other works by Smiles include a biography of railway pioneer George Stephenson (1857), the three-volume economic history text Lives of the Engineers *(1874), the books* Character *(1871),* Thrift *(1875), and* Duty *(1880), and a life of potter Josiah Wedgwood (1894). An autobiography was published after his death in 1904.*

The Phenomenon of Man

1955

"Modern man no longer knows what to do with the potentialities he has unleashed . . . Sometimes we are tempted to trample this super-abundance back into the matter from which it sprang without stopping to think how monstrous such an act against nature would be."

"We have said that life, by its very structure, having once been lifted to its stage of thought, cannot go on at all without requiring to ascend even higher. This is enough for us to be assured of the two points of which our action has immediate need. The first is that there is for us, in the future, under some form or other, at least collective, not only sur-vival but super-life. The second is that, to imagine, discover and reach this superior form of existence, we have only to think and to walk always further in the direction in which the lines passed by evolution take on their maximum coherence."

"In such a vision man is seen not as a static center of the world—as he for long believed himself to be—as the axis and leading shoot of evolu-tion, which is something much finer."

In a nutshell

By appreciating and expressing your uniqueness, you literally enable the evolution of the world.

In a similar vein
Abraham Maslow, *Motivation and Personality* (p236)

CHAPTER 48

Pierre Teilhard de Chardin

Pierre Teilhard de Chardin wrote the final words of *The Phenomenon of Man* in 1938, but it was not to break on the world until after his death 17 years later. As well as being a famous paleontologist, Teilhard was a Jesuit priest and the Church believed that he went beyond orthodoxy in his philosophical writings; their publication was consistently disallowed. Anyone else might have left the priesthood or at least become embittered, but Teilhard did neither. Perhaps strangely for such a liberated mind, he kept to his vow of obedience.

The effect of his isolation, intellectual and physical (he was "banished" to China to pursue scientific work), was a fermentation of thoughts that are incredibly free-ranging and radical, and some of his ideas are only just beginning to make sense. The worth of visionaries is only proved by the passage of time, but as we enter the twenty-first century there can be few people who provide us with a more compelling vision of the human race.

The Phenomenon of Man is not a self-help book in any conventional sense and many readers will find it too "Christian," but its influence on writers in the human potential and personal development fields is significant. Although abstract, its ideas about mental and spiritual evolution are enjoying a renaissance because they tie in perfectly with the questions that many of us are beginning to ask about ourselves and how we might fit into the larger scheme of things.

The evolution of us

Teilhard's evolutionary theory was about the mind as well as the physical world. He believed it was not enough for us to have worked out that we evolved from the apes—our task was to reach the point where we knew *why* we had evolved. Today's evolutionary biologists have ample evidence that the human brain has not changed in thousands of years, but merely because we have the same brain structure does not mean that we are the same beings. Teilhard believed that when humankind began living in the state of reflectiveness, our progress was inevitable; we would enjoy "not only survival, but super-life."

Teilhard was perhaps uniquely suited to the task of applying evolutionary science to the bigger questions of human destiny. Regular scientists were afraid to speculate, and not many men of the cloth had his scientific background and sheer intellect. As a paleontologist and anthropologist, Teilhard was intent on discovering the origins of man, but it seemed obvious to him that the more we know of the past, the further we could look into the future.

Humankind as phenomenon

Although he saw *The Phenomenon of Man* as a scientific treatise, he was impatient with overspecialization and took the paradoxical position that science could only come of age when it went beyond seeing man only in terms of the physical body:

"The true physics is that which will, one day, achieve the inclusion of man in his wholeness in a coherent picture of the world."

Teilhard's human being was a phenomenon that had yet to be properly explained either in the sciences or the humanities, and the quests, achievements, and events of human history had to be looked on as one whole movement. We are now so used to the word "humankind" that it has almost ceased to be an idea, yet it is a very young concept, based on the recognition of unity, despite all the wars, division of territories, and cultural differentiation.

For Teilhard humankind was not the center of the world, but the "axis and leading shoot of evolution." It is not that we will lift ourselves above nature, but in our intellectual and spiritual quests dramatically raise its complexity and intelligence. The more complex and intelligent we become, the less of a hold the physical universe has on us. Just as space, the stars, and galaxies expand ever outwards, the universe is just as naturally undergoing "involution" from the simple to the increasingly complex; the human psyche also develops according to this law. "Hominization" is what Teilhard called the process of humanity becoming more human, or the fulfillment of its potential.

Personality = evolution

Though he delved into the physics of the cosmos and the subterranea of the earth, Teilhard always came back to the human personality. In an address to UNESCO in 1947, discussing the possibility of a new Declaration of the Rights of Man, he urged provision not for the autonomy of individuals, but for "the incommunicable singularity of being which each of us possesses." This sounds lofty, but means that the human race is never going to progress by people seeking to transcend it, or through individualism, but rather that we will move forward as a race by making room for everyone to express their personalities to the full.

As humankind becomes more technologically advanced, it also becomes more interested in the spiritual dimension (Teilhard called this "interiorization"). Yet evolution does not work impersonally and at an even speed; it happens by leaps, and it always comes back to *someone*.

The noosphere and Omega point

In 1925 Teilhard coined the word "noosphere." Just as the biosphere is the living shell around planet Earth, the noosphere is its mental counterpart, an invisible layer of thought around the earth that is the sum total of humankind's mental and spiritual states, all culture, love, and knowledge. He foresaw that each person would eventually need the resources of the whole planet to nourish them both materially and psychologically. It would work the other way as well, for the influence of each person would defy time and space, when once their impact would have been restricted to their physical locality. As the world shrunk, we would cover it with our thoughts and relationships.

The noosphere concept has clearly come of age in the networked society. It has had a huge influence on computer and internet theorists, who recognize that Teilhard saw the internet 50 years before it happened. The concept also preceded James Lovelock's "Gaia" concept, by which we understand the planet as one living organism.

Teilhard said that as humanity became more self-reflective, able to appreciate its place within space and time, its evolution would actually start to move by great leaps instead of a slow climb. In place of the glacial pace of physical natural selection, there would be a super-charged refinement of ideas that would eventually free us of physicality altogether. We would move irresistibly toward a new type of existence, at which all potential would be reached. Teilhard called this the "omega point."

Final comments

The Phenomenon of Man is not an easy book to read. Some of the language may be impenetrable, but let's remember that Teilhard never had a proper audience to test his ideas and give feedback. (Those wanting bite-sized essays may prefer *The Future of Man* or *Le Milieu Divin*.) This is nevertheless his most important and well-known book, and its influence only seems to grow.

Teilhard's idea of super-life may seem like a castle in the air, but he was of the view that a truth seen by only one person was still a truth, and would eventually be accepted by all. Though his book was a best-seller after his death, the terrible realities of life in the twentieth century naturally and understandably undermined the idea that we were steadily moving toward some marvelous omega point in our destiny. Spiritual progress and intellectual advancement can nevertheless exist simultaneously with evil, and Teilhard in fact saw things like totalitarianism as a natural part of social evolution, which would be superseded by better forms of organization and community.

The Phenomenon of Man is a self-help book of the highest order. Its author supplied a set of ideas that can lift us beyond the place and time of our individual lives. By thinking big about the whole race, we can face our personal task with greater clarity and force. It is a cliché for people to say when gazing up at the cosmos, "You realize how insignificant you are." This is a sentiment that Teilhard would not have shared. In his philosophy, every soul has a vital role to play in the evolution of the world and, aware of the humility of Teilhard himself, we know that this does not have to mean having a big ego. Rather, it requires a person's utmost expression of their personality and abilities.

Pierre Teilhard de Chardin

Born in 1881 in the Auvergne region of France, Teilhard was fourth in a family of eleven. He became a boarder at a Jesuit college and at age 18 entered the Jesuit order for six years. At 24 he was sent to teach physics and chemistry at a college in Cairo, where he stayed for three years, followed by four years of theological study in Sussex, England. During this time Teilhard became a competent geologist and paleontologist, and was finally ordained as a priest in 1912. His return to Paris to pursue geological studies at the Museum of Natural History was thwarted by the outbreak of the First World War. He became a stretcher bearer, receiving a Military Medal and the Legion of Honor.

After completing a doctorate at the Sorbonne, in 1923 Teilhard went to China for a year on behalf of the Museum of Natural History. He was to spend 20 years there from 1926, virtually exiled by the church for his teachings on original sin and evolution. He made significant contributions to the paleontological and geological knowledge of China, and was in the group that found Peking Man.

He was allowed back to Paris just after the war, enjoying its intellectual life until a heart attack in 1947 brought a forced convalescence in the country. Teilhard's pile of writings was left with a friend to be published after his death.

Walden

1854

"*I went to the woods because I wished to live deliberately, to front only the essential facts of life, and see if I could not learn what it had to teach, and not, when I came to die, discover that I had not lived.*"

"*It is something to be able to paint a particular picture, or to carve a statue, and so to make a few objects beautiful; but it is far more glorious to carve and paint the very atmosphere and medium through which we look, which morally we can do. To affect the quality of the day, that is the highest of arts.*"

"*If you have built castles in the air, your work need not be lost; that is where they should be. Now put the foundations under them.*"

"*When we are unhurried and wise, we perceive that only great and worthy things have any permanent and absolute existence—that petty fears and petty pleasures are but the shadow of the reality. This is always exhilirating and sublime.*"

In a nutshell

Make sure that you have time in your life just to think.

In a similar vein
Ralph Waldo Emerson, *Self-Reliance* (p150)
Thomas Moore, *Care of the Soul* (p242)

CHAPTER 49

Henry David Thoreau

Though about an actual experience—two years in a log cabin in the woods—Thoreau's *Walden* is now usually read as a journal of personal freedom and awareness. It is a treasure on both levels. Thoreau walked into the woods on July 4th, 1845. They did not take long to reach, being only a couple of miles from the center of Concord, Massachusetts, where he had lived most of his life. Yet solitude could still be had and Thoreau wanted to strip life to its core, away from the lies and gossip of society. After building a 10 by 15 foot cabin, his time was pretty much free. He did grow some beans to sell at market, but even this he enjoyed, continuing with it only as long as necessary to cover some very modest costs. An idyllic life ensued, of walks, reading, watching birds, writing, and simply being.

The *Walden* life and attitude

This is a concept so foreign to most people, then as now, that it seems either a waste of time or subversive. Yet Thoreau felt that he was richer than anyone he knew, having everything he materially needed and the time to enjoy it. The average person, with all their things, had continually to labor to afford them, meanwhile neglecting nature's beauty and the gentle work of the soul, which solitude brings.

Thoreau lived in the time of slavery. He once spent a night in jail for not paying his taxes to the government that maintained it. But his objection was not merely to the slavery of the negro, but to the slavery of all people. As Michael Meyer noted in *Walden and Civil Disobedience*, *Walden* could be seen as an emancipation narrative, the chronicle of an escape from delusion. For Thoreau, the metaphorical Deep South was two miles away; Concord, though it contained friends and family, was a sort of prison that people did not know they were in, enslaved by materialism and conformity. Thoreau famously declared to his blank page, "The mass of men lead lives of quiet desperation."

His time by Walden Pond was a conscious exercise in what modern self-development would call "de-scripting." He wanted to recover the total freedom of mind that was his at birth but that he suspected (despite his education) had been warped by "conventional wisdom" and the prejudices of his upbringing. He withdrew in order to stop himself being a social reflection, to realize what being a free individual meant. Discussing the great explorers of the day, he mused over John Franklin, the Englishman who was lost on an expedition, and Grinnell, the American who went looking for him:

"Is Franklin the only man lost, that his wife should be so earnest to find him? Does Mr Grinnell know himself where he himself is? Be rather the Mungo Park, the Lewis and Clarke and Frobisher, of your own streams and oceans; explore your own higher latitudes."

The impact of *Walden*

With his friend Ralph Waldo Emerson, Thoreau now stands as a pillar of what might be called the ethic of American individualism. The irony of this is that they both railed against so much of what the United States and other western countries have arguably become: rich consumer playgrounds shadowed by a lack of personal meaning. Yet *Walden*, and the writings of Emerson that so influenced it, is as attractive as ever to those seeking something more. Many of the thoughts and ideas in it have entered the public consciousness, and it has been one of the key inspirations for the modern generation of personal development writers. For example, among the descriptions of nature and people we find:

"If one advances confidently in the direction of his own dreams, and endeavors to live the life which he has imagined, he will meet with a success unexpected in common hours."

And:

"I know of no more encouraging fact than the unquestionable ability of man to elevate his life by a conscious endeavor."

And this, which could have been written by Norman Vincent Peale or Deepak Chopra:

"The universe constantly and obediently answers to our conceptions; whether we travel fast or slow, the track is laid for us. Let us spend our lives in conceiving then."

Walden was also ahead of its time in environmental sensibility. It roughly follows the sequence of the seasons. Thoreau enjoyed the winter (having built himself a fireplace and chimney) but particularly looked forward to the power and grace of spring's renewal. Nature was worth saving for its own sake, but few things were more instructive to the examined life than the trees, the water, and the creatures. In one classic confession he remarked, "A match has been found for me at last: I have fallen in love with a shrub oak."

In some of the more poetic lines, Thoreau conveyed a feeling of oneness with his environment:

"This is a delicious evening, when the whole body is in one sense, and imbibes delight through every pore. I go and come with a strange liberty in Nature, a part of herself."

Yet what the author saw in nature is never long left unrelated to what he saw in us:

"I should be glad if all the meadows of the earth were left in a wild state, if that were the consequence of men's beginning to redeem themselves."

Progress and prosperity

A railroad passed by the other end of Walden Pond and its busy comings and goings amused and fascinated Thoreau. Technological progress reflected the nation's glory—or did it?

"Men think that it is essential that the Nation have commerce, and export ice, and talk through a telegraph, and ride thirty miles an hour . . . but whether we should live like baboons or like men, is a little uncertain."

This poke against the obsession with innovation and newness is also spot on for today's culture.

It comes as no surprise that Thoreau dismissed the Benjamin Franklin style of up-by-the-bootstraps hard-work heroism. Social standing was unimportant and prosperity was less something to be achieved than to be witnessed in the bounty of nature. Thoreau did not "do much" in his 20s. Work was only necessary to buy time to read, write, and enjoy nature.

However, this does not mean that we have to go and live in a hut and sow beans. Thoreau's woods are symbolic of the abundance of nature generally, which provides everything when we make the decision to act true to ourselves. By staying in the "village" of our minds, fearing what the next person will say about us, we will only see evidence of lack, pettiness, and limited horizons. His oft-quoted lines on staying unique are:

"If a man does not keep pace with his companions, perhaps it is because he hears a different drummer. Let him step to the music he hears, however measured or far away."

Final comments

Walden is the collective musings of a free spirit, deeply knowledgeable about the classics, eastern religion, Native American lore, and nature itself, sketched out against a background of great physical beauty and stillness. What better vacation for the reader's mind? The book invites you to become Thoreau's companion, enjoying the woods and Walden Pond as he does, and delighting in his commentary on people and society.

Near the end of *Walden* there is the story of a beetle that emerged from an old table, resurrected after a 60-year hibernation, thanks to the heat of an urn placed on it. The story sums up Thoreau's philosophy, in that he felt that all of us have the potential to emerge from the "well-seasoned tomb" of society, like the beetle, to enjoy the summer of life.

Henry David Thoreau

Thoreau was born in Concord, Massachusetts, in 1817. After graduating from Harvard in 1837 he took a position as a schoolteacher, but objected to the required use of corporal punishment so went to work in his father's business manufacturing lead pencils. He began his serious attention to the natural world in 1839 with a voyage down the Concord and Merrimack Rivers, related in a book published ten years later. Thoreau spent two years (1841–3) as a member of Emerson's household, and was much loved by the latter's children.

Walden Pond was on land owned by Emerson. In the years following the experience, Thoreau worked as a land surveyor, whitewasher, and gardener, as well as lecturing and writing for magazines, including the transcendentalist journal Dial. *In 1849 he wrote "Civil Disobedience," an essay provoked by opposition to the Mexican war that was to influence Martin Luther King and Gandhi. The essay "Slavery in Massachusetts" was published in 1854, the same year as* Walden. *Cape Cod (1865) and* A Yankee in Canada *(1866) followed his death in 1862. Emerson's essay "Thoreau" marvels at his friend's phenomenal knowledge of nature and practical skills.*

A Return to Love

1994

"A certain amount of desperation is usually necessary before we're ready for God. When it came to spiritual surrender, I didn't get serious, not really, until I was down on my knees completely. The mess got so thick that all the king's horses and all the king's men couldn't make Marianne function again. The hysterical woman inside me was in a maniacal rage, and the innocent child was pinned to the wall. I fell apart."

"Love taken seriously is a radical outlook, a major departure from the psychological orientation that rules the world. It is threatening not because it is a small idea, but because it is so huge."

"Relationships are assignments. They are part of a vast plan for our enlightenment, the Holy Spirit's blueprint by which each individual soul is led to greater awareness and expanded love."

In a nutshell

Miracles start to happen when we resolve to depend fully on God and decide to love ourselves.

In a similar vein
Wayne Dyer, *Real Magic* (p144)
M. Scott Peck, *The Road Less Traveled* (p260)
Florence Scovell Shinn, *The Game of Life and How to Play It* (p272)

CHAPTER 50

Marianne Williamson

Marianne Williamson was in her mid-20s, a self-destructive product of the "me generation," when she made a discovery that changed her life. In 1965 Helen Schucman, a professor of medical psychology at Columbia University, had started transcribing a "voice." The result was the massive *A Course in Miracles*, a self-study psycho-spiritual philosophy based on love and forgiveness that gave birth to discussion groups around the world. Williamson's full embrace of the *Course* led her to give talks and lectures on it, which eventually resulted in the publication of *A Return to Love*.

As a masterful summation of the *Course* the book is worth reading, but it is the passionate baring of the author's soul and spiritual awakening that pulls in readers. Initially, it was Oprah Winfrey's liking of the book that helped project it to the top of the *New York Times* bestseller list, where it spent over six months. A recent revised edition notes sales of over a million copies.

Sweet surrender

In Chapter 1 Williamson tells of the nervous breakdown that brought a total reorientation of her life. She had always considered herself a fighter—for causes or against injustice—and even liberation from her demons was seen as a forceful "breaking free." However, as her breakdown progressed and then slowly lifted, she discovered that freedom is more like melting into one's real nature and personality. This part of her story is captivating, given her previous skepticism and unwillingness to give up anything of herself. Like any normal person, she was wary of giving away any power. Yet that struggle between the ego and the purer, real self gives the book its pull. Only in getting as low as she did was she willing to try anything, in this case a spiritual surrender.

The ego loves great highs, Williamson says, but also manufactures calamities, and we are brought up to expect that events and circumstances can make or break our sense of wellbeing. The enlightened person, however, sees that their internal state determines how they see external things. Things happen to them as well, but without the fear and gravity attached. When we have internal security, she says, thrills abound, but they are of a different type; there is the thrill of perceiving the world clearly, without our normal emotional baggage. There are still dramas and crises, but they all contribute to personal growth: We have left behind the "cheap drama" of a non-spiritual life.

Relationships

A major part of *A Return to Love* is devoted to relationships. You may find yourself going back to this section again and again, if only to remember the person you could be. It should strike chords in anyone, particularly the fine distinctions made between "special" or ego relationships and "holy" ones. The ego is characterized as "the great faultfinder." But criticism only increases the insecurity of the other person, making them even less likely to change. Our attention to the fault blinds us to what is great about the rest of them. Unconditional love may be hard to cultivate, but it brings rich rewards, being the only way we stay at peace with ourselves.

According to the Course relationships are assignments, each one providing us with the maximum opportunity for growth. This means that the romantic idea we have of a soul mate is incorrect, as our true soul mate may be the person who pushes all our buttons and makes us grow by learning how to be patient and humble, and to love more. The people who make us angry can often be our most important teachers. The ego, on the other hand, will direct us to people who will give us the least problems and the most obvious pleasure, seductively pulling us away from the possibility of deeper relationships.

Williamson is happy talking about her own relationships and we can easily relate to the tales of heartbreak and angst that she recounts, of the longing for a special person to makes things right. We keep turning the page because it seems that it is our life she is talking about, asking the questions we ask. The answers, nevertheless, are often not what we expect.

Work and achievement

A Return to Love is equally interesting about work. We always talk about our career, our job, our pay. By our own efforts, we carve out a working life according to what interests us or how much we would like to earn. The book says that this is not the route to real success. If we offer our working life to God, He will reveal to us precisely what will best suit our talents and temperament and the way in which we can help the world the most. What we create by our own will might be good, but genius only happens when we become cleaner instruments for divine expression. We are not so much afraid of failure, but of the brilliance that might shine through us if we allow it to. With this mentality, we can no longer be slaves for money.

Goal setting is all very well, but it is the prime example of the ego trying to shape the world according to its pleasing. Because our minds are so powerful, we usually can accomplish any goals we set, but whether happiness ensues from their reaching is never certain. With God's work we're not only ecstatic to achieve the goals set before us, we're happy merely enjoying the journey. The *Course* says, "As we spread love, we climb naturally." That will not be taught on any MBA programs, but be courageous enough test it for yourself. Williamson says that we can't go wrong, because trust in God is like "trusting gravity."

Miracles

Personal development is usually about how we can engineer ourselves into better ways of acting and thinking; it seems to involve a great deal of responsibility. Yet if we have surrendered ourselves to the beneficence of the universe, or to God, suddenly it's not so hard. Williamson says that she used to put miracles in the "pseudo-mystical-religious garbage category." She later realized that it is in fact reasonable to ask for them.

A miracle does not have to mean turning water into wine. It is simply the occurrence of anything that was previously considered impossible. When we decide to have a certain openness of mind and are committed to change, anything that seems beyond us can be offered up for transformation. If it is not an ego want but a genuine part of that transformative frame of mind, the miracle will happen. Where once we saw our partner as guilty on a number of counts, today we see their innocence and treat them accordingly. Where we had an addiction, fueled by fear and self-hate, today that hole is filled up.

The title of *A Course in Miracles* is catchy because it is contradictory, combining something mundane (a course) with something divine. It promises not the usual human–divine relationship but a co-creating partnership. Remember that when Jesus performed his miracles, he told the disbelieving gathered around him that they, too, could do what he did—and even better than him. The Church may define a miracle as a physical happening that cannot be explained in any normal way, but this definition prevents the rest of us from knowing that miracles can happen through us. It is sad, Williamson remarks, that we so willingly give up power.

Final comments

With the strong eastern influence in self-help writing the Christian stance of *A Return to Love* stands out, but it is best seen as a spiritual work that happens to use the Christian terminology of the *Course*. Williamson is quick to admit that all ideas about God are expressions of a single reality (she herself has a Jewish background) and that people do not have to consider that they have a personal relationship to "God" to be an advanced *Course* student. Its students proceed according to how they treat other people.

While at first glance *A Return to Love* may seem like a baby boomer's indulgent search for the self, it is for the most part a beautiful summary of the *Course*, carrying its authority and timelessness. It is a spiritual self-help classic of great practical worth.

Marianne Williamson

Williamson grew up in Houston, Texas, the child of left-wing lawyers. At 13 her father took her to Vietnam to see the "military-industrial complex" in action. She spent two years at Pomona College in California, majoring in philosophy and theater, followed by a laid-back existence lasting several years. She began giving lectures on the Course *in 1983, which became increasingly popular. Between 1987 and 1989 Williamson founded the Los Angeles and Manhattan Centers for Living, non-profit counseling and support organizations for people with life-threatening illnesses, including AIDS.*

A Return to Love *was her first book.* A Woman's Worth *(1994) was also a bestseller, followed by* Illuminata, *a book of prayers and meditations.* Enchanted Love *is an exploration of "holy relationships," blending Christianity, myth and goddess studies, and feminism.* The Healing of America *is a blueprint for America's political rejuvenation via a spiritually tuned-in citizenry. Recent books include* The Law of Divine Compensation *and* Tears to Triumph: Spiritual Healing for the Modern Plagues of Anxiety and Depression.

50 More Classics

1 **Alfred Adler, *What Life Could Mean to You* (1931)**
Adler formed an entire new branch of psychology (individual) but with this book brought his insights to a popular audience. It covers adolescence, feelings of superiority and inferiority, the importance of cooperation, work, friendship, love, and marriage.

2 **Horatio Alger, *Ragged Dick* (1867)**
Probably the most famous of Alger's poor-boy-makes-good stories that made the American dream come alive for millions. Set in the cityscapes of nineteenth-century America, they carry an earnest message of ethical striving for success, but are still great fun to read.

3 **Muhummad Al-Ghazali, *The Alchemy of Happiness* (11th century)**
Al-Ghazali was an esteemed philosopher in medieval Persia who became a wandering Sufi mystic. *The Alchemy of Happiness* is a superb expression of the self-help ethic in Islam, and an abridgment of his masterwork *The Revival of Religious Sciences*, in which readers have delighted for centuries. Its basic premise is that that self-knowledge comes from knowledge of God.

4 **Roberto Assagioli, *Psychosynthesis* (1965)**
Assagioli, an Italian humanistic psychologist, believed that Freud's focus on the libido, complexes, and instincts was incomplete. In *Psychosynthesis* he set about integrating the soul and imagination into psychology. Somewhat of a heavy read but influential.

5 **Eric Berne, *Games People Play* (1964)**
This was written for an academic audience but became a best-seller. The major influence on Harris's *I'm OK–You're OK*, it presented the idea that we all have "life scripts" that determine our actions. The good news is that we can change them.

6 **Frank Bettger, *How I Raised Myself from Failure to Success in Selling* (1950)**
Bettger was a salesman in the America of the 1920s and 1930s and a friend of Dale Carnegie. His book has remained popular because everyone needs selling skills—and it tells a good story.

7   **John Bradshaw, *Homecoming: Reclaiming and Championing Your Inner Child* (1992)**
    The "inner child" concept has been ridiculed as a feeble expression of a victim culture. Bradshaw's bestseller is in fact a serious work showing why knowledge and acceptance of the past are crucial in making us responsible adults.

8   **Nathaniel Branden, *The Power of Self-Esteem* (1969)**
    An apostle and lover of Ayn Rand, Branden helped kick off the self-esteem movement with this book.

9   **Claude M. Bristol, *The Magic of Believing* (1948)**
    Its references are dated, it may be repetitive, and its ideas on visualization and affirmation may seem old hat today, but many in the last 50 years have attested to this book's power to change.

10 **Leo Buscaglia, *Love* (1972)**
    Buscaglia is a popular self-help figure. This is one of his earlier works on a subject that we take for granted and is probably his most appreciated.

11 **Jack Canfield & Mark Victor Hansen, *Chicken Soup for the Soul* (1993)**
    Not a self-help philosophy but a collection of heart-warming inspirational stories that has enjoyed vast sales, the formula endlessly repeated in *Chicken Soup* books for the teen soul, pet soul, global soul, etc.

12 **Chin-ning Chu, *Thick Face, Black Heart* (1994)**
    Promoting a warrior philosophy with eastern overtones, this has been a success with both business and personal development readers who see regular self-help as "wimpish."

13 **Confucius, *Analects* (6th century BC)**
    This collection of 2,500 aphorisms, anecdotes, and dialogs came from one of the most influential sages in history. Published after the author's death, the *Analects* guided Chinese civilization for 2,000 years and can still have a profound impact on readers.

14 **Russell H. Conwell, *Acres of Diamonds* (1921)**
    Originally an inspirational lecture, this book was so much in demand that the proceeds funded a university. Stories and anecdotes illustrate the idea that people go looking for their fortunes elsewhere when "acres of diamonds" are to be found in their own backyard (literally and metaphorically).

15 **Emile Coué, *Self-Mastery through Conscious Autosuggestion* (1922)**
Contains the famous autosuggestion mantra, "Every day in every way I am becoming better and better," which started the ball rolling for personal success affirmations. Influential but not widely read now.

16 **Edward De Bono, *The Use of Lateral Thinking* (1967)**
De Bono did not invent lateral thinking, but the term only entered the public vocabulary with this book. In offering an alternative to the starched logic of conventional "vertical" thinking, this and De Bono's later books have taught us to think about thinking itself.

17 **Stephanie Dowrick, *Intimacy and Solitude* (1996)**
A work showing how the abilities to be intimate and happily alone are related. Dowrick is an Australian-based psychotherapist whose *Forgiveness* has also been popular.

18 **Albert Ellis, *A Guide to Rational Living* (1975)**
Ellis's "rational emotive" approach showed how to control our emotional life through altering our beliefs. This book continues to find devoted new readers who appreciate its transformative effect on relationships.

19 **Marsilio Ficino, *The Book of Life* (15th century)**
A Renaissance life guide applying spiritual ideas to everyday matters. Harder to read than a modern classic, but strongly influenced *Care of the Soul*'s Thomas Moore.

20 **Eric Fromm, *To Have or to Be* (1976)**
A great social philosopher, Fromm made the distinction between the "having" approach to life (materialistic, ironically fostering scarcity and misery) and "being" (the basis of satisfaction and peace). Still gets rave reviews as societal commentary and self-help.

21 **Les Giblin, *How to Have Confidence and Power in Dealing with People* (1956)**
An enduring people skills manual from a former top salesman. In focusing on how people actually respond and why, its aim is friction reduction and the creation of goodwill.

22 **Kahlil Gibran, *The Prophet* (1923)**
Gibran was a Syrian who emigrated to the US. Though an artist in several media, it was this 20-million-copy seller that made him famous. Beautiful and profound verses on love, loss, marriage, etc.

23 **William Glasser, *Reality Therapy* (1965)**
This surprising bestseller put forward the idea that mental illness

comes from a person's unwillingness to face reality and make commitments. Based on clinical work.

24 **Thomas A. Harris, *I'm OK—You're OK* (1967)**
Many people's idea of a self-help classic. Popularized the transactional analysis model of seeing our actions and words as expressing either a Parent, Adult, or Child mentality.

25 **Tom Hopkins, *Official Guide to Success* (1982)**
A modest but powerful work by one of America's most respected personal development speakers and authors.

26 **Elbert Hubbard, *Message to Garcia* (1899)**
In 1895 Hubbard founded a community based on self-sufficiency and positive thinking in New York State. Its press published *A Message to Garcia*, a pamphlet (estimated printing 40 million copies) recounting a tale of heroism during the Spanish-American war. Still popular with army officers and employers for its message of "getting the job done" no matter what.

27 *The I-Ching*
The Chinese "Book of Changes" has been around for 3,000 years but is still a compelling tool of self-understanding. Its ability to make the reader aware of other possibilities in times of great change makes it relevant in the twenty-first century.

28 **Harold Kushner, *When Bad Things Happen to Good People* (1984)**
Kushner, a rabbi, wrote this as a response to his child's fatal illness. About the things you can't control and how to deal with them, it is intellectually sound and practical, and has remained popular.

29 **Muriel James and Dorothy Jongeward, *Born to Win* (1971)**
Transactional analysis bestseller (four million copies), analyzing communication styles and providing Gestalt exercises in order to reveal ego states standing in the way of full mental health.

30 **William James, *The Will to Believe* (1907)**
James may be the "father of American psychology," but as a practical philosopher he has been very influential in self-help. *The Will to Believe* gets to the heart of personal questions about motivation and belief, and essays such as "Is Life Worth Living?" provide some of his finest and most life-expanding thoughts.

31 **Orison Swett Marden, *Pushing to the Front* (1894)**
Considered the founder of the success movement in America, Marden (1850–1924) published numerous books inspired by the character and hard work ethic of Samuel Smiles. This was his huge bestseller.

32 **Rollo May, *Freedom and Destiny* (1981)**
May argues that attaching ourselves to a particular end (destiny), instead of tying us down, provides the right amount of freedom to create and prosper. The theme of personal responsibility has influenced Stephen Covey and others.

33 **Og Mandino, *The Greatest Success in the World* (1981)**
Familiar self-help themes of goal setting and self-realization put into the form of a story set in New Testament times. Mandino was a friend of Norman Vincent Peale and delivers a similar have-faith-in-yourself message.

34 **Earl Nightingale, *The Strangest Secret* (1955)**
The late Earl Nightingale was known as the "Dean of Self-Development." This is his classic inspirational recording that sold over a million copies and made the audiotape central to the motivational industry.

35 **Robin Norwood, *Women Who Love Too Much* (1988)**
Talk-show bestseller that still enjoys readership with its useful distinctions about self-love and dependency, and the traps into which people fall when choosing partners.

36 **Fritz Perls, *Gestalt Therapy: Excitement and Growth in the Human Personality* (1951)**
Perls was a key figure in the Human Potential movement of the 1960s and this was his key work. Influenced by psychoanalysis and existentialism, Gestalt therapy emphasized the need for people to see "outside the box," focusing on the present moment.

37 **Robert J. Ringer, *Looking Out for No. 1* (1977)**
A 1970s bestseller. Not as bad as it sounds, it shows readers how to avoid needless sacrifice and pursue what they want without guilt.

38 **Carl Rogers, *On Becoming a Person* (1961)**
Rogers helped revolutionize psychotherapy by replacing psycho-analytic "interpretation" with empathic listening by the therapist. Though an emblematic work of the self-discovery ethic of the 1960s, *On Becoming a Person* is still popular.

39 **Bertrand Russell, *The Conquest of Happiness* (1930)**
This famous Oxford philosopher's venture into self-help territory. While dated, Russell's wit and insights still make it an enjoyable read. The first part discusses what makes people miserable, the second what makes them happy.

40 **Robert H. Schuller,** *Tough Times Never Last, But Tough People Do!* (1984)
Tool for creating a rock-hard self-image from the Minister of the Crystal Cathedral, California. Schuller coined the phrase "possibility thinking."

41 **Gail Sheehy,** *Passages* (1976)
Garish 1970s bestseller that navigates the reader through the stages of adult life. Translated into 28 languages, it has featured on Library of Congress lists as one of the most influential books of all time.

42 **José Silva and Joseph Miele,** *The Silva Mind Control Method* (1977)
Former audio repairman Silva became interested in mind-control techniques and developed a famous course involving theta brainwaves. This was the bestselling book on the method.

43 **W. Clement Stone and Napoleon Hill,** *Success Through a Positive Mental Attitude* (1960)
Stone was Hill's mentor and business partner, and this book was a combination of Hill's *Science of Success* and Stone's Horatio Alger-style American optimism. Selling well even after 40 years.

44 **Deborah Tannen,** *You Just Don't Understand* (1991)
An examination of men's and women's communication styles that came out of Tannen's work as a linguist. An alternative to John Gray.

45 **Brian Tracy,** *Maximum Achievement* (1995)
Many connoisseurs of self-help put Tracy at the top of their list. A good synthesis of the genre's ideas and techniques but in Tracy's own style.

46 **Kevin Trudeau,** *Mega Memory* (1995)
Simple steps for impressing friends and yourself through memory power. Trudeau is one of the original infomercial kings, but his techniques actually go back to the seventeenth century.

47 **Theodore Zeldin,** *An Intimate History of Humanity* (1994)
Panoramic view of the human condition by an Oxford historian, spliced with fascinating profiles of contemporary women. Its theme is that the quality of your life is vastly improved by appreciating it within the context of all of human history.

48 **Zig Ziglar,** *See You at the Top* (1975)
Old-school motivational work based on the belief that "You can get everything you want if you help others to get what they want." Enjoyable, but its Christian values won't appeal to everyone.

49 **Danah Zohar,** *The Quantum Self* (1990)
An application of quantum physics to how we see ourselves and our connection with the universe. Ahead of its time and will remain influential.

50 **Gary Zukav,** *The Seat of the Soul* (1990)
Perhaps more New Age than self-help, this presents a schema for understanding human evolution in terms of the shift from sensual awareness to soul awareness. Millions attest to its life-changing ideas.

Chronological
List of Titles

The Bhagavad-Gita
The Bible
The Dhammapada
Lao Tzu *Tao Te Ching* (5th–3rd century BC)
Marcus Aurelius *Meditations* (2nd century)
Boethius *The Consolation of Philosophy* (6th century)
Benjamin Franklin *Autobiography* (1790)
Ralph Waldo Emerson *Self-Reliance* (1841)
Henry David Thoreau *Walden* (1854)
Samuel Smiles *Self-Help* (1859)
James Allen *As a Man Thinketh* (1902)
Florence Scovell Shinn *The Game of Life and How to Play It* (1925)
Dale Carnegie *How to Win Friends and Influence People* (1936)
Norman Vincent Peale *The Power of Positive Thinking* (1952)
Abraham Maslow *Motivation and Personality* (1954)
Pierre Teilhard de Chardin *The Phenomenon of Man* (1955)
Viktor Frankl *Man's Search for Meaning* (1959)
Maxwell Maltz *Psycho-Cybernetics* (1960)
Joseph Murphy *The Power of Your Subconscious Mind* (1963)
Shakti Gawain *Creative Visualization* (1978)
M. Scott Peck *The Road Less Traveled* (1978)
William Bridges *Transitions: Making Sense of Life's Changes* (1980)
David D. Burns *Feeling Good: The New Mood Therapy* (1980)
Louise Hay *You Can Heal Your Life* (1984)
Joseph Campbell with Bill Moyers *The Power of Myth* (1987)
Susan Jeffers *Feel the Fear and Do It Anyway* (1987)
Stephen Covey *The 7 Habits of Highly Effective People* (1989)
Ellen J. Langer *Mindfulness: Choice and Control in Everyday Life* (1989)
Robert Bly *Iron John* (1990)
Mihaly Csikszentmihalyi *Flow: The Psychology of Optimal Experience* (1990)
Anthony Robbins *Awaken the Giant Within* (1991)
Martin Seligman *Learned Optimism* (1991)

Wayne Dyer *Real Magic: Creating Miracles in Everyday Life* (1992)
Clarissa Pinkola Estés *Women Who Run with the Wolves* (1992)
John Gray *Men Are from Mars, Women Are from Venus* (1992)
Thomas Moore *Care of the Soul: A Guide for Cultivating Depth and Sacredness in Everyday Life* (1992)
Paulo Coelho *The Alchemist* (1993)
Deepak Chopra *The Seven Spiritual Laws of Success* (1994)
Marianne Williamson *A Return to Love* (1994)
Daniel Goleman *Emotional Intelligence: Why It Can Matter More than IQ* (1995)
James Hillman *The Soul's Code: In Search of Character and Calling* (1996)
Alain de Botton *How Proust Can Change Your Life* (1997)
Richard Carlson *Don't Sweat the Small Stuff. . . and It's All Small Stuff* (1997)
The Dalai Lama & Howard C. Cutler *The Art of Happiness: Handbook for Living* (1998)
Richard Koch *The 80/20 Principle: The Secret of Achieving More with Less* (1998)
Charles Duhigg *The Power of Habit* (2011)
Brené Brown *Daring Greatly* (2012)
Clayton Christensen *How Will You Measure Your Life?* (2012)
Marie Kondo *The Life-Changing Magic of Tidying Up* (2014)
David Brooks *The Road to Character* (2015)

Credits

Please note that many titles have had different publishers in the US and the UK. The editions below were the ones mostly consulted in researching the book.

Allen, J. (1998) *As You Think*, ed. with introduction by M. Allen, Novato, CA: New World Library.

Aurelius, M. (1964) *Meditations*, trans. M. Staniforth, London: Penguin.

The Bhagavad-Gita (1973) trans. J. Mascaró, London: Penguin World's Classics.

Bly, Robert (1992) *Iron John*, New York: Vintage Books.

Boethius (1999) *The Consolation of Philosophy*, trans. with introduction and explanatory notes by P.G. Walsh, Oxford: Clarendon Press.

de Botton, A. (1998) *How Proust Can Change Your Life*, London: Picador.

Bridges, W. (1996) *Transitions: Making Sense of Life's Changes*, London: Nicholas Brealey Publishing.

Brooks, David (2015) *The Road to Character*, London: Penguin Random House.

Brown, Brené (2012) *Daring Greatly*, London: Penguin Random House.

Burns, D. (1992) *Feeling Good: The New Mood Therapy*, New York: Avon Books.

Campbell. J. with Moyers, B. (1991) *The Power of Myth*, New York: Anchor Books.

Carlson, R. (1997) *Don't Sweat The Small Stuff... And It's All Small Stuff: Simple Ways to Keep the Little Things from Overtaking Your Life*, London: Hodder & Stoughton.

Carnegie, D. (1994) *How to Win Friends and Influence People*, New York: Pocket Books.

Chopra, D. (1996) *The Seven Spiritual Laws of Success*, London: Bantam Press.

Christensen, Clayton (2012) *How Will You Measure Your Life?*, London: HarperCollins.

Coelho, P. (1999) *The Alchemist*, trans. Alan R Clarke, London: HarperCollins.

Covey, S. (1990) *The 7 Habits of Highly Effective People*, New York: Simon & Schuster.

Csikszentmihalyi, M. (1991) *Flow: The Psychology of Optimal Experience*, New York: Harper Perennial.

His Holiness the Dalai Lama & Howard C. Cutler (1999) *The Art of Happiness: A Handbook for Living*, London: Hodder & Stoughton.

Dhammapada: The Path of Perfection (1973) trans. J. Mascaró, London: Penguin Classics.

The Dhammapada: Sayings of Buddha (1995) ed. T.F. Cleary, New York: Bantam Wisdom.

Duhigg, Charles (2011) *The Power of Habit*, London: Random House.

Dyer, W. (1993) *Real Magic: Creating Miracles in Everyday Life*, New York: HarperCollins.

Emerson, R.W. (1993) *Self-Reliance and Other Essays*, Dover Publications.

Estés, C. P. (1993) *Women Who Run with the Wolves*, London: Rider.

Frankl, V. (1984) *Man's Search for Meaning*, preface by Gordon W. Allport, New York: Simon & Schuster.

Franklin, B. (1993) *Autobiography and Other Writings*, ed. O. Seavey, Oxford: Oxford University Press.

Gawain, S. (1985) *Creative Visualization*, New York: Bantam Books.

Goleman, D. (1997) *Emotional Intelligence: Why It Can Matter More than IQ*, New York: Bantam Books.

Gray, J. (1992) *Men Are from Mars, Women Are from Venus: A Practical Guide for Improving Communication and Getting What You Want in Your Relationships*, London: HarperCollins.

Hay, L. (1999) *You Can Heal Your Life*, Carlsbad CA: Hay House.

Hillman, J. (1997) *The Soul's Code: In Search of Character and Calling*, New York: Warner Books.

Jeffers, S. (1991) *Feel the Fear and Do It Anyway*, London: Arrow Books.

Koch, R. (1998) *The 80/20 Principle: The Secret of Achieving More with Less*, London: Nicholas Brealey Publishing.

Kondo, Marie (2014) *The Life-Changing Magic of Tidying Up*, London: Vermilion/Random House.

Langer, E. (1990) *Mindfulness: Choice and Control in Everyday Life*, Cambridge, MA: Perseus Publishing.

Lao-Tzu's Tao Te Ching (2000) trans. T. Freke, introduction by M. Palmer, London: Piatkus.

Maltz, M. (1960) *Psycho-Cybernetics*, Los Angeles: Wilshire Book Company.

Maslow, A. (1987) *Motivation and Personality*, ed. R. Frager, New York: Addison Wesley.

Moore, T. (1992) *Care of the Soul*, New York: HarperCollins.

Murphy, J. (1995) *The Power of Your Subconscious Mind*, London: Pocket Books.

Peale, N.V. (1996) *The Power of Positive Thinking*, New York: Ballantine Books.

Peck, M.S. (1990) *The Road Less Travelled: A New Psychology of Love, Traditional Values and Spiritual Growth*, London: Arrow Books.

Robbins, A. (1993) *Awaken the Giant Within*, New York: Simon & Schuster.

Scovell Shinn, F. (1998) *The Game of Life and How to Play It*, Saffron Walden: C.W. Daniel.

Seligman, M. (1998) *Learned Optimism*, New York: Simon & Schuster.

Smiles, S. (1996) *Self-Help: With Illustrations of Conduct and Perseverance*, London: Institute of Economic Affairs; also (2002) ed. P.W. Sinnema, Oxford: Oxford University Press.

Teilhard de Chardin, P. (1970) *The Phenomenon of Man*, introduction by J. Huxley, London: Collins Fontana.

Thoreau, H.D. (1986) *Walden and Civil Disobedience*, introduction by M. Meyer, New York: Penguin.

Williamson, M. (1993) *A Return to Love: Reflections on the Principles of A Course in Miracles*, New York: HarperCollins.

About the Author

A graduate of the London School of Economics and the University of Sydney, Tom Butler-Bowdon was 25 years old and working as a political advisor in Australia when he read his first personal development book: Stephen Covey's *The 7 Habits of Highly Effective People*. Captivated, he came to the view that this was an underrated field of writing. At 30, he left his career to write the bestselling *50 Self-Help Classics*, the first guide to personal development literature and winner of the Benjamin Franklin Award.

The follow-up, *50 Success Classics*, celebrated the great writings in motivation and success, from Horatio Alger to Napoleon Hill to Anthony Robbins. Tom completed the personal development trilogy with *50 Spiritual Classics*, which provides insights into the thinking of Gandhi, Mother Teresa, Carl Jung, and Eckhart Tolle, and 46 other great minds.

USA Today described Tom as "a true scholar of this type of literature." His award-winning *50 Classics* series has sold over 300,000 copies and has been translated into 23 languages.

Visit his website www.Butler-Bowdon.com

THE GREATEST BOOKS DISTILLED

by Tom Butler-Bowdon

The *50 Classics* series has sold over 300,000 copies

50 Economics Classics 978-1-85788-673-3

50 Philosophy Classics 978-1-47365-542-3

50 Politics Classics 978-1-47365-543-0

50 Psychology Classics, **2nd ed** 978-1-85788-674-0

50 Self-Help Classics, **2nd ed** 978-1-47365-828-8

50 Success Classics, **2nd ed** 978-1-47365-835-6

50 Spiritual Classics 978-1-47365-838-7

50 Business Classics 978-1-85788-675-7 (coming 2018)

50 PHILOSOPHY CLASSICS

Your shortcut to the most important ideas on being, truth, and meaning

Tom Butler-Bowdon

For over 2000 years, philosophy has been our best guide to the experience of being human and the true nature of reality. From Aristotle, Plato, Epicurus, Confucius, Cicero and Heraclitus in ancient times to seventeenth century rationalists Descartes, Leibniz and Spinoza, from 20th-century greats Jean-Paul Sartre, Jean Baudrillard and Simone de Beauvoir to contemporary thinkers Michael Sandel, Peter Singer and Slavoj Žižek, *50 Philosophy Classics* explores key writings that have shaped the discipline and had an impact on the real world.

From Aristotle to Wittgenstein, *50 Philosophy Classics* provides a lively entry point to the "king of disciplines". It seeks to enlighten and explain rather than merely instruct, helping readers comprehend some of the key questions – and possible answers – at the centre of human existence. Insightful commentaries on famous texts, biographies of each author, "In a nutshell" summaries and representative quotes give a taste of the writings that have changed the course of intellectual history – and keep changing minds today.

> "Explains with remarkable lucidity ideas of fifty philosophical thinkers from ancient times to the present day. Complex views on a range of important and enduring issues are made accessible to the general reader. … Enjoyable and instructive."

C.L. Ten, Professor of Philosophy, National University of Singapore

Trade paperback 978-1-47365-542-3
320pp 216x135mm

50 PSYCHOLOGY CLASSICS
NEW EDITION

Your shortcut to the most important ideas on the mind, personality, and human nature

Tom Butler-Bowdon

In a journey spanning 50 books, hundreds of ideas and over a century, *50 Psychology Classics* looks at some of the most intriguing questions relating to what motivates us, what makes us feel and act in certain ways, how our brains work, and how we create a sense of self. This brand new edition includes commentaries on new classics suach as *Thinking, Fast and Slow; Quiet* and *The Marshmallow Test*.

50 Psychology Classics explores writings from iconic figures including Freud, Adler, Jung, Skinner, James, Piaget and Pavlov, but also highlights the work of contemporary thinkers such as Gardner, Gilbert, Goleman and Seligman. *50 Psychology Classics* will further your understanding of human nature and yourself.

"At long last a chance for those outside the profession to discover that
there is so much more to psychology than just Freud and Jung.
50 Psychology Classics offers a unique opportunity to become acquainted
with a dazzling array of the key works in psychological literature almost
overnight."

Dr Raj Persaud, Gresham Professor
for Public Understanding of Psychiatry

"This delightful book provides thoughtful and entertaining summaries
of 50 of the most influential books in psychology. It's a 'must-read' for
students contemplating a career in psychology."

VS Ramachandran, Director, Center for Brain and Cognition,
University of California, San Diego

Trade paperback 978-1-85788-674-0
320pp 216x135mm